TEMPTATIC

Other titles in the series

National Fictions
Literature, film and the construction of Australia narrative
Graeme Turner

Myths of Oz
Reading Australian popular culture
John Fiske, Bob Hodge, Graeme Turner

Australian Television
Programs, pleasures and politics
Edited by John Tulloch and Graeme Turner

Fashioning the Feminine
Girls, popular culture and schooling
Pam Gilbert and Sandra Taylor

Dark Side of the Dream
Australian literature and the postcolonial mind
Bob Hodge and Vijay Mishra

From Pop to Punk to Postmodernism
Popular music and Australian culture from the 1960s to the 1990s
Philip Hayward (ed.)

Stay Tuned
An Australian broadcasting reader
Albert Moran (ed.)

Framing Culture
Criticism and policy in Australia
Stuart Cunningham

Australian Cultural Studies
Editor: John Tulloch

Temptations
Sex, Selling and the Department Store

Gail Reekie

ALLEN & UNWIN

First published 1993
Allen & Unwin Pty Ltd
9 Atchison Street, St Leonards NSW 2065 Australia

National Library of Australia
Cataloguing-in Publication entry:

Reekie, Gail.
Temptations: sex, selling and the department store

Bibliography.
Includes index.
ISBN 1 86373 342 6.

1. Women consumers. 2. Department stores – Sociological aspects.
3. Sales promotion – Sex differences. I. Title.

658.8348

Set in 11/12pt Garamond by DOCUPRO, Sydney
Printed by Kin Keong Printing, Singapore

10 9 8 7 6 5 4 3 2 1

General Editor's Foreword

Nowadays the social and anthropological definition of 'culture' is probably gaining as much public currency as the aesthetic one. Paticularly in Australia, politicians are liable to speak of the vital need for a domestic film industry in 'promoting our cultural identity'—and they mean by 'cultural identity' some sense of Australianness, of our nationalism as a distinct form of social organisation. Notably, though, the emphasis tends to be on Australian *film* (not popular television); and not just *any* film, but those of 'quality'. So the aesthetic definition tends to be smuggled back in—on top of the kind of cultural nationalism which assumes that 'Australia' is a unified entity with certain essential features that distinguish it from 'Britain', the 'USA' or any other national entities which threaten us with 'cultural dependency'.

This series is titled 'Australian Cultural Studies', and I should say at the outset that my understanding of 'Australian' is not as an essentially unified category; and further, that my understanding of cultural is anthropological rather than aesthetic. By 'culture' I mean the social production of meaning and understanding, whether in the inter-personal and practical organisation of daily routines or in broader institutional and ideological structures. I am *not* thinking of 'culture' as some form of universal 'excellence', based on aesthetic 'discrimination' and embodied in a pantheon of 'great works'. Rather, I take this aesthetic definition of culture itself to be part of the *social mobilisation of discourse* to differentiate a cultural 'élite' from the 'mass' of society.

Unlike the cultural nationalism of our opinion leaders, 'Cultural Studies' focuses not on the essential unity of national cultures, but on the meanings attached to social difference (as in the distinction between 'élite' and 'mass' taste). It analyses the construction and mobilisation of these distinctions to maintain or challenge existing power differentials, such as those of gender, class, age, race and ethnicity. In this analysis, terms designed to socially differentiate people (like 'élite' and 'mass') become categories of discourse, communication and power. Hence our concern in this series is for an analytical understanding of the meanings attached to social difference within the *history* and *politics* of discourse.

It follows that the analysis of 'texts' needs to be united from a single-minded association with 'high' culture (marked by 'authorship'), but must include the 'popular' too—since these distinctions of 'high' and 'popular' culture themselves need to be analysed, not assumed.

The field of cultural studies embraces the practices, patterns of meaning and symbolic systems of everyday life; and in particular it focuses on the way in which social divisions are made meaningful—or, alternatively, effaced. As Gail Reekie argues in this book, the 'portrayal or retailing as a harmonious, even romantic, activity has obscured the sexual politics of selling, the femininity of shoppers and the masculinity of retail owners, managers and publicists'. Behind the practices and discourses which have naturalised this relationship, and disguised the systems of power and inequality on which it is based, Reekie discerns the ways in which 'sex and gender . . . were primary ways of signifying relationships of power within the department store . . . This study argues that the department store created a sexual culture which formulated and reinforced men's power over women . . . Retail men's sexualisation of selling and formulation of sexual difference had, by the 1920s, created standardised ideals of womanhood and manhood that continue to shape the sexual organisation of the contemporary world.' As such, the sexualisation of selling has contributed in a major way to the ongoing divisions and inequalities within Australian culture.

Culture, as Fiske, Hodge and Turner say in *Myths of Oz*, grows out of the divisions of society, not its unity. 'It has to work to construct any unity that it has, rather than simply celebrate an achieved or natural harmony.' Australian culture is then no more than the temporary, embattled construction of 'unity' at any particular historical moment. The 'readings' in this series of 'Australian Cultural Studies' inevitably (and polemically) form part of the struggle to make and break the boundaries of meaning which, in conflict and collusion, dynamically define our culture.

JOHN TULLOCH

Contents

Illustrations

Acknowledgements

My thanks to all those teachers, colleagues and friends at Murdoch University, the State University of New York, Binghamton, the University of Sydney, and Griffith University who in various ways inspired, challenged and sustained me during the intellectual travels which led to this book. More directly, Carole Adams, Judith Allen, Peter Cochrane, Ann Curthoys, Jenny Lee, Bronwyn Levy, Heather Radi, John Spierings and Gillian Swanson offered valuable suggestions, and Anne-Maree Collins helped me reconceptualise the original thesis and interpret my sources in new and stimulating ways. I am also grateful to Pat Hodgkinson, previously of the Grace Brothers Archives, and the staff of the Mitchell Library for their assistance. My study depended heavily on the rich collection of material preserved in the David Jones Archives, and especially on Barbara Horton's archival and historical expertise. The State Library of New South Wales and David Jones (Australia) Ltd have kindly given me permission to reproduce photographs from their collections.

Introduction

The vast majority of the world's shoppers have been women. An observer on any of the main shopping streets of London, Paris, New York or Toronto anywhere between the middle of the nineteenth century and the middle of the twentieth would see crowds of women entering and leaving shops, walking or travelling by carriage or tram between shops, looking in the windows of shops, and talking to each other about shopping. In late nineteenth-century Sydney, women bargained with stall-keepers selling produce and fancy goods at Paddy's Market, carried home parcels and baskets of shopping on trams, omnibuses and trains, purchased groceries for the family's meals in suburban shops at Newtown or Bondi Junction, carefully compared prices in the milliners, watchmakers, stationers and haberdashers of Pitt and George Streets, or visited the dressmaker and bought a matching parasol and pair of gloves at one of the city drapery houses.

Although the nature and extent of shopping may have varied considerably for women of different classes, it was invariably women who were charged with either buying or managing the purchase of clothing, household goods, food, drink and other daily necessaries for themselves and for their families. It is still common knowledge and conventional marketing wisdom that supermarkets and department stores are predominantly female worlds. Research into a proposed shopping-centre development in inner Melbourne in 1991, for example, found that 'The Myer [department store] shopper is 25 to 45, married and a destination shopper, so for her it's a bit of a treat and a shopping experience'.[1] This book explores the implications of the retail and marketing industries' recognition of a sexed market and its significance to the sexual organisation of everyday life.

The portrayal of retailing as a harmonious, even romantic, activity has obscured the sexual politics of selling, the femininity of shoppers and the masculinity of retail owners, managers and publicists. The simple fact that it was women who shopped appears to have escaped the notice of economists, historians and other analysts of the retail industry. Despite the occasional perfunctory remark that department stores were 'women's stores', conventional retail histories failed to pursue retailers' consistent observation that most shoppers were female, and even the most recent publications inaccurately refer to the customer as a universal 'he'.[2] Silence has, until very recently, also surrounded the activities, standpoints and sexualities of men and their efforts to protect and promote the interests of their sex.[3] Although store histories were typically written as celebratory tales of benevolent male paternalism, individual male achievement and male managerial perspicacity, retail historians have been reluctant to specify the sex of those who collectively attempted to woo the female consumer, and who ultimately profited from her seduction.[4]

Neither do traditional retail histories reveal the fraternal nature of the retail and marketing industries. According to Carole Pateman, civil individuals (men) constitute a fraternity because they 'share a common interest in upholding the original [sexual] contract which legitimizes masculine right and allows them to gain material and psychological benefit from women's subjection'.[5] Retailers, managers and marketing experts formed a fraternity, bound together by a bond *as men*, whose primary object was to reap profits from the compliance of the female customer.

Scholarly histories—business histories of department stores, economic histories of the retail trade, social histories of shopping, urban histories and accounts of the development of mass marketing in the United States and Australia—also attribute little consequence to the radical differences of sex that existed between managers and consumers, and within department-store culture. European, American and Australian department stores have been presented in this literature as institutions critical to the formation of a democratic ethic, urban culture and middle-class tastes, aspirations and lifestyles.[6] The contribution of retail establishments to *sexual* cultures—that is, institutions in which notions of masculinity, femininity and sex were forged, learned and negotiated—has thereby been missed. While the historical studies of mass marketing, consumer culture and commodity aesthetics that emerged in the 1980s generally acknowledged the femininity of the consumer, they remained largely uninterested in men, masculinity and sexual difference.[7]

Gender featured more prominently in feminist studies of consumer capitalism and the history of shop assistants.[8] The predominance of socialist-feminist approaches to the study of women, and a focus on women as wage-earners rather than consumers, however, pushed female customers—not to mention men—into the background. As Rosemary Pringle pointed out in 1983, feminists were preoccupied with production at the expense of consumption.[9] Male managers and female customers were present in Susan Porter Benson's 1986 account of saleswomen, managers and customers in American department stores before 1940, but her study represented sales and display spaces as a predominantly female space, an 'Adamless Eden'.[10]

Retail histories which approached the department store primarily as a workplace, an arena of class conflict or an institution of bourgeois hegemony could not fully accommodate questions of sexual difference and sexuality. Sex and gender, to adopt Joan Scott's argument, were primary ways of signifying relationships of power within the department store.[11] Retailing and commerce were not beyond questions of sex and sexual difference, but constituted by them. The department store, then, is most usefully analysed as a site of sexual culture in which men and women shaped and contested historically-specific formulations of masculinity and femininity and relations between the sexes. David Chaney has argued that the physical form of the nineteenth-century department store, similar in cultural resonance to other urban monuments and festival sites, required and depended upon new and specifically modern forms of conduct.[12] On this consumer stage were developed and articulated not only the new social and economic relationships outlined by Chaney, but new codes of heterosexuality, new formulations of sexual identity and new bodily regimes. Sheila Jeffreys has appropriately defined heterosexuality as 'a political institution through which male dominance is organised and maintained'.[13] This study argues that the department store created a sexual culture which formulated and reinforced men's power over women.

The bodies that became the objects of mass-marketing policies were not neutral but sexed bodies, with distinctly sexed experiences and meanings.[14] The recognition that historically the body has been distinctly segregated into male bodies and female bodies seriously disrupts conventional explanations of the process of mass marketing based on class or economic factors. The significance of the department store as a cultural institution lies in its implicit management of male and female bodies and sexual relations. New methods of display, advertising, customer surveillance and departmental organisation introduced after the turn of the century ascribed increasingly explicit cultural meanings to male and female bodies. Mass marketing methods also articulated with greater clarity differences between the sexes.

These new sales techniques and knowledges provided unambiguous and frequently tangible models of appropriate modes of heterosocial conduct. Like the superficially rational but deeply sexualised environment of the modern office, department store culture was saturated with the dynamics of sex.[15] The department store was an institution of everyday culture which touched the lives of every woman who shopped there, and those of the thousands of women who regularly read the mail-order catalogues widely distributed throughout the city and country; hence its potential to shape popular values and ideas about sex and gender was incalculable. The department store in effect created modern manhood and womanhood and, as a heterosexual space, crucially influenced the ways in which women and men viewed and related to each other as sexes.

The sexual culture of the department store was marked by complex rituals of sexual power, accommodation and transaction that suggest that male retailer and female customer were engaged in a relationship very similar to that established within courtship conventions of the late nineteenth and early twentieth centuries. Rachel Bowlby has identified in the discourse of consumer culture a model of female seduction:

> The essential point is that the making of willing consumers readily fitted into the available ideological paradigm of a seduction of women by men, in which women would be addressed as yielding objects to the powerful male subject forming, and informing them of their desires.[16]

The male sexuality implicit in metaphors of seduction was

not directly exposed, however, but respectably masked by forms of courtship.

Courtship is usually taken to mean a fairly decorous, relatively innocent and chaste period of intimacy between individual women and men which served as a pleasurable prelude to their eventual marriage. But the term courtship, especially in a working-class context, also stands for more coercive forms of sexual interaction between single men and women in private spaces, and between groups of single men and groups of single women in public spaces. Masculine street cultures, such as the larrikin pushes of late nineteenth and early twentieth century urban Australia, revealed what John Gillis describes as the 'essentially ritual character of the antagonism between young men and women'.[17] Courting implied male conquest and female passivity, and might have involved male sexual attentions and intentions not always welcomed by women: its primary object for many men was not necessarily marriage but gratification achieved by women's submission. Women petitioning foundling hospitals to admit their illegitimate infants in the second half of the nineteenth century, for example, described as part of normal courtship behaviour sexual encounters to which they had not consented.[18] The male suitor's desire for possession and governance over the female body was sometimes consummated, sometimes not; sometimes reciprocated, sometimes violently resisted. Similar expressions and negotiations of sexual power can be detected in the attempts of retail and marketing men to seduce female customers into their stores. Changing codes of courtship and heterosexual practice thus provide a useful model through which to interpret sales techniques and discourses and the tensions existing between retailers and their female customers in the period 1880 to 1930.

Codes of conduct and the physical location of courtship changed significantly in this period as courtship moved from the private to the public sphere. Until the 1890s it was usual for a man to 'call' upon his chosen partner at her home and on her initiative. Their conduct was strictly governed by rules of etiquette and propriety over which the woman had some measure of control. Gradually, between 1890 and 1925, this female-controlled calling tradition was replaced by the male-initiated dating system. A man's invitation to a woman to join him in 'going somewhere' entailed, as Beth Bailey argues, a more hazardous invitation into the world of men. Dating, a universal custom in America and probably Australia by the 1920s, also signalled a new perception of courtship as an economic system. Women's company was seen as a commodity to be bought or traded, and in which a man invested his money. Twentieth-century courtship became 'more and more a private act conducted in the public world'.[19]

The history of sexuality in the period 1880 to 1930, according to John D'Emilio and Estelle Freedman, was characterised by the commercialisation of sex and an increased emphasis on consumption, gratification and pleasure. New public spaces for courtship—theatres, dance halls, restaurants, pleasure boats, amusement parks and movie houses—were part of the same urban landscape as the department store. Working class forms of sexual interaction were projected outward on to a wider society and began to influence middle-class courtship norms and practices. As public leisure activities and entertainment became part of a mass commercialised culture, courting and consumption became inextricably intertwined. Women needed to have an up-to-date wardrobe and to purchase the goods that would make them sexually attractive in an increasingly competitive environment. Catching a mate or simply seizing a momentary escape from work and poverty, especially for working-class women, became a matter of wearing stylish clothes and knowing the latest dance step. Young working women devised strategies whereby they traded sexual favours for a night's entertainment paid for by their male partner without necessarily losing their self-respect or respectability.[20]

Sex had become a more open and explicit component of premarital relations between women and men by the 1920s. From the turn of the century, but especially after World War I, sexuality was decisively put into discourse by a range of reformers with diverse political agendas. The writers of marriage manuals, psychologists, sexologists, free-love advocates, sex educationists, birth-control promoters, eugenicists, and social purity crusaders contributed in different ways to the open discussion and greater social acceptance of heterosexuality, at least within marriage.[21] Feminists in Australia and in other western nations publicly criticised forms of heterosexual conduct and male sexuality that degraded women, whether prostitutes or wives. As sexual fulfilment came to be seen as crucial to a happy marriage, as Ellen Rothman argues, it also became important in the transition to marriage. Whereas couples courting in the nineteenth century had been united in domestic concerns, those in the twentieth sought compatibility in the realm of the sexual.[22]

The promotion of marital sexual happiness and the sexualisation of courtship after 1900 had both advantages and pitfalls for women. Married women were perhaps allowed more freedom of sexual expression and greater access to contraceptive advice, and female sexuality generally began to be acknowledged. But feminist campaigns conducted since the 1880s against forms of male sexuality detrimental to women were seriously undermined by repressive legislation designed to control female sexuality during World War I. The repeated pronouncements of psychologists and sexologists that it was unhealthy for women to repress their sex instinct may have allowed men to persuade women unwillingly or precipitatively into premarital sexual relationships. Single women who refused to play the courtship game risked being called old maids, frigid, lesbian or otherwise deviant women.[23]

Many of the new sexological statements, according to Margaret Jackson, eroticised women's oppression. Havelock Ellis, widely read in Australia as well as elsewhere after the turn of the century, and extensively drawn on by the writers of marriage manuals, represented courtship as men's aggressive pursuit and conquest of an unwilling and submissive female object. Female resistance was not real, but all part of the game. Marie Stopes' widely distributed *Married Love* employed more romantic imagery but embodied the same message that it was a man's duty to 'rouse, charm and stimulate' his wife and to take responsibility for her sexual fulfilment. Man was the hunter who experienced the desires and thrills of the chase; woman needed to be wooed and won.[24]

The persistent tensions which surfaced between retail managers and customers, and between managers and shop assistants in the same period suggests that, like courtship, selling entailed a series of negotiations between the sexes premised on the assumption that man was the hunter and woman his legitimate prey. Both selling and courtship scripts of the early twentieth century were structured by clearly demarcated sex roles predicated on the assumption of a man's right of conquest and female passivity. Man was the pursuer, woman the pursued; man the active initiator, woman the pliant respondent.

There were times in the department store, as in the parlour

or on the street, when men's attentions to women were unwanted or coercive. Celebratory retail histories commonly featured anecdotes designed to present the Napoleon of Commerce or Merchant Prince in question in a favourable light but which, read differently, indicate retail men's misogyny. This story from *The Romance of the House of Foy* illustrates the point. Francis Foy one day noticed one of his male assistants unsuccessfully attempting to sell some material to a 'difficult lady customer'. Foy instructed his assistant to serve another customer and when the woman protested, told her to 'go home and tell your husband to give you a jolly good hiding for wasting my man's time'.[25] Retailers' efforts to educate un-cooperative women customers into appropriately submissive consumer behaviour constituted, at its extremes, a subtle form of sexual harassment.

Women were not entirely powerless as the consumers of men's sexual attentions. Despite the liberalisation of middle-class sexual codes in the period 1870 to 1920, women were still expected to 'post the do's and don'ts' in their intimate relations with men. Under the dating system, a woman could still invoke her traditional authority as sexual arbiter without losing her femininity. The woman who smoked in public, danced the latest jazz step and spooned with the boy who drove her home was considered to be quite within her feminine rights to sleep only with the man who promised to marry her.[26] In the sexual relations of consumerism, equally, women had certain rights and privileges. The customer, as numerous articles and advice literature have pointed out since the late nineteenth century, was always right. Any retailer who dared to suggest otherwise risked losing not only her custom but his reputation within the female community as a fair trader.

This is not to imply that the sexual culture of the department store, any more than relations between women and men, was unchanging in this formative period in Australian consumer society. Retail entrepreneurs and managers effected radical transformations in the physical form and sexual ambience of their stores between 1880 and 1930. The story of Anthony Hordern & Sons, universal providers, epitomises the rise of the late nineteenth century retail enterprise. Anthony Hordern & Sons began in 1825 as Ann Hordern's single-storey bonnet shop and stay-making establishment. This small specialty shop became a general drapery business in 1838 and by 1854 had grown into a three-storey shop. By

1876 Anthony Hordern & Sons had diversified into 'universal providers', stores which sold drapery and other commodities such as hardware, fancy goods, china and cutlery, leather goods, trade tools and supplies, furniture and furnishings. Ten years later Samuel Hordern became proprietor of the six-storey Palace Emporium complex selling 'everything made or manufactured'. When fire spectacularly destroyed the Palace Emporium in 1901, it was replaced by a truly monumental building, encompassing a large clothing factory, with a total floorspace of nearly 20 acres extending over an entire city block. Anthony Hordern & Sons claimed in 1922 to serve 30 000 customers each day.[27]

Drapery businesses such as David Jones (established 1838), Mark Foy's (1885), Farmer's (1840), Grace Brothers (1885), Hordern Brothers (1879), and Marcus Clark (1883) grew in similar fashion.[28] When they began trading in the mid to late nineteenth century, shopping consisted of a series of individualised transactions conducted between proprietor and customer within a bourgeois and easily monitored environment. By the early twentieth century, with several thousands of women roaming freely over twenty acres of floorspace each day, retailers such as Samuel Hordern and their managers and marketing advisers had established more effective and scientific strategies to regulate the conduct of female shoppers. In devising these management strategies, the men in the retail and advertising industries drew on and gave discursive form to modern configurations of male and female character. Retail men's sexualisation of selling and formulation of sexual difference had, by the 1920s, created standardised ideals of womanhood and manhood that continue to shape the sexual organisation of the contemporary world.

Modern sexualised consumerism, then, had its beginnings in the culture of the department store and the entrepreneurial activities of retailers and their marketing assistants in the key period between the turn of the century and the 1920s. By 1930, the major patterns of a consumer culture structurally supported by definitive sexual boundaries and rules of heterosexual conduct were securely in place. The argument of this book is that, by providing popular and accessible models of sexual identities and conduct, the department store reformulated and gave specifically modern meanings to male and female bodies, to definitions of manhood and womanhood, and to models of heterosocial and heterosexual

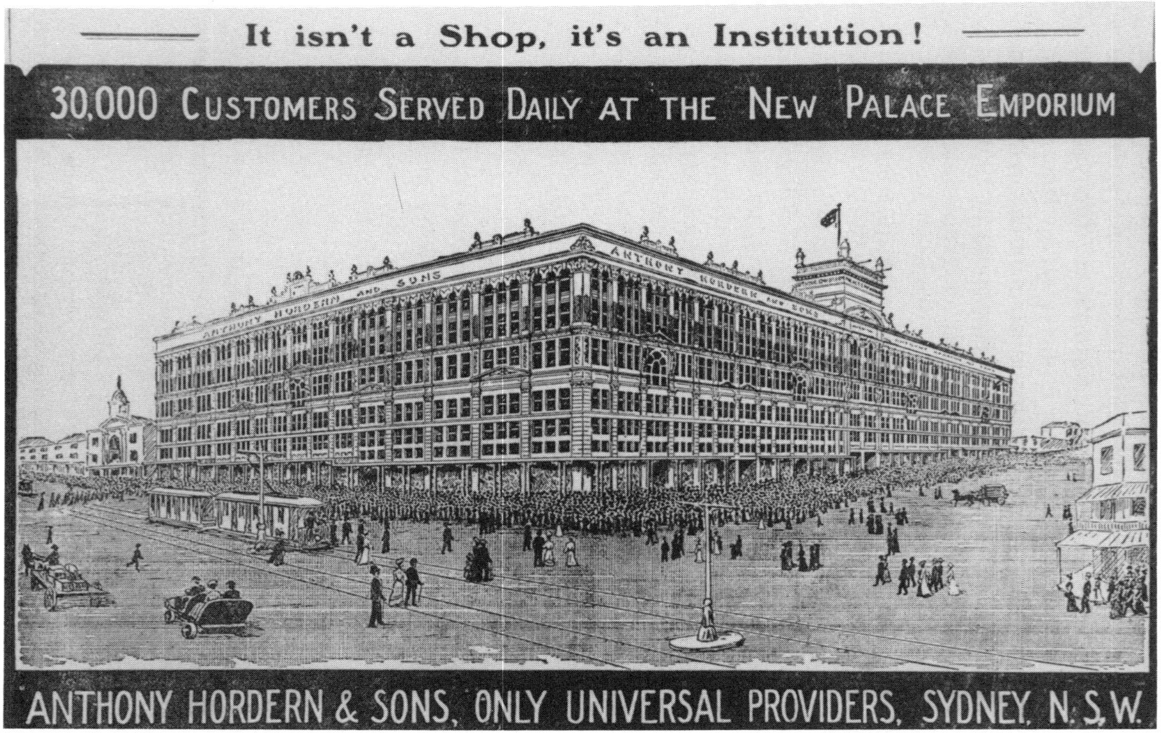

Anthony Hordern & Sons, New Palace Emporium, Sydney, c. 1905. This store covered an entire city block and was reported to be the largest in the southern hemisphere. Trams transported home the Anthony Hordern customer with her shopping. (MITCHELL LIBRARY, STATE LIBRARY OF NEW SOUTH WALES)

interaction. The changes that took place in sales knowledges and practices between the late nineteenth century and 1920, as the following chapters show in more detail, resembled transformations occurring over the same period in codes of courtship.

In this book I use the term 'sex' to denote bodily (but not necessarily biologically determined) differences between women and men. I have also used sex to stand for expressions of heterosexual behaviour. While this appears to conflate two distinct meanings of sex, there are significant conceptual continuities between the two. Sex is both the bodily marker of sexual difference and that set of culturally regulated activities that constitute acceptable forms of interaction between those bodies. Heterosexuality is here broadly defined as a code of conduct governing relations between the sexes and maintaining male dominance, both at the individual and collective level. Sexualisation denotes the cultural process by which objects and activities are invested with unambiguously sexual meanings.

Taking Sydney as representative of similar retailing developments in Australia and elsewhere, this book surveys the major changes in the sexual organisation of the drapery store and the increasing sexualisation of selling as it expanded from an emporium or universal provider in the 1880s into the department store of 1930.[29] Part I sketches the characteristically bourgeois, personalised and domestic sexual arrangements and forms of sexual politics evident within the late nineteenth century emporium. Part II details the development of mass marketing techniques and the sexualisation of selling as retailing was rationalised after the turn of the century. Chapter 2 begins by looking at changes in the class and sexual composition of the mass market for drapery goods and suggests that consumption was well established as a female sphere by the 1920s. Chapter 3 shows how more coherent and explicit sales techniques and knowledges (particularly psychology) and the more effective political organisation of the retail industry in the first three decades of the twentieth century constructed ideas of male and female nature. The inscription of manufactured commodities with sexual meanings and the implications of the sexual organisation of commodities for the sexual division of labour in selling are examined in Chapter 4. Chapter 5 suggests that display spaces—both interiors and window displays—became more definitively sexed and carried more explicit sexual meanings in the period from 1900 to the 1920s.

Part III looks more closely at the crucial years 1915 to 1930, a period in which the sexualisation of selling not only intensified but increasingly standardised and institutionalised notions of masculinity, femininity and heterosexual attractiveness that continue to characterise contemporary relations between the sexes. Chapter 6 assesses retailers' success in attempting to cultivate and then manage women's consumer desires, whether expressed legitimately in shopping or illegitimately in the peculiarly female offence of shoplifting. Women's resistance or manifest opposition to retailers' practices was also evident in various forms of female consumer politics, examined in Chapter 7. Chapter 8 suggests, however, that by the 1920s retailers had created culturally homogeneous and relatively fixed models of the sexually-attractive woman and man through store mannequins, fashion photography, catalogue illustrations and the marketing of beauty products and services. Chapter 9 shows how, after the 1930s, the locus of production of sexual messages shifted from the physical site of the department store to a more amorphous and ubiquitous mass marketing industry.

Part I: 1880–1905

1 Private desires

John L. Hordern opened his drapery business in Sydney's Pitt Street in 1878. Joined by his brothers in 1882, the store rapidly expanded from a one-room shop into one of the largest retail stores in the city. When new and larger premises were opened in 1886, the *Australian Town and Country Journal* described Hordern Brothers' lavish and seductively beautiful interior. 'Silks and satins, velvets and plushes, all in endless variety and almost innumerable colors and hues are here laid bare to tempt and fascinate the aesthetic eye.' Mirrors were lavishly distributed throughout the store. The shopper ascended from the ground floor to the ladies' showroom by stairs bordered with exotic plants, flowers and ferns. Upstairs, millinery was displayed in an 'irresistably attractive way'. The writer wondered 'Where is the lady who could withstand such a temptation to invest in something for nature's adornment?', confident that the reply would be: none.[1]

This brief glimpse inside the doors of one of Sydney's major drapery houses provides a wider window into the world of the big city stores and the ways they were perceived in the late nineteenth century. By the 1880s, the principal drapery businesses were significant urban landmarks and architectural symbols of the growing stability and prosperity of Australian urban culture. They provided visible proof that Sydney had entered an emerging international consumer culture, and was well qualified to join the ranks of the great cities of Europe and North America. This civic pride was evident in a report in the *Sydney Morning Herald* of 20 May 1887 of the progress of four visiting Chinese dignitaries through Sydney's leading factories, warehouses and stores. At Lassetters they were 'astonished' at the lifts, at Farmer's they 'eagerly scanned' the departments, and at David Jones they gave an 'impression of wonderment' and 'greatly admired the dresses for evening wear, and the gold tinsel broche of which some of this kind of apparel is made'. Like other public buildings such as banks, post offices, theatres, railway stations, commercial buildings and town halls, these palaces of consumption were outstanding examples of a monumental and masculine Victorian vision of public progress, wealth and enterprise.

Photographs and drawings of late nineteenth century drapery stores demonstrate how architecture celebrated and legitimated the retail industry in general, and the power and prestige of individual retailers in particular. These retailers were all men, with the exception of Harriette McCathie, who opened a hat shop in 1886 and continued to run the business as a general drapery store until her retirement in 1905.[2] The sheer size of the buildings, particularly as additional storeys were added as business increased and lifts allowed buildings to grow higher, marked the drapery store out from and eventually enabled it to dwarf the smaller specialty shops such as tailors' and millinery establishments. The prominent display of the store name and establishment date was a common and cheap form of advertising which provided customers with reassuring evidence of the company's reliability and longevity. Store architects had to ensure that the building would attract the female shopper. A functional and solid business-like facade that was masculine in appearance was combined with ornate and florid embellishments such as arches and colonnades, decorative windows and floral or leafy brickwork motifs. Among the most prominent of these architectural extravagances were Grace Brothers' clock towers surmounted by large copper globes, and Farmer's Victoria House, which featured a colonnade supported by pillars of white marble with fanlights in the roof, the name of the firm in red and white Worcester tiles, stone carvings decorating the two upper storeys, and a bust of Queen Victoria prominently displayed in an upstairs window.[3] David Jones advertised the Italian Classic style of architecture, four storeys, fine shop windows and elegant iron verandah of its expanded George Street store opened in 1887, and Mark Foy's store opened in 1908 was modelled on the European grandeur and ornate piazza-style Bon Marché store of Paris.[4]

Retailers had a number of ways of enticing customers in to their stores. Advertisements were placed in newspapers, journals and other printed material such as trade directories. Circulars, sale

Farmer & Company, Sydney, c. 1882. Even in the 1880s the major drapery stores dwarfed their smaller competitors and dominated the urban landscape. On the right, in Pitt Street, is the original Victoria House (built 1873), with its distinctive granite colonnade and a bust of Queen Victoria in an upstairs window. The new premises, featuring large plate glass windows, were erected on the corner of Pitt and Market Streets. Many women were brought to shop in the store by private carriage. (MITCHELL LIBRARY, STATE LIBRARY OF NEW SOUTH WALES)

notices and price lists were distributed by the 1880s and 1890s, and posters by the turn of the century. Farmer's and perhaps other drapery stores employed an advertising manager in the 1890s.[5] Sales were held from the 1840s and were common by the 1890s. Women reportedly flocked to the Pitt Street drapery stores at sale time, eagerly seizing on 'the remnants of silk, the odd lengths of ribbon, the chaotic piles of damaged artificial flowers, the showy hats that previous customers have rejected, and all the wreckage and sediment of the season'.[6] These early sales were advertised as festive public events. Francis Foy held 'fairs' that attracted such large crowds of women that the police were reportedly called in to ensure order and protect the plate-glass windows from being smashed.[7]

Other forms of entertainment presented by stores attempting to attract a more refined female clientele reflected private and domestic forms of leisure and recreation popular among the late nineteenth century urban bourgeoisie. Anthony Hordern & Sons staged an exhibition and promenade concert to celebrate the opening of the Palace Emporium in 1881, and a musical conversazione and spring show in 1884. Piano and pianola recitals, such as those given at David Jones and Lowes, would have been popular forms of family entertainment in the drawing rooms of Sydney around the turn of the century.[8]

The most noticeable aspect of the store exterior to the shopper on the street was the show windows. Improvements in glass and lighting technology allowed store windows to become larger and more expansive in the late nineteenth century, and male window dressers were employed from the 1880s. The windows were more cluttered with goods than is usual today. Conservative retailers disapproved of 'the showman propensities of the proprietors of drapery establishments', implying that such retailers were inappropriately attempting to attract a mass, or working-class trade.[9] Some retailers used their windows as stages for animated displays using live performers. These live displays were frequently racist or imperialist in theme. Lowes' menswear store, for example, advertised its 'fast black hats' in 1903 by employing two black men to perform various 'antics' in the window, and Hordern Brothers hired an Irishman to dance a jig on the roof of its Pitt Street awning for an 'All Nations Sale'. Other stunts involved live monkeys and a Sudan veteran flourishing a sword accompanied by the slogan 'Horderns Slash Prices'. All of these displays featured men, suggesting that in this early period it would have been improper to have placed women on public display. The word 'display' was not used in reference to the systematic treatment of goods before the 1890s, and did not become part of common marketing language until World War I.[10]

The typical late nineteenth century shop window contained lengths of dress material, household drapery such as curtains and tablecloths, and streamers of lace and trimmings, displayed higgledy-piggledy on boxes, rods or shelves. Women's dress materials and ready-made articles of clothing were either displayed in lengths or rolls, or draped on headless dressmakers' dummies. Although the sexual character of windows containing dress materials and unmanufactured goods was not particularly marked, nineteenth century retailers rarely placed women's (including household and children's) goods and men's goods in the same window.

This segregation of space was also evident to the shopper when she entered the store. As far as we can tell from the available sources, the typical drapery store customer in the nineteenth century was a middle-class or wealthy woman who spent her days organising her household, arranging her home and taking sole responsibility for the welfare of her husband and children. Urban middle-class and wealthy women began to be seen in public more frequently by the 1880s, leaving their homes to pay formal calls on friends and acquaintances, engage in charity or philanthropic work, or manage domestic affairs including shopping for clothes or household goods.[11] The shopping woman's unpaid labour constituted the essential link between the home and the increasing range of manufactured foods, clothes, household tools and home furnishings which were coming onto the markets of western societies in increasing numbers in the second half of the century.

Shopping also represented a form of female recreation and enjoyment sanctioned by the demands of the private sphere.[12] City dwellers and women living in isolated rural areas looked forward to the rare visit to the city emporiums in which they could find all of their requirements under one roof. Rachel Henning marvelled at the convenience of being able to choose material in the dresses department, have it made up into a fashionable garment in the dressmaking department, and purchase bonnet, mantle, underclothes, carpets and upholstery all at Farmer's drapery store. 'It is a wonderful save of time and trouble', she wrote enthusiastically to her sister in 1875.[13] A visit to one of the city drapery houses such as David Jones or Hordern Brothers which catered to the 'carriage trade' during the respectable shopping hours between mid-morning and 5 or 6 p.m. represented both work and pleasure for the middle-class female shopper. David Jones was anxious to employ saleswomen who had the required refinement and style to serve the ladies of Sydney's ruling class such as Mrs Darley, Lady Carrington and Lady Jersey. Working-class women may also have visited the big stores if they were dressmakers, to buy an occasional inexpensive article, or simply to look around and enjoy the luxurious surroundings.

Arriving at the main entrance of her preferred drapery establishment, the female shopper would alight from her carriage to be greeted by a shopwalker, formally dressed in morning suit, who would courteously ask her which departments she would like to visit. The shopwalker would then usher the customer into the store and personally escort her to her chosen department, where he would make sure she was comfortably seated at the counter and call on a saleswoman to attend to her. As the shopwalker was charged with the job of making sure that the customer received all the attention, service and satisfaction she required, he was primarily responsible for disciplining and monitoring the conduct of shop assistants, many of whom were, by the late nineteenth century, female. He commanded assistants to serve customers, reprimanded them for suspected idleness, made sure they did their job properly, and exacted fines and punishments for lateness or other lapses in conduct. Eugenie McNeil recalled 'a shopwalker in frock coat and striped trousers would hurry forward with chairs, to see if we were receiving every courtesy and to reprimand the girl if her attention happened to wander for a moment'.[14] The shopwalker was in ultimate charge of his department or departments, and therefore frequently responsible for hiring and firing staff. The customer may have enjoyed the courtly and deferential attention paid to her by the gentlemanly shopwalker, but many female shop assistants had good reason to fear and dislike this patriarchal embodiment of proprietorial authority.

Seated on her side of the counter, the shopper might ask the assistant to show her a range of coloured ribbons, try on gloves of different sizes or hats of different styles, match buttons or sewing silks to fabric, or unroll for her inspection a selection of velvets or calicos. The skills expected of the male draper's assistant of the 1880s included the arrangement of stock and showing the contents of shelves, drawers and boxes, handling haberdashery, measuring, and 'rolling and blocking' dress materials, and tying parcels.[15] Women shop assistants would have carried out similar tasks, with the exception of the handling of heavy bolts of material typically required in the manchester or dresses departments. Once the customer was satisfied with her choice, the assistant would wrap the goods into a parcel, complete a sales docket and call for a 'cash boy'. Some stores used a hollow ball and track system and, later, pneumatic tube cash-delivery systems, to take the docket and money to a central cash desk. The cashier would register the sale and return the change to the customer. As a standard service to female customers for whom it would have been most unladylike to emerge from the store carrying an armful of heavy goods, most stores offered a parcel collection and home-delivery service.

The male draper's assistant found in the mid-nineteenth century drapery store was, by the 1890s, being joined by the female shop assistant. The nineteenth-century drapery house was a paternalistic institution in which the proprietor exerted direct and generally authoritarian control over his workers in much the same way as the Victorian father ruled over his wife and children. The store was viewed as a large family in which male and female employees were expected to demonstrate filial duty and loyalty to the head of the firm, who would reciprocate by personally guaranteeing their security and welfare. The proprietor would either personally, or through his shopwalker or departmental head reward or punish his employees at his discretion. Female employees, especially dressmakers, milliners or other skilled workers who were in considerable demand in late nineteenth-century Australia, frequently resisted this paternal authority by renegotiating the terms of their contract, refusing to cooperate, or simply resigning.[16]

Interactions between customer and sales assistant were also shaped by the sometimes dangerous intimacy characteristic of domestic sexual and class relations. The customer was, like the mistress of the household, in a commanding position, with license to treat the person on the other side of the counter as a servant employed to meet her wishes and treat her with respect and deference. Susan Porter Benson suggests in *Counter Cultures* that a considerable degree of class antagonism was manifest over the counter between the middle-class customer on one side and the working-class salesgirl on the other. Sexual tension was also evident in these often personalised sales transactions. Women customers may have viewed well-dressed and attractive female shop assistants, particularly those in charge of the fashion departments such as millinery and costumes, as intimidating role models and rivals in the process of constructing a feminine sexual identity.[17]

Sales transactions between female customers and male assistants were of a more potentially flirtatious nature. Male assistants were instructed by their employers to treat women customers as if they were courting them: to be deferential but not servile, pleasant and knowledgeable but not patronising, to flatter them within moderation, and above all to treat them with gentleness and a 'manly civility'. One English advice text of 1878 listed the qualities considered necessary in the male draper's assistant. He must demonstrate courtesy, cleanliness, punctuality, honesty and duty to God. The successful draper's assistant avoided the temptation to be idle, thoughtless or vicious, and should amuse himself in athletic sports rather than resort to the bar or the taproom.[18] In the tailoring, glove or shoe departments, male employees discretely, and within the bounds of propriety, verbally referred to and made contact with women's bodies. We do not know how women responded to the physical intimacy demanded by this kind of shopping: like other forms of heterosexual interactions, it could equally have been the source of pleasure or discomfort.

The female shop assistant was, like the barmaid, represented in contemporary writing, drawings and cartoons as an object of glamour and male fantasy. Beatrix Tracy was told by the proprietor of a confectionery business that he was looking for striking girls, 'the sort a man thinks about after he goes out'. An illustration of 'A Typical Saleswoman Off Duty' in the *Woman's Budget* of 1908 showed her bare shouldered, gazing seductively at the camera to give her likeness to her 'Best Boy', suggesting the ways in which selling and desire were intermingled in the figure of the shop girl. Separated from the public by the shop counter, she embodied a distant and unobtainable form of male sexual pleasure which could legitimately be experienced simply by looking, listening or speaking.[19] Correspondence concerning the appointment of senior personnel in the David Jones Archives confirms the impression that retailers preferred saleswomen with an attractive and stylish appearance.

Just as the nineteenth-century customer would have been assured of attentive and personal service in her chosen emporium, the goods which she bought were frequently individually tailored to meet her private desires. Drapery stores tended to stock goods of a sufficient variety to accommodate the requirements of the specialty customer by ordering small numbers of a wide range of lines. Many of these goods were sold in their unmanufactured state: sheets, for example, would be made up by a woman at home from sheeting material, or a hat created from a frame and trimmings purchased from the drapery store. A wide range of manufactured goods such as boots and shoes, household utensils and fancy goods, and some ready-made clothing such as blouses, skirts, men's suits and shirts, were carefully selected to make sure that every taste and size was catered for. Clothing that was 'made-to-order' that is, made in a store's manufacturing workroom from measurements provided by the customer—ensured at least some degree of fit with individual bodies and desires.

As efficient millinery and dressmaking departments were crucial to the success and reputation of the high-class drapery business, dressmakers, milliners and tailors were key personnel in the nineteenth-century emporium, commanding relatively high salaries and status. They and their workers were employed in the manufacture—largely by hand, although power-driven sewing machines were commonly used for routine stitching by the 1890s—of exclusive and personally fitted garments of special design. Despite the use of standard patterns, fashion plates and fabric types, each woman could order a new spring hat or a ball gown, confident in the knowledge that her model was personalised. The wealthy woman's pleasure in the garments sold 'upstairs' in the drapery store were, however, achieved at the expense of the health and well-being of many hundreds of sewing women working away in less pleasant conditions 'downstairs' in the store's workrooms. An estimated 1300 workers, 900 of them female, were employed in the tailoring workrooms of Sydney's retail establishments in 1891.[20]

A visit to the store's dressmaker or milliner was a specifically feminine pursuit. It was a social event as well as an opportunity to exchange fashion knowledge and exercise consumer skills in the selection of styles, colours, fabrics and trimmings. These feminine interactions took place in salons designed to make the customer feel as comfortable and relaxed as she would be in her own home. One well-known dressmaker was reported to have presided over a department that was 'more of a reception room than a salon', and another offered a personal service to her favoured country clients by engaging domestic servants on their behalf.[21] The nineteenth-century drapery store in some ways, therefore, continued an older private tradition of clothing manufacture used by the wealthy, in which dressmakers made personal visits to

COSTUME DEPARTMENT.

Costume Department, David Jones, George Street, Sydney, 1887. The ladies' showroom was traditionally the most lavishly decorated sales area. While consulting the head of the showroom, always dressed in black, the wealthy women who patronised David Jones enjoyed floral carpets, pot plants, framed pictures and comfortable seats. Display dummies were headless until the 1910s. (DAVID JONES LTD, A SOUVENIR, 1887. DAVID JONES (AUSTRALIA) PTY LTD)

women in the comfort and convenience of their own homes. Retailers attracted custom by offering lady customers retiring rooms and boudoir retreats equipped with various toilet requisites designed to refresh them after a day's travelling and shopping exertions.

If the dressmaking room was the boudoir of the drapery store, its public spaces and selling departments were the drawing room or front parlour. The 'riotously overdecorated' and overcrowded late-Victorian parlour was, as Karen Halttunen has shown, believed to be the most important room of the house because of its capacity to communicate the occupant's moral and genteel character to the outside world.[22] Like many domestic interiors, the typical drapery store was divided into departments trimmed with dark polished wood and linked by a series of archways, decorative ceilings and cornices, elegant gaslight fittings, wooden counters and shelves that had to be constantly dusted and polished, and a

TAILORING DEPARTMENT.

Tailoring Department. In contrast to the women's costume department, this is a more sparsely decorated and clearly masculine space. The pictures on the wall provide models of acceptable male body display.
(DAVID JONES LTD, A SOUVENIR, 1887. DAVID JONES (AUSTRALIA) PTY LTD)

few strategically placed glass cabinets for the display of treasured commodities. A trade journal suggested that a woman would look for the same qualities in a draper's shop as she would in her home: 'cleanliness, neatness of arrangement, and artistic display of their goods'.[23] Many of the domestic accessories considered appropriate to the well-dressed parlour were common features of drapery store interior decoration: ferns and large pot-plants in brass planters and arranged on cane plant stands, carpets with floral designs, horsehair sofas and cane chairs, ornate mirrors, decorative pelmets and lace curtains, occasional tables draped with soft coverings, framed prints on the walls. Premium fashion goods were displayed on dummies, in large glass casements, or arranged on small tables which allowed the customer to move freely around, touch and inspect from all angles any article that appealed to her.

The men's departments, by contrast, presented a restrained masculinity. David Jones' tailoring department lacked the carpeted floor, decorative ceilings, glass cabinets, storage fixtures and display models characteristic of the store's costume department. Instead, the space was filled with bolts and drapes of material,

THE MILLINERY DEPARTMENT.

Millinery Department, David Jones, George Street, Sydney, 1887. Millinery was a fashionable and highly profitable drapery store commodity. Here it is temptingly displayed in a parlour-like environment which encouraged women to walk around, touch and try on the hats. (DAVID JONES LTD, A SOUVENIR, 1887. DAVID JONES (AUSTRALIA) PTY LTD)

storage boxes and dark wooden cabinets. Where ladies' gowns and millinery resembled a 'riot of hothouse blooms', the men's hat department looked more like the sparse and functional space of a public bar.[24] Other departments such as manchester and fancy goods were decorated somewhere in between these masculine and feminine extremes: not as plush as the showroom, but less austere than the men's departments. The display of drapery goods such as lace, ribbons and sheetings in the manner of washing on a line added a domestic touch to the manchester and haberdashery counters.

These gendered spaces provided the backdrop to a drama involving male and female characters with different, sometimes conflicting roles in the drama of consumption. Relations between men and women within the drapery store both reflected and contributed to late nineteenth century formulations of masculinity, femininity and domesticity. Women customers were constructed in much of the early retail trade literature as irrational, unpredict-

THE MEN'S HAT DEPARTMENT.

Men's Hat Department. Although serving a similar function to millinery, men's hats were presented in a more utilitarian fashion. Men were assisted to select a hat as quickly and effectively as possible. The male customers are seated at the counter much as men lined up at a public bar. (DAVID JONES LTD, *A SOUVENIR*, 1887. DAVID JONES (AUSTRALIA) PTY LTD)

able and easily led into temptation. The common belief that women's susceptibility to the 'love of finery' enticed them into the ranks of fallen women permeated nineteenth-century fiction and medical and political debates surrounding prostitution. Criminal discourse after the turn of the century also constructed adult women as lascivious, easily tempted and complicit in men's seduction.[25]

Drawing on popular medical theories of women's nature, the trade paper the *Draper and Warehouseman* argued that women (and young people) were attracted to the city by their highly-strung, nervous temperaments, fits of depression, craving for constant change, and the excitement and bustle of the shopping crowds. Women shopped around because 'the chance of getting a bargain appeals irresistably to the female mind'. Women, agreed the *Australian Storekeepers' Journal* confidently in 1900, were 'unable to resist the temptation' of tables strewn with delicate dress materials and snow-white damasks. Pretty and artistic things had a charm for women who would admire, then want to possess them. They simply 'follow like sheep in the path marked out for them by the softgoods merchant'.[26]

The language of temptation permeated publicity writing for the big stores from the 1880s. Silks and satins tempted ladies at Hordern Brothers in 1886; a 'tempting profusion' of goods was displayed in Lassetters' store in 1894; and Anthony Hordern & Sons' Palace Emporium was 'a veritable Garden of Eden' in 1907.[27] A writer for *Australia* magazine attempted to capture the allure of this fairyland:

> Here a hint of delicate audacity; there a shimmering seductiveness; yonder a creation highly ornate; and everywhere pervading an all-absorbing, bewildering, fascinating atmosphere of artistic conceptions that suddenly make one feel old-fashioned, dissatisfied, and dowdy, and out-of-date—and—and—and—that a new hat is an absolute necessity.[28]

The central focus of the emporium was the creation and embodiment in 'woman' of consumer desire. The late nineteenth-century belief in woman's childish and 'natural' propensity to submit to momentary temptation made her the automatic target of retailers' attempts to cultivate consumer desire.

In addition to their susceptibility to suggestion and inability to make rational choices, women customers were criticised as thoughtless, difficult and unethical. The *Australian Storekeepers' Journal* advised its readers on 'The Best Way to Handle a "Cranky" Shopper', the *Draper* was critical of women known as Tabbies who never knew what they wanted except to cause trouble, and J.W. Hayes reprimanded the thoughtlessness of women with the reprehensible habit of 'turning over a draper's stock merely for their own amusement'.[29] Women were accused of depressing the wages of shop workers by bargaining with retailers, keeping shops open late at night and a 'careless neglect or indifference' towards the sweated worker.[30] The *Australian Worker's* misogyny emerged clearly in this description of women shoppers in 1906:

> Women sweating, struggling, swarming round the damaged gloves; snarling, gesticulating over the eighteen-penny muslins. Scratch a bargain-hunter and you get a Tartar every time . . . Their fat, bulging, gloating eyes are twinkling with greed. Their hands lovingly fondle the prizes they are losing their self-respect

> to win. Never once do they pause to realize that someone must go short that their insatiable greed may be satisfied.[31]

Conflict between retailers and women customers is evident in store correspondence detailing customers who left their accounts unpaid, bought large amounts of goods on their husband's or father's account without their permission, or presented dishonoured cheques.

Retailers were also sorely tried by women who exploited the approbation system. They complained that a cloak given to a potential customer on approval would be returned to the shop the next day with a lace handerchief and a theatre ticket in the pocket, indicating that it had been 'borrowed' free of charge for a special occasion.[32] Shoplifting represented the most vexatious form of this recalcitrant female consumer behaviour. One of the earliest reported cases was that of a mother and daughter team who stole drapery goods using a special pocket in their dresses in 1893. Despite persistent grumbles about the extent of shoplifting in drapery trade journals from the 1890s, retailers had no systematic or effective means of controlling customer theft. Some of the big stores employed a detective by 1900, but generally customer monitoring was left to busy shop assistants, shopwalkers or the cashiers in their elevated cash desks.[33]

Retail proprietors' and managers' ambivalent relationship with their female customers reflected wider tensions in late nineteenth-century masculinity. Social custom demanded that the man must take the lead in courtship by expressing his interest, devising trysts and pursuing his beloved. Yet the middle-class man was also expected to control his bestial nature and reign in his passions. The ideal man was therefore 'a contradiction in terms': he must be aggressive, masterful, and self-assured; but also deferential, gentle and courteous.[34] His position was similar to that of the retailer who knew that to survive economically he must be both masterful and obliging. Retailers could not afford to lose women's custom. Like the courting male described in one marriage manual of the 1890s, the retailer was haunted by the fear of losing his mate before consummation and therefore must be 'humble and pliable'.[35]

Despite their surface chivalry, retailers were secure in the knowledge of their superiority over the weaker sex. The incomprehensible nature of the female shopper's mind was the subject of male gossip within the retail industry. One partner of David Jones wrote to another:

> . . . the Millinery productions of recent seasons are almost outside the comprehension of the masculine mind—they are fantastic vagaries, grotesque and highly fanciful elegancies, with no standard of fashion, style or construction—it is only the feminine mind which can rise to such lofty heights of beauty and nothingness.[36]

Trade experts considered that, in contrast to women, men were stable, regular and predictable customers who preferred to shop at the same place. Rather than waste time inspecting and comparing goods, men typically decided outside the store exactly what they wanted, dashed in, bought it, and rushed out again.[37] Women were critical of men's inability to shop. As one journal put it: 'Men take what is given them regardless if it is really what they want; pay what is asked for it, without the least consideration as to its actual worth; and as to counting their change, they would think that unmanly in the extreme.'[38] Shopping was, by the turn of the century, clearly defined as a female activity associated with the private sphere and hence socially devalued.

These different characterisations ascribed to men and women were given graphic form in the store catalogues of the late nineteenth and early twentieth century. Widely distributed in both the city and in regions otherwise remote from sources of fashion information from the late 1880s, mail-order catalogues advertised and gave visual form to the retail industry's construction of 'man' and 'woman'. The dominant female form that found its ideal expression in the catalogues until the mid-1910s was the voluptuous and buxom matron. Women's bodies were presented as an S-shape in which corsetting pushed the top part of the torso forward and the bottom part back. This unstable and asymmetrical female body, propped up with the aid of a parasol or the back of a chair, lacked balance and created an illusion of dependence. Catalogue men, by contrast, gave an impression of balance, body symmetry and reliability. Men's bodies were presented as rectangular and upright, feet placed solidly apart, a walking cane providing additional security.

The precarious tilt of the women's bodies was heightened by the placing of both feet close together. Arms and hands were arranged decoratively in balletic poses and either pointed outwards in a gesture of appeal, or directed narcissistic attention to the woman's own clothing, hair, body contours or accessories. Women clasped the symbols of femininity: necklaces, scarves, handkerchieves, parasols, fans, flowers and mirrors. Their smiles were enigmatic: simultaneously demure and coquettish. Despite the standard posture, women's faces exhibited a degree of individual characterisation. Catalogue artists used the fashion line drawing to show a variety of ages, facial types, features, and hairstyles. This attempt to show bodily diversity and individuality, consistent with the emphasis on tailor-made and personally-fitted clothing, suggests that nineteenth-century consumption embodied a set of private and individual desires.

These desires were evident particularly in the discourses of fashion.[39] To retailers, fashion represented increased saleability and a high rate of gross profits. John McDowell of McDowell and Hughes, for example, believed that fashion goods virtually sold themselves. Fashions in his store in the early years of the twentieth century changed twice a year in all departments, but especially in the women's sections of dresses, millinery and mantles. A subtle change in colour from, say, a wine shade close to purple in one season to a wine shade closer to red in the following season enabled the retailer to charge women higher prices for the more fashionable fabric.[40] The expansion of the retail industry in the second half of the nineteenth century, and the popularity of trade journals after the turn of the century formalised and gave greater visibility to the view of fashion as a trivial and essentially feminine pursuit.

Women's periodicals of the period were equally concerned with fashion, although they reveal a greater diversity of viewpoints which frequently conflicted with retailers' interpretation of fashion as profit. Dress held a particularly significant place in women's private pleasures. Beatrix Tracy compared women's love of fashionable drapery goods with men's potentially more damaging leisure activities: 'Drapery is a feminine luxury, almost exclusively. It is the object on which we spend our drink-money, our tobacco-cash—it is our means of intoxication, of forgetfulness, or contentment . . . The dress counter is our bar.'[41]

The fashionable garments women purchased from the drapery emporium held a variety of meanings. For many shoppers, fashionable goods literally constituted the material with which they could enhance their personal attractiveness, physical identity and sexual selves. The purchase of a fashionable hat or dress occupied a central place in what Valerie Steele has described as the individual's search for the ideal self, a self defined by socially-constructed notions of heterosexual attractiveness and erotic appeal.[42]

While women clearly derived considerable personal pleasure from buying fashionable drapery goods, they were not necessarily the easily tempted and slavish followers of fashion that retailers imagined them to be. The rise of the women's rights movement and campaigns for female suffrage lent a critical flavour to Australian women's responses to fashion in the late nineteenth century. Women active in the women's movement and those who contributed to the growing number of women's journals from the 1890s expressed a distinctively female rationale for buying beautiful clothes and furnishings for the home. It was important, argued *Happy Homes*, for women to demonstrate neatness, order and pride in their dress at home in order to maintain self-respect and fulfil their duty to 'beautify, to ornament the world'. Young women should, consequently, study seriously the rules of colour and ornament and the art of being well-dressed.[43]

Dress was seen by some women as an explicitly political form of female resistance to the sexual order. Dress could be empowering for women, a potent weapon in the fight for women's rights.[44] Feminism and the rational dress movement were natural allies, as much of Louisa Lawson's writings in the *Dawn* between 1888 and 1895 suggest. Lawson believed that too much female clothing was extravagant, restrictive, and over-embellished with frills and tucks. Critical of 'the masses of lace, feathers, frippery, and even parts of deceased fowls, that partly cover, or are skewered to the many female heads' sporting fashionable millinery, Lawson advocated good quality, plain and untrimmed bonnets. Rather than buy a new hat each season, Lawson advised her readers to refurbish last year's old straw hat by buying ready-made trimmings such as wired bows. A clever woman could use remnants, fresh flowers and her own dressmaking skills to make a pretty dress.[45] Contributors to the *Woman's Voice* argued in 1894 and 1895 that women should unite to resist the tyranny of ornament and embellishment and the evil of extravagance in dress. Instead, women should choose clothing that was well cut and made of good quality material.[46] By sewing, improvising, matching and making-do, women effectively subverted retailers' attempts to sell them costly fashion goods while simultaneously creating highly-individualised garments that reflected their personality and skills.

In the course of their project of redefining ethical consumer behaviour, feminist adherents of the rational dress movement came into direct contact with retailers. The retail trade papers were well aware of this 'revolution in ladies' dress' and advised drapery proprietors to capitalise, for example, on the demand for specialised bicycling clothes. Although concern was expressed in some articles that the New Woman and her claims for equality and preference for male attire represented a disturbing deviation from desirable models of womanhood, in general retailers saw the fashion for rational dress as a profitable development.[47] Many women themselves encouraged their sisters to patronise the drapery emporium, but to exercise discretion. Louisa Lawson helpfully informed correspondent 'Anti-Corset' that pure wool combinations and the Neglige Corset could be purchased from Messrs David Jones & Co.

Some feminists, while they condemned the frivolous excesses of fashion, gently criticised rational dressers and bluestockings for neglecting the aesthetics of dress in their search for a practical and ethical wardrobe. The New Woman was certainly clever and independent, but her cleverness could not excuse her from being 'unkempt, untidy or unbecoming'. American historian William Leach argues that the emerging culture of consumption exemplified in the department store provided emancipation and a new world of individual expression for women in which feminism merged with a cosmopolitan, heterogeneous culture of consumption.[48] The statements of Australian women's rights advocates on dress, however, represented a distinctly feminist politics of consumption. Women claimed for themselves the private pleasures of shopping, while arguing that dress and fashion could serve explicitly political purposes in giving the New Woman credibility and attractiveness.

Some feminists explicitly charged men with reaping the profits from women's desire for fashionable clothing:

> . . . we wear cashmere or serge, or we are puffed up or flattened as it suits the maker of fabrics and Worth to decide. Isn't it comical? Hundreds of women getting into this, or that, or the other

> extraordinary rig, in order that men may grow rich by trading on their love of novelty.[49]

Feminists such as Rose Scott supported members of the anti-plumage movement in their attempts to stop the killing and torturing of birds and animals whose feathers and skins were used in women's fashionable clothing. They pointed out, however, that men controlled the fashion and retail industry. Too often women were blamed for the slaughter, rather than 'the men who set the fashions [and] displayed the tempting feathers in shops'. The women's periodical the *Wardrobe* was critical of newspaper advertisements which attempted to seduce women into buying clothes which they could not afford.[50]

Feminists were critical, too, of retailers' treatment of their female employees. The younger and less skilled of the shop assistants had little bargaining power with which to improve the conditions of a poorly-paid job that demanded that they be on their feet and remain courteous to customers in hot and stuffy buildings well into the night. The wages, hours and working conditions of saleswomen were matters of considerable concern to a number of female reformers from the 1890s. The first female inspectors appointed under the New South Wales Factories and Shops Act of 1896 and members of the early closing movement of the 1890s attempted to end the sweated labour and exploitation of female shop assistants. In pressing for early closing legislation (passed in New South Wales in 1899) and openly criticising male employers in the retail industry, women like Annie Duncan and Rose Scott placed themselves in explicit opposition to the masculinist and paternalist work culture of the drapery store.[51]

Such feminists frequently likened shop employment to a form of white slavery, a phrase strategically used by a variety of concerned individuals and organisations in the nineteenth century to denote the seriousness of the female shop assistant's situation. The white slavery rhetoric had been used by English feminists and supporters since at least the 1820s to describe the general sexual subjugation of women to men and, after 1885, when W.T. Stead published the *Maiden Tribute to Modern Babylon*, more particularly to the traffic in young girls abducted and coerced into prostitution. The early closing movement's adoption of the white slavery metaphor, current among Australian groups involved in campaigns to eradicate or control prostitution in the late nineteenth century, suggests that its members identified women shop assistants' exploitation as sexual as well as economic. Like the innocent girls who were supposedly bought and sold in the white slave trade, women employed in shops were assumed to be in moral danger. An article on early closing by British reformer Margaret Irwin, quoted in the *Woman's Voice* in 1895, concluded:

> We cannot wonder that some of the weaker [shop girls], girls whose whole life is one long despairing struggle with weariness and poverty, should be tempted by the galling spectacle of their sisters attired in silk, bedecked with jewellery, and faring sumptuously, to make a fatal plunge into the social maelstrom.[52]

Retailers' preference for attractive female shop assistants also suggests the sexual politics of shop employment. Rose Scott criticised retailers not only for keeping assistants on their feet late into the night, but for employing girls for their 'Good Looks, merely to add to the other shop decorations'.[53]

The shopwalker's masculine authority over younger, female subordinates contributed to the sexualisation of power relations between male store management and female workers. Annie Duncan drew attention to the intimidation suffered by tired saleswomen who would never dare to sit down in the 'awful presence of the shopwalker'; a saleswoman referred more critically to him in the *Australian Worker* as a 'savage monarch' who bullied, abused and insulted saleswomen; and, in a speech on early closing, Scott expressed sympathy for saleswomen 'with sometimes insulting and brutal men as task Masters'.[54] The language used by Scott and her contemporaries hints at the possibility that shopwalkers used their power to harass and extract sexual pleasures from their interactions with the saleswomen in their charge. Relations between the shopwalker and female customers were also sexualised. On witnessing the shopwalker's 'detestable' persuasive sales techniques directed at women who found it hard to resist, Beatrix Tracy concluded that 'shopwalkers combined the morals of the magsman [storyteller] with the manners of a policeman'.[55] In targeting men and masculinist forms of behaviour, rather than the class 'employers', feminism made a distinctive contribution to the early closing movement of the 1890s.

The sexual politics revealed in feminist interventions into retailing in the late nineteenth century suggests that women wanted to incorporate a distinctively female sensitivity to sexual ethics and morality into the emerging culture of consumption. They argued for more rational, economical and ethical forms of dress that enhanced women's claims for equality with men. Some directly challenged a masculinist sexual culture which sanctioned men's right of access to the young women in their charge. But few wished to deny their sisters the aesthetic satisfactions and private pleasures of consumption.

Before the first decade of the twentieth century, the drapery store catered to and managed individual desires. Because women shopped, and because women were believed to be irrational and infinitely temptable, these consumer desires were viewed in practice as essentially female desires. Although in polite society, sex and sexual matters were rarely spoken of outside (perhaps even within) marriage, the sexual relations typical of family, marital and non-marital interactions between men and women were clearly reflected and created in the public world of the late nineteenth century drapery store. Retailers courted their female customers with the same ambivalent mix of deference and superiority, and with the same ritualised set of heterosocial conventions that governed male–female relations outside the store. The sexual forms of interaction, display and enticement they initiated were couched in the language of respectability and domesticity deemed appropriate for a limited and predominantly bourgeois female market. The efforts of retail organisations, advertisers and marketing experts to cultivate a mass market in Australia after the turn of the century brought sex and sexual difference out from the shadows and into popular discourse.

Part II: 1900–1930

2 Sex, class and the mass market

The growth of some of Sydney's small drapery shops into the monumental department stores of the 1920s marked a shift from local retailing to mass marketing. Mass marketing was not a natural response to rising levels of working- and middle-class demand, as some historians have implied, but a self-conscious and active process engineered by retailers and other men of capital and business expertise.[1] After about 1900, successful retailers effectively capitalised on and helped shape the changing character and spending capacity of the Australian consumer population. Economic historians have tended to represent the consumer who participated in this twentieth-century marketing revolution as a male wage-earner. Historians of the department store, meanwhile, have stressed the middle classness of its customers. A closer look at the history of women and the family in the period between 1900 and 1930 suggests that these assumptions need scrutiny. This chapter looks at the sex and class characteristics of those who patronised the big stores as they grew into dominant institutions of mass marketing.

It is difficult to state confidently who shopped in the big stores. Retailers of this period did not keep detailed profiles of their customers, and market research did not begin to provide some of the answers until after World War II. Estimating changes in the distribution of disposable income is also hazardous.[2] As Jean Baudrillard cautions, there is no universal or material basis of human need: all cultures socially construct notions of what are considered to be 'essential' food, clothing or shelter requirements.[3] Fashionable drapery goods were considered by some (perhaps many men) to be luxuries, but viewed by others (mostly women) as necessities. Individuals of different sexes, classes, races and ethnic groups had different ideas of what constituted a frivolous indulgence and what was essential to maintain a respectable appearance and a reasonable family standard of living.

There was nevertheless a material basis to the rapidly expanding sales of drapery goods. A customer needed to have the money—either her own or that of her husband or father—with which to buy a shirt, a pair of hose or a roll of linoleum. Her income, or that portion of her husband's income over which she had control, determined the quality and quantity of the goods she bought. To find out who shopped, then, we need to know who had the capacity, motivation and opportunity to spend, and who was expected to do the spending.

Whether married or single, widowed or separated (or deserted), women as a sex have historically had less money at their disposal than men. Unless they were fortunate enough to have an independent income, or took on part-time income-producing work as laundresses, seamstresses or boarding-housekeepers, married women were largely dependent for spending money on the goodwill of their husbands. Working women's wages were maintained in this period consistently and deliberately at approximately half the level of men's on the erroneous assumption that they had no dependents and were supported financially first by their fathers and eventually by their husbands.

Despite these persistent inequalities, a gradual improvement in women's economic status from the late nineteenth century made it increasingly likely that women would have money to spend in the big stores. Under the Married Women's Property Acts passed in New South Wales in 1879 and 1893, property such as earnings, investments, savings and real estate was declared to be the wife's separate estate as a matter of law.[4] Such measures clearly benefited only those women who had property to claim as their own in the first place, and did not necessarily give them more immediate spending power. Nevertheless the Acts were significant legislative markers of a growing recognition of women's economic rights within marriage.

Working-class married women almost certainly benefited from a general rise in the standard of living between 1880 and 1914. With the exception of the 1890s depression, Australian wage-earners (more than three-quarters of them men) enjoyed relatively high levels of expendable income relative to prices, with wage rates in

New South Wales and Victoria rising faster than prices between 1909 and 1913.[5] If few families gave savings and home ownership a high priority before 1914, as one historian suggests, much of this income would have been available for immediate consumption.[6] Spending in the big stores appears to have increased significantly in the first decade of the twentieth century. Employees of some of Sydney's largest retail establishments told the Royal Commission into the Alleged Shortage of Labour that there had been a general rise in prosperity in the years preceding 1911. The Commonwealth *Labour Report* of 1912 also recorded increased levels of consumption since 1903, particularly in 'luxury' commodities. High prices after 1914 temporarily increased the cost of living, but conditions for wage-earners again improved in the 1920s. The relative cost of living, expressed as a proportion of the average weekly adult male wage, declined from 128 per cent in 1914 to 100 per cent in 1927.[7]

Increases in men's wages, of course, did not necessarily flow on to their wives. But because women were in charge of managing household expenditure, the escape from poverty and larger housekeeping allowances would have made their lives as consumers considerably easier. Married women in the 1920s probably had more household income to spend in the big stores than those shopping in the 1890s. Apart from the period of high prices around World War I, average daily expenditure per person on clothing and drapery goods increased from 15.3 per cent in 1900 to 23 per cent by 1920.[8]

Married women of the 1920s may have had more housekeeping money at their disposal than their sisters had had fifty years before, but did not necessarily have complete freedom to buy as they pleased, or to buy goods for their own pleasure. Despite the tempting displays created by retailers, there were strong social and economic disincentives for married women to pursue personal needs and desires. Only if she had an allowance to spend purely on herself could a woman buy a fashionable hat or a new spring costume with a clear conscience. The right of a married woman to her own allowance was a matter of some debate after the turn of the century, suggesting that men were being placed under pressure to give their wives more money to spend on themselves. Retailers, not surprisingly, strongly supported a woman's right to a personal allowance on the assumption that most of it would be spent on the highly profitable fashion articles of personal and home adornment they were trying to sell.

An editorial on the subject in Mark Foy's magazine-style catalogue, the *Magnet*, suggested that the 'unrest of women' evident in 1910, was because for so long 'their lords and masters denied them the privilege of even a certain amount of financial independence'. The refusal of such 'miserably mean men' to give their wives an allowance not only created marital unhappiness but, according to one woman, encouraged women to run into debt. 'What is more humiliating and undignified than for a woman to be compelled, as it were, to ask her husband for a few shillings to buy some new handkerchiefs, a new veil, a pair of gloves, or it may be some underclothing.'[9] This woman argued for an allowance on the grounds of both economic independence and sexual propriety: men, she suggested, had no right to control a woman's purchase of intimate feminine articles of clothing.

A wife's access to her husband's income was also publicly questioned in several London court cases reported in the *Journal of the Retail Traders' Association of New South Wales* in July 1922. The judge in one case upheld the husband's right to restrict his wife's expenditure; in the other the judge ruled that 'a wife living with her husband as manager of his household has presumptive right to pledge his credit for what were called necessaries'. Such necessaries might include, according to the judge's definition, an evening dress. Retailers were likely to have been pleased with the judicial sanction given wives' entitlement to claim expenses from their husbands for the purchase of an evening dress.

The increased tendency towards smaller family size in the early twentieth century facilitated consumer spending. Australian women, in common with women in most western societies since 1870, appear to have used the arguments of voluntary motherhood and various means of contraception and fertility control (babyfarming, infanticide, desertion, adoption and abortion) to reduce the number of children they reared during their reproductive lives. Married women born in the years 1841–46 endured an average of 6.8 births during their lifetime. This declined to 4.2 births for women born 1871–76, and 2.6 births for women born 1903–08.[10] In releasing large numbers of women from the extreme physical, emotional and economic burdens of motherhood, this dramatic decline in family size had a major impact on women's options and life choices.

The fewer children a woman had, the greater the improvement in her own and her family's standard of living. Women and their husbands appear to have increasingly made the decision that the pleasures of consumerism and the comforts of a smaller but better-off family were preferable to the physical dangers and impoverishment of unregulated motherhood. They made that decision in the face of extreme male hostility when fears of race suicide were at their height in the late nineteenth and early twentieth centuries. The New South Wales Royal Commission on the Decline of the Birthrate included among its findings in 1904 that women's increasing 'love of luxury and of social pleasures' had contributed to their reluctance to bear children. By the 1920s, however, women appear to have convinced some male officials of the negative social and economic effects of large families. Referring to the 61 per cent increase in the cost of living between 1914 and 1920, Commissioner A.B. Piddington concluded that families with more than one child had been forced to live 'at a standard below what is reasonable'.[11]

At the same time as married women were exercising their right to determine acceptable levels of family expenditure, increasing numbers of women chose to have no children or to remain unmarried. Many of these came from the growing band of educated and independent 'new women' determined to support themselves and pursue a career. The proportions of women who never married or who married but had no children reached unprecedentedly high levels for the generation of women born 1871–76, 17 per cent of whom never married, and 25 per cent of whom remained childless during their lifetime.[12]

Although the spinster had her enemies, social acceptance of the career woman slowly increased in the 1920s. The *Shop Assistants Magazine*, for example, championed the rights of single women, particularly those with a college education, to work on an equal footing with men. One writer believed that the term 'old maid' was no longer popular, and that no social stigma now attached to the woman who chose to remain unmarried and pursue her chosen work. Another proudly reclaimed the title of 'Old Maid', asserting in a letter to *Woman's World* that spinsters were not necessarily unattractive, but simply single by choice.

'Callisto' in her 'Woman to Woman' column looked forward to the day when 'all women shall be economically independent of men, and so have nothing to gain by marriage'.[13] The economically independent women of whom Callisto and Old Maid wrote constituted a considerable portion of the shopping public by the 1920s.

The single female wage-earner was becoming more visible in the streets of Sydney. While factory and domestic employment continued to be significant into the early twentieth century, there was at the same time a comparatively greater expansion of service-sector white-collar jobs such as teaching, nursing, sales, typing, stenography, clerical work and public service employment. This opened up new and welcome opportunities for educated middle-class, and some working-class, women to whom the traditional areas of women's work were unattractive or socially unaccceptable.[14] Not only did more women become wage-earners, but occupations which brought women into the public eye rather than closeted away in factories and workshops required female employees to spend part of their incomes on good quality and smart work clothes. Retailers were themselves instrumental in creating a large body of female consumers from the late nineteenth century by employing women as shop assistants.

Retailers deliberately targeted the female wage-earner or 'business girl' as consumers after World War I. Farmer's, for example, staged a special 'Smart Business Girls Campaign' in the wake of publicity surrounding a 1918 New South Wales Board of Trade enquiry into the cost of living for adult women workers. Farmer's advertisements in the *Sydney Morning Herald* promised to let the business girl know 'how she can dress with all the grace and individuality her social and business status calls for, at the same time safeguarding her necessarily limited dress allowance'. The promotion used the dramatic talents of Mlle d'Alroy, store mannequins, lectures, and a special lunchtime playlet set in the office of a costume and millinery showroom to attract working women into the store. Coordinated window displays included life-size photographs of the business girl, dressed in the featured garments, arriving at the office, sitting at the typewriter, and leaving the office.[15]

Manufacturers recognised the potential for profits to be made from the working-girl market in the 1920s. Berlei organised special demonstrations which showed models wearing corsets while typewriting. Free shows with names like 'Her Grace—the Lady of Line', staged in the theatres of the country's major cities from the late 1920s, included a Special Business Girls' Session each evening.[16] Trade literature also named the business woman as a recognisable type of female customer with her own particular needs and consumption patterns. Proprietors were advised that as the business woman 'comes into contact with more people in her hours in the city than in her home at weekends', she generated a constant demand for clothes to enable her to dress sensibily but well throughout the year.[17]

State intervention into the wages system had some, if limited, benefits for women workers. Although Arbitration Court decisions after 1901 rarely awarded women more than two-thirds of the male wage, the fixing of minimum wages and the establishment of union grievance mechanisms were an improvement on unregulated nineteenth-century paternalism.[18] Government officials, unionists and female reformers argued that the basic wage for women should be sufficient to enable to her to buy a decent wardrobe. Reporting on the fixing of the living wage for working women in New South Wales in 1922, the *Woman's World* suggested that the working girl still had to struggle to make ends meet. Wanting simply a 'chance to buy, buy, buy, and to be able to have a frock just by wishing', the poor working girl had to be content with making over an old muslin frock:

> No sparkling jewels, no softly falling georgettes, or clinging jersey silks for Miladi, and she went back to sucking that worn-down finger-nail, and shuddered as she thought of the 9s 3d allowed for dress, and pondered how, without stinting herself more, she could beat the basic wage, which gave her £1 2s 4d for board and lodging, 9s 3d for clothes, and 7s 11d for fares and extras. And this little girl, who had to support herself, who had to go to work each day, clad respectably, and tidily shoed and stockinged, not to mention all the bits of underwear, sat and puzzled her little head.[19]

The average working woman employed in one of the traditionally female occupations such as dressmaking, millinery, food processing, laundry work or domestic service may have had little left from her pay packet each week to spend in the big stores. But her rights as a consumer as well as producer had entered a number of discourses by the 1920s.

Women's ability to consume was further enhanced by the extension of credit facilities. Most of the big stores, initially those courting a working-class trade, but by the turn of the century even the 'first class houses', operated on a cash basis. Credit was typically restricted in the nineteenth century to account customers patronising the better class houses such as Farmers and David Jones. However, big stores selling high-expenditure items like furniture, pianos and sewing machines offered formal time payment arrangements for poorer customers from the 1880s.[20] Time payment facilities were supplemented by lay-by and cash-order systems, popular with and often essential to working-class patrons of the big stores after World War I. Cash-order companies specifically targeted married women, even though they usually took a guarantee for repayments from the man of the house.[21] The cash-order, lay-by and time-payment systems together represented a significant extension of credit to the working-class housewife by the 1920s.

The housewife became firmly entrenched as a female role in the first two decades of the twentieth century. As women moved into new fields of employment from the 1890s, domestic service gradually retracted as a major employment area for women. Responsibility for the labour and smooth running of middle-class households previously dependent on the domestic servant fell on the shoulders of wives and daughters. The housewife combined the administrative work previously performed by the upper- or middle-class mistress with the domestic labour previously performed by the maid. The rise of the housewife was coincident with a reorganisation of unpaid domestic, including consumer, activities within the home as the marketplace reached into both working-class and middle-class homes to alter the nature of women's work. The work of the modern housewife who emerged in the years between the wars revolved around the purchase and transformation of commodities into goods and services which the family consumed.[22] The rise of the housewife made shopping unambiguously women's work.

Various groups of reformers, educationists, family welfare experts and feminists attempted to regulate family life and elevate housework into a scientific and professional activity in the early twentieth century. These attempts were part of a more general move, popular within the world of work, to incorporate the rhetoric of 'efficiency' and technical rationality into the domestic sphere. Domestic efficiency promised to improve family nutrition, domestic management, infant welfare, and childbirth and childrearing practices. Kerreen Reiger and other historians have shown how a range of professionals produced advice literature, coordinated educational campaigns, set up special schools and clinics, and lobbied governments to take women's work as housewives and mothers more seriously.[23] Governments themselves were keen to encourage better habits of industry in the housewife. Inspectors attempting to enforce 1899 New South Wales Government legislation requiring the early closing of shops, for example, condemned the 'slip-shod' practices of working-class housewives 'devoid of any education in the economy of household management, born to wastefulness, negligence, and the lack of system'.[24]

Implied within these campaigns to improve household efficiency and elevate the status of the housewife was a legitimation of the female role of consumer within an emerging market economy. A number of individual women, women's periodicals and women's organisations, pre-eminently the Housewives Association of New South Wales, stressed woman's crucial role as scientific manager of the home and household economy and, ultimately, of the nation. The professional housewife's skills included thrift, good domestic management and the ability to buy wisely. Shopping, according to the *Shop Assistants Magazine* in 1926, could be reduced to an 'exact science' in which the application of vital principles, such as selecting one well-known house to benefit from being a regular customer, proved more efficient than random bargain-hunting.[25] The men of the retail and marketing industries therefore found support from feminists and family welfare experts in their attempts to formalise women's unpaid work in consumption as an occupational role ideally suited to female nature.

The changing status of women's consumption activities can be detected in the development of new shopping habits after the turn of the century. The wives and daughters of Newcastle miners had since the 1880s flocked into town on 'Pay Friday' night and 'Pay Saturday'. Local shops were allowed, under Early Closing legislation, to remain open late on Friday nights so that the breadwinner would not be tempted to leave home early on Saturday morning for what Ellen McEwen has called 'the old Geordie habit of a fortnightly spree' and perhaps forget to leave his wife the money for settling accounts.[26] By 1907, the heaviest trading day was not Pay Friday but the following Monday. The reason, according to the local factories and shops inspector, was that Saturday was increasingly devoted to family leisure pursuits such as picnics and visits to the seaside: '. . . on the Monday the miner has gone back to work, the children are at school, the good wife comes into town and leisurely, without any bustle, makes the purchase she requires.'[27] The inspector's observation suggests that working-class women and their families were redefining shopping, not as a family activity to be carried out at leisure, but as domestic labour most properly performed by women during the breadwinner's working hours.

It is probable that this shift to female weekday shopping in the Newcastle area occurred in other urban working-class communities in the early years of the twentieth century. As wages stabilised through arbitration and basic wage rulings, and the average standard of living for working-class families rose, fewer married women needed (or wanted) to engage in paid employment outside the home. Supported ideologically by the rhetoric of family reformers, the working-class wife and mother was increasingly likely to be a full-time housewife responsible for buying most of the family's food and clothing. Many witnesses called before the 1920 enquiry into the cost of living indicated that it was the usual practice for married women to manage the family income and buy household commodities; or, as a male gardener succinctly put it, 'the wife buys my clothes'. The perception that women spent the bulk of their husbands' earnings was evident in trade journals and women's periodicals from the first decade of the century and continued into the late 1920s.[28]

Trading hours, regulated in New South Wales from 1899, made it extremely difficult for men and women engaged in full-time waged labour to shop in the big city stores. With the exception of one late shopping night a week, the opening hours of drapery stores broadly conformed with the working week. There were therefore strict time constraints on full-time wage-earners, 78 per cent of whom were men in 1901, wishing to patronise the big stores.[29] Most married women, and some single middle-class women, on the other hand, were not engaged in the full-time or formal labour force. They consequently had more flexibility than men with which to arrange their daily domestic tasks in ways that accommodated shopping. Women, too, were more likely than men to spend their leisure time and any disposable income on clothing and drapery goods. Men had a wider range of socially-acceptable public leisure and consumption activities to choose from. By the 1920s, men preferred to spend their spare cash on motoring and holidays rather than on clothes.[30]

Women, then, had the motive, opportunity, social sanction and increasingly the material means with which to be department store shoppers. Retailers and marketing experts have been unwaveringly of the opinion that women constituted the majority of shoppers for household goods and clothing from the 1890s until relatively recently. The main change in the nature of these comments was that the unstatistical impressionistic remarks on the predominance of women in the early years was gradually replaced by percentage estimations in the post-World War I enthusiasm for scientific approaches to selling. Women, according to retailers' reports in the 1920s, constituted somewhere between 70 per cent and 95 per cent of all shoppers.

Women not only bought goods for herself, but those for her home, her children, and—significantly—for her father, husband, sons, brothers and other male relatives. The *Shop Assistants Magazine* reported in 1926 that 75 per cent of men's personal wear was bought by women: a mother bought items such as shirts, pyjamas, underwear, handkerchieves, ties and socks (but not apparently collars or hats) for her son until his late teens, and when he married, his wife took over the job. Even when men bought goods such as suits and coats for themselves, they frequently did so with their wife or mother present, or on female advice given at home. Sales expert Herbert Casson estimated that women directly or indirectly purchased 90 per cent of men's suits, and generally spent more than three times as much money as men. Overall, retailers were convinced that 'Man is essentially the earner, woman the spender'.[31]

If there was consensus within the industry on the sexual composition of shoppers, retailers were unable to describe the class characteristics of their clientele with the same confidence. Were the female customers on which the mass market was based predominantly middle class or working class? Some historians have assumed that department stores attracted mostly middle-class and wealthy customers, while others imply than shopping was a more

Mercery Department, David Jones, George Street, Sydney, 1927. When David Jones opened its Elizabeth Street store in 1927, a large sale was held in the old George Street store. The men's and boys' mercery department is clearly self-service, with large numbers of women buying goods for the men of their family. (DAVID JONES (AUSTRALIA) PTY LTD)

popular, even democratic, experience. It is important to distinguish between the class status of customers and the bourgeois forms of opulence, display and luxury that motivated the marketing strategies of the big stores. As centrally-located public institutions to which admission was not only free but actively encouraged, men and especially women of all classes could enter and browse in the big city stores. A working-class woman might buy cheaper goods in smaller quantities, and buy less frequently, than her wealthier sister, but she was nevertheless an equally valued customer.

Certainly there were alternative options open to those of limited means to meet their clothing and household needs. The poorer suburbs had their small drapery, second-hand clothes and 'Johnny-all-sorts' shops. Street stalls and local markets such as Paddy's Market were also important sources of clothing, crockery, fancy, haberdashery, drapery and ironmongery goods. Of the 338 stalls at Paddy's Market in 1909, 34 sold new clothing, 39 sold used clothing, 28 sold fancy goods, and twelve sold haberdashery. As the Town Clerk submitted to the Royal Commission on the Saturday Half-Holiday, 'the continuance of the "Paddy's Market" business is almost an imperative necessity in the interests of the poorer classes of the city and immediate suburbs'. Many working-class women made their family's clothes themselves, or altered 'hand-me-downs' from relatives and neighbours.[32]

While working-class women made many of their own garments at home, the market for ready-made clothing was also predominantly working class. Women engaged in full-time waged labour, for whom the distinction between work time and leisure time was clearer than it was for women who saw themselves as full-time housewives, found it more difficult to devote the necessary time and energy to needlework. Twopeny observed disapprovingly in 1883 that, whereas it was common for upper- and middle-class girls to sew their own clothes, the servant class invariably had their hats made up at extravagant cost by milliners. Single women employed as kitchenhands and factory workers gave evidence at the 1918 enquiry into the cost of living for female workers that they bought all their clothes ready-made, and the four-woman advisory committee established to determine the costs of essential clothing for female workers recommended that minimum wages should be based on the assumption that a working girl's wardrobe would contain ready-made clothing. Some women stated that they made their own underclothes and blouses, but not their costumes or 'best dresses'.

Purchasing manufactured clothing was a much cheaper alternative to having it made up by a dressmaker or tailor. A woman could buy a ready-made costume for around seven guineas in 1920, considerably less than the eight to 21 guineas asked by ladies' tailors for a comparable article.[33] Working-class women would therefore have found the large drapery stores convenient sources of manufactured clothing.

Female wage-earners shopped at department stores because they needed a cheap, smart and durable wardrobe, and the stores stocked a good range of manufactured clothing. They were also likely to be regular customers. As one female witness told the 1920 cost of living enquiry, a working woman wore out boots and blouses more rapidly than 'a lady of leisure'. Another told the 1918 enquiry that a working woman needed a good costume because it saved on wear on other clothing and could be worn on cool summer days and in winter without an overcoat.[34] The need to buy clothes as cheaply as possible without sacrificing the quality they deemed necessary brought many working women through the doors of the city's emporiums. An advocate for the employers at the 1919 hearing commented: 'I think it can be well expected that the working class can appreciate a bargain whenever they see it . . . One has only to go to Newtown on any Friday night to see the trams crowded coming into Sydney.'[35] The big city stores were a considerable attraction to any woman compelled to compare prices.

Working-class women, moreover, were just as interested as middle-class women in fashion, beauty and personal adornment. Janet McCalman found in her study of the working class in Richmond that working men and women needed to own at least one good set of clothes. Young women, in particular, 'almost as a gesture of insane defiance at their poverty . . . would allow themselves one absurd luxury such as an expensive hat'.[36] Working-class women pursued such apparently extravagant items frequently in the face of strong middle-class disapproval. There were, then, strong material and psychological reasons why working-class women as well as middle-class women shopped in Sydney's big stores.

Class distinctions evident between the big stores in the nineteenth century tended to become less significant in the common drive to capture a mass market. Some stores were perceived by retailers and the general public as conducting a predominantly working-class trade (Grace Brothers, Mark Foy's, Marcus Clark, Lassetters, Hattes and Gowings, Sweet Brothers and Sydney Snow), others conducted a high-class business (David Jones and Farmer's), and others such as Anthony Hordern & Sons had a mixed clientele.[37] However, stores known for their working-class trade served customers 'from factory girls to the very best of customers', and working- class women at least occasionally bought clothes from stores such as Farmer's.[38] Anthony Hordern & Sons apparently catered to both a working-class and a 'better' trade. As a representative for the employees claimed in 1919, 'If Anthony Hordern & Son do not depend on [the families of working men], where do they get sufficient people in and around Sydney to keep a large emporium of that kind going?'[39]

Retailers often deliberately courted a mixed trade. Anthony Hordern & Sons, like other city stores, opened at 8 a.m. to serve working men, dressmakers' assistants and 'girls going to business'. The 'ladies' trade' began mid-morning and ended when it began to get dark. Retailers deliberately stocked a wide variety of merchandise at different prices and presented ready-made clothing as suitable wear for women of all classes in their attempts to attract a wider market. The *Draper* observed in 1926 that it was often difficult to tell mistress from maid, 'both evidently very good customers of the draper'.[40]

David Jones instituted a revealing policy change in 1916 that captures this shift towards a mass market. What had previously been 'an exclusive, largely personality business' selling a wide range of goods to meet the individual requirements of customers, became a 'Trading House' designed to 'hold the majority of men'. The store planned to sell a smaller range of standard goods, but in larger volume. Where a department may have previously stocked 200 lines, it now had only 100, and instead of ordering 50 dozen of an individual line, buyers now ordered 100 dozen. This change, the executive hoped, would lead to 'less loss, more stable profit rates and bigger turnover'.[41] Once a high-class drapery shop catering exclusively to the 'carriage trade', David Jones was a mass retailer aiming at a mass market by World War I.

The state regulation of shop trading hours after 1899 contributed to the standardisation of what were previously different class patterns in shopping. Working-class men and women, used to shopping late at night after work, had to conform to shop opening hours based on the daily routines of middle-class women without full-time employment. This created problems for working women such as tailoress Elizabeth Daw, who pointed out to the 1918 cost of living enquiry that, because she could only shop on Friday nights, she frequently missed out on the best bargains.[42] The continuing popularity of late-night shopping well into the 1920s caused suburban shopkeepers to complain that the major retailers had pushed the working-class trade away from smaller shops in the suburbs towards the big city stores which were more convenient to those travelling to or from work.

This increasing concentration of middle-class and working-class customers in the shopping districts of the large cities suggests that, after the turn of the century, shopping was increasingly tied to urban patterns of work and leisure. The restriction of late-night shopping to one evening a week turned shopping from an every-day routine practice into a special outing in the city viewed as an occasion of pleasure as much as business. The crowds of finely-dressed individuals who had since the 1880s enjoyed window shopping, or simply promenading in the city streets, appeared to comprise men and women of all classes.[43] Retailers encouraged *all* Sydney inhabitants—and, through the mail-order business, those further afield—to view the big city stores as a focal point for their leisure and consumer activities.

Retailers thus helped create a mass market in which qualitative differences of class status were reduced to quantitatively measurable differences in the economic capacity to consume. The mass market not only eroded class differences in a lifestyle increasingly defined by consumption, but diminished the longstanding differences between city and rural cultures through the widespread distribution of mail-order catalogues and by attracting country dwellers into the big city stores on their visits or business trips to Sydney.[44] More than this, the department store was a cross-cultural institution. In a 1922 article entitled 'Cosmopolitan Shopping', a well-travelled woman compared department stores in London, Paris, Berlin, Athens, the United States and Australia. She concluded that department stores were more alike than dissimilar, and that a woman could 'in any of the world's big cities buy anything she needs at a varyingly reasonable price, and with the minimum of difficulty'.[45]

Department store shopping was an experience common to women and a few men of all classes by the 1920s. Although it was the middle-class trade that retailers tried hardest to attract, and appeals to middle-class values and aspirations that they incorporated into their marketing policies, a poor woman's coin was just as welcome and eagerly sought as that of a rich woman. Store managers attempted to increase the turnover of their stores in the first two decades of the twentieth century by extending their market, whether it was the new wage-earning woman or the professional housewife. The class differences in the market for drapery goods evident in the late nineteenth century had been substantially eroded and replaced by a feminised mass market by the 1920s.

The men of the retail trade noticed differences of sex in consumer behaviour more consistently than differences of class. As the big stores assumed a monopoly of the city retail trade and the retail industry became politically organised after the turn of the century, these perceived sexual differences in shopping behaviour were articulated with greater clarity. The next chapter shows how a retail managerial culture based on an adherence to scientific principles and new knowledges such as psychology facilitated constructions of masculinity and femininity based on a predominantly female market.

3 Scientific selling

The desire to create a mass market in Australia made the more effective organisation of the retail and marketing industries imperative. The individualism and informality characteristic of the nineteenth century drapery trade was replaced between 1900 and 1920 by a more systematic and institutionalised retail industry. Major retailers realised the political and economic advantages of sharing sales expertise and acting as a united body against unions, employees, suburban competitors and recalcitrant shoppers. They combined forces within trade associations, developed their own journals, and used these organisations and organs to articulate and circulate shared business principles and scientific knowledges about consumer behaviour. This modern retail culture created mass marketing techniques which relied on a more openly sexualised approach to selling.

The big city stores physically and economically towered over smaller competitors and dominated the local market for drapery commodities by the 1920s. Anthony Hordern & Sons' giant Palace Emporium, opened in 1905, symbolised to many observers this dangerous tendency for the large stores to monopolise the retail trade. Future Labor prime minister William M. Hughes told the Women's Political Education League that this mammoth store 'pronounced the doom of the small trader, whose day was done in Sydney. Let a small store spring up within its blackening shadow, and that flower dies!' It was perhaps no coincidence that Hughes had opened a small suburban shop himself in the 1890s. George Beeby, Hughes' colleague and counsel for the Shop Assistants Union, was equally critical of the growth of the big stores in the years preceding the first shop assistants hearing before the New South Wales Arbitration Court in 1907. Listing the main Sydney retail firms and their recent extensions, he concluded that 'All of them have grown up in the last few years and assumed gigantic proportions'. Factories and shops inspector, Annie Golding, reported in 1912 that the old established stores were almost double their original size, while the *Australian Worker* carried a cartoon portraying the large retailer as 'Monopoly' being carried on the backs of the small traders and sweated shop employees. Even the conservative *Sydney Morning Herald* cautiously greeted the new Palace Emporium as a sign of the 'concentration of an enormous proportion of the retail trade of a growing community in one hand'.[1]

This expansion of the retail trade became noticeable around 1905 with the return of prosperity and revived building activity after the years of depression and drought. The large stores survived the depression of the 1890s relatively unscathed: as the *Draper and Warehouseman* commented in its first issue, produced in the height of the depression, those Australians who could afford to do so continued to want to 'clothe themselves well and comfortably'.[2] All of the major drapery stores, and many of the smaller ones, expanded between 1902 and 1908 by extending or building new premises. Sydney's population roughly trebled in the period between 1880 and 1914 as the result of natural increase, migration from the country into the city, and state-assisted migration from Great Britain. Immigrants not only helped supply the stores' considerable demand for labour, but also constituted a greater market for drapery goods by bringing consumers and expendable income into the stores. The factory managers of David Jones and Grace Brothers suggested at the Royal Commission on the Alleged Shortage of Labour in 1911 that the increase in demand their stores were experiencing was the result of the increased numbers and prosperity of the country's consumers.[3]

The resilience of the big stores continued during the trade disruptions of World War I, which their managements weathered by careful stock management and the use of their own factories or local manufacturers as suppliers. Although inconvenienced by the restrictions on and increased costs of imports, retailers were able to pass on many of these added costs to consumers in the form of higher prices. Evidence given by retailers at enquiries into alleged profiteering suggest that the stores' public image was affected more than their profit levels.[4] The stores consolidated their position and continued to grow steadily in the post-war period, most extending or rebuilding their premises again in the 1920s.

The New South Wales Government's intervention into the retail industry in the form of factories and shops legislation (1896), early closing legislation (1899) and compulsory arbitration (1901) provoked the major retailers to join forces against common threats and facilitated the more systematic organisation of the retailing and marketing sectors in the early twentieth century. While such laws did little to challenge the workplace prerogatives of the large city retailers, they were harbingers of an ongoing struggle for control between the state and the retail industry. The establishment of the New South Wales Arbitration Court in 1901, in particular, convinced retailers of the need to combine for their own protection. The Master Drapers and Clothiers' Association was established in 1902, changed its name in 1903 to the Master Retailers' Association of New South Wales, and from 1921 was known as the Retail Traders' Association of New South Wales. The name changes suggest significant shifts in the nature of the drapery trade between 1900 and 1920 from small-scale craft to large-scale industry.

The Retail Traders' Association and the men, all of them large employers, who filled its executive positions rapidly became the dominant and coordinating voice in the New South Wales retail industry. The Association absorbed the membership of its rival organisation, the City and Suburban Shopkeepers Association, in 1921 and was well represented on Sydney employer bodies such as the Employers Federation, the Sydney Chamber of Commerce and the Clothing Industries Employers Council.[5] Because they were not only distributors but manufacturers, wholesalers, and importers, the big stores were uniquely placed to play a leading role in the dissemination of a common business culture based on shared principles of labour management and mass marketing.

The large retailers and their brothers in the advertising industry were in confident command of the Sydney retail scene by the end of World War I. This retailing and marketing fraternity acted cooperatively in a number of promotions. The New South Wales Advertising Men's Institute joined with Anthony Hordern & Sons, David Jones, Lassetters, Marcus Clark, Snows and McCathies to introduce Mother's Day to Australia in 1918 with a two-week campaign of newspaper advertisements, rubber stamps and window displays.[6] When the *Draper* reviewed in 1922 the major changes that had occurred in the 21 years of its existence, it listed the lack of secrecy in business methods and the 'growing spirit of friendly rivalry' created by trade associations and journals.[7] Members of the Retail Traders' Association cooperated in special sales campaigns such as the 1925 'Spring Shopping Week', the inaugural 1929 Father's Day promotion, and a 'Balance the Budget Sale' designed to counter declining trade in 1930.[8]

Retailers were agreed on the importance of science and scientific principles to the success of their enterprises. Major retailers were convinced by the first decade of the twentieth century that scientific rationalisation and the dissemination of marketing ideas, techniques and theories were essential to economic success. Writers and publishers discerned a profitable market for an industry-specific literature, prolific by the 1920s, aimed at retailers, retail managers and their employees. Trade journals, notably the *Draper of Australasia* (from 1901), employer association journals such as the *Journal of the Retail Traders' Association of New South Wales* (from 1919), manuals designed to educate salespeople or show retail entrepreneurs the road to success, and advertising trade journals with a particular interest in retail advertising provided a forum in which retailers and their growing band of experts in sales techniques, store layout, stock management, merchandising, window display, advertising, industrial relations and customer management could articulate and communicate their theories of successful selling.

Retailers' common project in the first two decades of the twentieth century was to make business amenable to rationalisation and scientific control. By 1930, business was seen by those in the trade as no longer a matter of trial and error or soothsaying and quackery, but 'a scientifically controlled adventure'.[9] Retail trade and advertising experts joined those attempting to improve mass production techniques, labour relations, maternal health, infant and child welfare and parenting in looking to science and technical rationality for answers to problems of population management.[10]

Retailers believed that salesmanship, in particular, demanded a more scientific approach. The intervention of the state into wage-fixing in the retail industry after the first shop assistants minimum wage case in 1907 impressed on retailers the need to monitor, manage and mould the activities of their staff.[11] Nineteenth-century methods of personal training and mentoring were appropriate only to small shops in which the proprietor could keep his eye directly on his apprentices' transactions. An inconsiderate, discourteous, unknowledgeable or even indifferent assistant could, unknown to the manager of the large business, alienate customers and do irreparable damage to the store's reputation and sales performance.

By the turn of the century, retail trade journals were calling for training in scientific salesmanship that emphasised personal qualities rather than the manual skills characteristic of the old draper's assistant. The cry for scientific and technical training intensified in the columns of the trade papers after 1914. Many of the large stores' welfare schemes in the 1920s incorporated salesmanship training or improvement classes which covered subjects such as store history, customer and merchandising policies, rules and regulations.

Stress was placed on the need for good presentation and keeping the customer happy, particularly for female assistants who were expected to be feminine and charming. Educational work and training in 'efficiency in business' for female shop workers was considered by women reformers and sales experts alike in the period after the war as a route by which women might achieve professional status.[12] There were, however, different expectations for female and male retail staff. The salesmanship and advertising course introduced after years of pressure by the Retail Traders' Association of New South Wales at the Sydney Technical College in 1935 was divided into one course for male students which focused on retail management, and another for women which dealt with stock, sales-floor duties and customer relations. Both courses included training in appearance, manner, voice and personality.[13]

The sexual differentiation in salesmanship training reflected the development of managerial structures in the large retail organisations in the second decade of the twentieth century. As drapery businesses became departmentalised and grew beyond the control of one individual, expert managers and 'executive control' came to be seen as necessary to the smooth functioning of the large department store.[14] The autocratic rule of the head of the firm and the decision-making power of his sales-floor representatives (shopwalkers, buyers and department heads) was gradually replaced by partnerships, boards of directors, and eventually trained managers. The managerial expertise on which retailers depended nevertheless continued to be located mostly in the hands of a few men from the same family until the late 1920s, when substantial losses forced many firms to appoint new specialist managers and consultants intent on reorganising store systems. The new rational system of retailing placed a premium on managerial talent and ability. Consumption, according to John Spierings, was no longer based on 'human intimacy and exchange, but was organised by new skills of analysis and planning'.[15]

This new rationalist regime replaced a retail patriarchy based on the rule of the father with a modern patriarchy in the form of a managerial fraternity. David Jones, for example, began to centralise its decision-making processes after 1906, and by 1913 operated under a fifteen-member executive, only two of whom were women (heads of advertising and the complaints office), and one of these was replaced by a man in 1914. Two years later the company established an exclusively male junior executive, and in 1924 the Board recommended training young men from prominent public schools and the University of Sydney for administrative positions.[16]

Retail management and retail success were clearly articulated as the province of men by the 1920s. Grace Brothers started a Boys Model Trader Club in 1923 to encourage boys to become 'men of business ability' by selling the store's catalogue on commission in the form of commercial education classes. *Rydge's Business Journal* in 1929 related the fictional success story of Jimmie, a working-class lad from Redfern, who worked in a large Sydney department store 'From the Ground Up' to become its advertising manager.[17] Thus, as the retail industry consolidated after 1900, retail management and retail careers became increasingly associated with men, while the lower status work of selling and shopping were viewed as feminine pursuits.

The advertising industry was also dominated by men. Those few women who did work in the industry faced opposition from some of their male colleagues. The Advertising Association of Australia and New Zealand agreed to admit women as members in 1925, but only 'after much discussion'.[18] One of these new members may have been Eleanor Donaldson, David Jones' advertising manager in the mid-1920s, reported to be the originator of the store's famous slogan 'David Jones for Service'.[19] Like retailing, advertising entered a new era of expert knowledge and scientific professionalisation around the turn of the century. Most major firms employed advertising managers by 1905, and a new journal called *The Reason Why*, devoted to the science of advertising and containing advice from men prominent in the Australian retail industry, was established in 1908. Retailers assumed a prominent position within the fledgling Australian advertising industry from its outset: more than one-third of the delegates to the first Australasian Conference on Advertising held in 1918 were connected with the retail trade, and the president of the New South Wales Advertising Men's Institute was Harrie Tear of Anthony Hordern & Sons.[20] An explicit attention to advertising and publicity was the keystone of the large retail institutions' mass marketing policies by the 1920s. The Retail Traders' Association claimed in 1929 that 'we have passed through a great production era and are on the threshold of an advertising and selling one'.[21]

Retailers were also enthusiastic participants in the industrial hygiene and industrial psychology movements that shaped the labour relations of most large business concerns in the years immediately following World War I. Between 1915 and 1930, most of the big stores instituted recreational, health and educational welfare programmes for their predominantly female workforce in the hope that it would improve productivity, forestall industrial unrest, curtail the power of unions, and make labour more efficient. Academic psychologists and industrial relations experts such as Elton Mayo, A.B. Fitt, Bernard Muscio, Irving Fisher and Tasman Lovell attended early advertising association conventions and published numerous articles on industrial psychology in retail trade literature after the war. Elton Mayo's faith in psychological research as the only solution to social unrest, whether in the factory or in the suburban home, may have brought to retailers' attention the need to understand human irrationality.[22]

Industrial psychology was seen as a useful tool in the personnel-management strategies often implicit in welfare schemes. It convinced retailers of the need to understand the 'human instincts in business'. Winifred Taylor of Farmer's welfare department used industrial psychology, in particular intelligence tests, to assess the abilities of junior boys and girls, and determine staff-training needs in stock, sales and office work in 1925. Psychology, she argued, made it possible to 'disentangle the various factors, and to measure or assess them on an exact and scientific basis'. The Retail Traders' Association of New South Wales was a member of the Institute of Industrial Psychology from its formation in 1928.[23]

Retailers, sales experts and advertisers began to use the language of psychology in their attempts to manage sales assistants and customers, and stimulate consumption around the turn of the century. Trade experts were keen to replace the inefficiency of individual approaches to selling with scientific methods, urging retailers to persuade assistants to use psychology to achieve better empathy with customers. The *Draper of Australasia* advised retailers as early as 1902 that a study of psychology was necessary because the sales assistant needed to be a 'mind-student' to recognise and deal with each customer as an individual.[24]

The same principles were applied to advertising and marketing. The *Reason Why* argued in 1908 that it was a 'psychological fact' that illustrations arrested the eye. One of the first advertising texts published in Australia, Gewurz's 1910 *Wisdom and Success in Advertising*, referred reverently to the 'recently discovered psychological laws' of advertising. The only scientific basis of advertising, claimed Gewurz, was the 'study of the mind you are seeking to influence'. Hence the advertiser needed to put himself in the shoes of the customer in order to 'feel as they feel, like as they like, and think as they think'.[25]

Despite impressive chapter headings such as 'The Psychological Effect of Environment', texts such as these did little more than make vague calls on the profession in order to legitimate sentiments which were already widely accepted in early twentieth-century business culture. The psychology adopted by the retail trade before 1930 was neither 'pure' nor 'applied', but a form of popular or common sense business knowledge. References to psychological principles which occur in the literature are typically unspecific, colloquial and rarely refer directly to the work of a named psychologist. The terms 'psychology' and 'psychological' tended to be used indiscriminately. Writers consistently referred vaguely, and without further explanation, to advertisements which 'used psychology', 'the psychology of woman', shopkeepers who had 'lost their psychological sense', the 'psychological effects' of certain marketing strategies, the need to seize the right 'psychological moment' for a sales campaign, or flatly asserted that certain forms of customer behaviour were 'psychological facts'.

This use of psychology as a kind of trigger to stimulate certain responses in the reader indicates that sales experts consciously deployed the term to lend scientific authority to their profession and its discourse. Retailers were concerned to impress on their customers and competitors that they were modern and progressive, and trade writers were scornful of retailers who refused to relinquish the ways of the past and failed to adapt to the changed conditions of contemporary retailing. Introducing the serialised version of Fitt's *Human Instincts in Business* and attempting to convince sceptical retailers of the value of the new science, the editor of the *Draper* reminded readers that psychology had superceded guesswork reliant on casual impressions.

> Psychology is based on accurate observations and experiments as to the way in which the human mind works. It takes into consideration all the facts that have been learned by previous workers and in previous generations. It reduces these observations to systematic order, and puts forward conclusions that can be tested in practice. The conclusions are often strange and unexpected to those who have given little attention to the subject, but they can all be put to the test.[26]

Retailers seized eagerly on psychology's promise to introduce rationality and scientific precision to their operations. An article on 'The Psychologist and the Business Man' in the *Retail Traders' Association of New South Wales Journal* explained that psychology was as necessary to the modern business-man as the chart and compass were to the sea captain. It helped advertisers to manufacture in the mind of the consumer new and acquired desires.[27] Whether or not retailers routinely adopted psychological principles in their day-to-day operations, the language of psychology was fully incorporated into marketing discourse by the 1920s.

Historians have argued that applied and industrial psychology promoted particular class and professional interests and facilitated the better management of labour. They have failed to notice psychology's fascination with the sexes. Retailers were perhaps more conscious than professional psychologists, industrial-relations experts or even advertisers, of the need to be sexually specific when analysing consumer behaviour. In the decade or two before surveys and statistical forms of measurement were devised to survey and measure these indicators of consumer behaviour, psychology offered a scientific and accountable means of knowing the female consumer. Like other mythical representations of woman—the 'dependent woman' or the 'housewife'—the 'female shopper' was a stock figure of trade literature by the second decade of the twentieth century.[28]

One of the earliest applications of psychology to retail problems was the construction of theories of customer 'types' which implicitly constructed sexual differences in shopping behaviour. The practice of 'naming' types of customer was prevalent in the retail trade well before the introduction of psychological theories. In addition to the 'Tabbies' well known to the turn of the century retail trade, journalist Beatrix Tracy, who posed as a shop assistant in 1908, catalogued the 'managing mother', the 'bustling spinster' and 'the dreadful person who became reminiscent, and enlarged upon bargains she had got elsewhere'. In 1915, the *Draper* distinguished between the 'homely matron' and the 'fashionable lady', each theoretically attracted to different types of merchandise. Psychology codified and legitimated these largely impressionistic constructions of female character. Systems of customer classification constituted part of the syllabi of several salesmanship training schemes discussed by the Retail Traders' Association of New South Wales during the inter-war period.[29]

The classification of customers helped retailers in their daily struggle to manage large customer populations by encouraging sales assistants to recognise different types of customer so that they could adapt their sales strategies accordingly. These classifications tended to institutionalise certain customer traits as specifically female characteristics. One of the earliest schemes, run by Bright and Hitchcock of Geelong, included a Study of Types of Customer. Three general types—the Sanguine, Nervous and Phlegmatic—were supplemented by the 'special' types: the calmly-indifferent, over-careful, grumpy, overbearing, argumentative, frigid, procrastinating, prejudiced, logical or emotional types of customer.[30] Although these types were not explicitly attributed to the female customer, the store's choice of adjectives strongly suggests that its managers had women in mind.

The 'frigid' category was unambiguously female. Retail-trade experts' use of the term suggests the influence of sexological knowledges. The new sexual knowledge concealed a traditional phallocentrism and deep mistrust of women's motives and behaviour in sex, increasingly codified after 1914 by Freudian psychology's stress on an innate sexual instinct. Women who failed to be appropriately responsive or pleasing to their husbands in sexual matters were dismissed as unfeminine, deviant or unhealthily repressed. Sheila Jeffreys argues that the category 'frigid woman' was invented and deployed by sexologists to control women in the 1920s. Sex experts attributed frigidity in women to ignorance, homosexuality, masturbation, feminism, or simply an unhealthy independence.[31] Retailers and sales experts may have consciously or unconsciously drawn on sexological knowledge in their attempts to rationalise selling. Although the *Draper* does not describe the 'frigid' type of customer in any detail, retail experts' use of the term as early as 1917 suggests that businessmen easily incorporated misogynist concepts of female behaviour derived from psychology, sexology and anti-feminism into their classificatory schema.

Lustre Hosiery Limited was more explicit in specifying the mental characteristics of male and female customers in its salesmanship manual of the 1920s. The nervous and querulous type, for example, was typically found among wealthy women. The irresolute and talkative type came in male and female varieties: men were simply ready to talk; women 'just love to shop'. All the examples given in the manual's discussion of sales talk were of female customers. Similarly, William Beable's *Practical Guide for Shop Assistants* advised shop assistants that customers could be, among other things, impulsive (the pronoun suggests this is a female type), deliberate (a male pronoun), vacillating (female) or suspicious (female). *Rydge's Retail Merchandising Course's* eight types (vacillating, hesitating, argumentative, quiet, quick-tempered, doubting, the customer who cannot say yes, and the customer who is 'just having a look around') were all female. Where male customer types were specified, such as the *Draper*'s sporting man, professional man and the 'Knut' (a fashionable man), they were generally more flattering.[32]

This psychologically-inspired recognition of customer variation contributed to a more general discursive specification of sexual difference. Perhaps the most persistent source of sexual difference in buying behaviour articulated in the literature was women's 'instinctive' shopping ability, love of fashion and bargain-hunting. Marketing men of the 1930s acknowledged their debt to the 'new psychology' and, in particular, to William McDougall's theory of native and acquired instincts.[33] However, the observation that women were instinctive shoppers occurred frequently in retail-trade publications without the ostensible benefit of psychological terminology. Mrs Bertha Fortescue Harrison, quoted in the *Reason Why* in 1909, stated confidently that 'woman's natural propensity for bargain-hunting' was aroused by the efforts of advertisers clamouring for her attention, and in 1921 the *Draper* instructed retailers that 'a bargain is only a bargain to the feminine mind when the value is unique'. Even in menswear stores, women were better bargain-hunters than men because of their 'natural instincts' as shoppers. Salesmanship writer Herbert Casson's 1928 text *The Art of Customer-finding* more clearly suggests the influence of psychology. In the course of his advice on 'Finding Out the Wishes of Women', Casson specified seven 'buying instincts': comfort, beauty, pleasure, fear, economy, imitation and self-preservation.[34]

'Kinduno' argued along similar lines in an article in the *Advertiser's Monthly* entitled 'Coy and Hard to Please: Appealing to the Woman Buyer'. Kinduno suggested that a woman lived to shop. She took herself and her buying activities very seriously, and would shop for days—yes, weeks—before making up her mind. Kinduno enlisted the literary support of Mark Twain:

> When a man goes into a store to buy a collar he comes out with a collar. When a woman goes into a store to buy a collar, she comes out with a new silk waist, a pair of gloves, ten yards of dress goods, several toilet articles, some window curtains, and a refrigerator.

Advertisements aimed at women should be domestic and personal, not technical or statistical. A woman's buying instincts, asserted Kinduno, were rooted in her natural attachment to her home, her domestic duties, and the well-being of her family:

> That is why I say sell her something beyond the product itself. Sell her the idea of a better home, better things for her family, healthier children, improved surroundings . . . If a woman is convinced that what you have to sell will help her to make life easier and happier—if it will add anything to the health and well-being of herself and her family—she will find a way to afford it even if she goes without many other things to do so.[35]

The sales experts' perception of women as instinctively concerned with the care of home and family reveals an unspoken assumption that women were naturally and biologically suited to mothering, and therefore to shopping. This form of biological determinism, in which men were perceived as producers and women as consumers, underpinned much of the new marketing psychology.

Men, on the other hand, were constructed in the literature as reluctant, unnatural and even 'peculiar' shoppers with a natural distrust of department stores, and a particular aversion to walking through the women's departments. The influence of psychology is less marked in these characterisations of the male shopper. Where instincts were mentioned in reference to men in the 1930s, they had a higher social value than women's shopping, bargain-hunting or nest-building instincts: male instincts listed in *Rydge's Business Journal* included sex, pride of possession and fighting. 'Shopping' in the sense used by those in the retail trade referred to carefully considered inspection, comparison and judgement of the goods offered for sale. It also implied a pleasurable but serious activity which kept customers in the store where they might be persuaded to buy more articles, or more expensive articles than they originally intended. Whereas the marketing experts of Lustre Hosiery assumed that women found shopping a pleasure and an excuse for a day's outing in the city, men were believed to generally dislike and be embarrassed by it. Anthony Hordern & Sons told readers of the *Sydney Morning Herald* that many men preferred not to buy their own clothes because they considered themselves to be bad judges of quality.[36]

In defining women's buying activities as instinctive, retail writers contributed to the social construction of women as naturally suited to the domestic sphere. In a similar manner, the trade construction of men as unnatural and hasty shoppers reinforced the notion that their proper role was breadwinner and their place was in the public world of work. Roland Marchand argues that the American advertising industry resolved the potential conflict inherent in consumerism's challenge to the work ethic by maintaining distinct and traditional social roles for the sexes: women belonged to the extravagant world of consumption; men to the world of work and rational control. The portrayal of men in advertisements as husbands or businessmen (and in Australia as rural workers) perpetuated the notion of polarised sexual spheres and countered the potential decadence of a consumption ethic associated with the feminine.[37] Psychology substantially assisted this project of sexual differentiation.

A second theme in psychologically-derived statements of sexual difference was women's 'natural' attraction to anything new or fashionable contrasted with men's inherent conservatism. Women, as Marchand suggests, tended to be characterised as the modern sex and men as the traditional sex. Psychology was not solely responsible for constructing women as the changeable sex. Nineteenth-century medical and psychological models of sexual difference stressed the greater sensitivity of the nerve centres in women, and their consequent irritability and susceptibility to nervous abnormalities such as hysteria.[38] The 'craving for change' distinguished woman's response to shopping from that of her male counterpart. Women were fickle. They shopped around and tried 'new pastures', whereas men 'stick to some shop they know, and where they are known.'[39]

Women's changeability was particularly evident in their affinity to fashion. The Journal of the *Retail Traders' Association of New South Wales* told retailers that women's chief motivation in shopping was to increase her own charm and reputation for good taste. Women, according to the *Draper*, 'greedily' absorbed fashion information and were readily attracted to advertisements, whereas men read advertisements less willingly and bought new clothes only when they needed them. Lustre Hosiery advised its salespeople that women were inclined to fashion, but men liked to conform and be uniform.[40]

Men's conformity frustrated retailers who wished, in this case, that men were more like women. The male customer, as the *Draper* exclaimed in exasperation in 1919, was 'as conservative as a Prussian'. The Retail Traders' Association of New South Wales made the same point a decade later when it reproduced in its journal a *Sydney Morning Herald* article stating that 'sartorially every boy that is born into this world alive is an ardent and impenitent conservative'.[41] Although retailers constructed men's conservatism as a sales 'problem', trade papers nevertheless gave the impression that it would have been most unmanly to have behaved otherwise.

Sales writers also agreed that women made better potential consumers because they were more suggestible and open to persuasion than men. Again the lines between common-sense and psychological forms of knowledge were blurred. Psychology frequently reinforced or lent credibility to informal knowledges of women's nature, while religious and sexological notions of woman's temptability provided ideological scaffolding for psychological insights. Trade writers suggested that women lacked the ability to plan, for example, in refurbishing their homes, and needed to be shown what to buy: 'Many women know what they like when they see it, but they cannot plan in imagination'. The answer was to show them a series of coordinated displays and they would have no hestitation in choosing the one they preferred.[42]

Psychology provided a 'scientific' formula for this female propensity to follow and imitate others. Lustre Hosiery advised sales personnel that the underlying motives for buying were: 'the inclination to imitate by following the lead of Fashion, with which is closely related regard for appearance and self-gratification; the matter of fact gain of utility; satisfaction of caution; yielding to weakness; and, with parents, an emotional regard for their children'.[43] This instinct-based statement appears gender-neutral, but it was obviously written with women in mind. Drawing explicitly on psychology, an article from *Printer's Ink* reproduced in the *Draper* in 1918 revealed how one advertising expert used modern psychology and the 'unconscious' in selling to women. Dr. B.L. Dunn, a psychologist employed in the advertising section of a large manufacturer, claimed that the female love of beauty was instinctive and that 'the mind of woman always responds more readily to the elemental, emotional appeal than the mind of man'.[44]

Local advertising experts also held that women responded to advertising emotionally rather than logically. 'Women, in that delightful illogical way of theirs, "just know" that they get the best value at David Jones.' Berlei's 'dramatic selling' technique was designed to play on the female consumer's emotional response to the spectacle of corsets presented by live models in a variety of theatrical settings. Women, according to Berlei's Phil Warner, were more susceptible to dramatic selling than men because they did not 'arrive at a conclusion by logical reasoning' but instead relied on their feelings. Women entered a theatre in a state of pleasurable anticipation that made them particularly receptive to efforts to sell them the ideas of figure beauty and health. Warner suggested that the success of the Berlei presentations was attributable to a coordinated sales plan that helped women avoid the 'time and bother of thinking and reasoning'. Warner was not alone in assuming that women had little capacity for critical thinking. 'Psychologist', writing in *Rydge's* journal, reported that a woman easily absorbed, believed and parroted sales messages because she had been taught by the slogan to believe them.[45]

Sales writers frequently remarked on this sexual difference in thought. They generally assumed that men were more likely to question, reason and think about advertising material than women. The *Draper* advised advertising men in the 1920s that advertisements aimed at male shoppers needed to use 'reason why' copy and headlines that made them 'sit up and think'. Men were interested in a 'boot to suit you' story rather than a 'hat you ought to have' message. Men were also more attracted by advertising themes linked to current affairs and, unlike women, could be persuaded to buy locally-made goods for patriotic reasons. The *Draper* warned retailers during World War I that women did not appreciate advertisements which referred to 'business ethics or lofty sentiments'.[46]

Experts agreed that women's thoughts were dominated by personal and domestic matters rather than technicalities. Casson told retailers that the world's greatest merchants knew better than to talk the language of finance, engineering or other masculine subjects to women.

> Women are not mechanical. They do not appreciate the value of ball bearings or six cylinders. They do not understand the technical language of the mill and the factory. They have a point of view of their own . . . A woman is most interested in a subject that relates to herself, her family, her duties, and her surroundings. She is not so much interested in general facts nor in abstract problems that do not personally concern her.[47]

Women's interests were 'mainly personal': comfort, style, personal appearance, health, lower prices, social position, the welfare of children, the people in her own family and social circle. Kinduno also cautioned advertisers to avoid technical or statistical facts in talking to the woman buyer. She would respond more to atmosphere, colour, human interest and 'friendly, human, readable and probable' facts.[48] Although both Casson and Kinduno claimed to employ psychology in understanding the female customer, their observations appear to be determined as much by contemporary perceptions of female nature as they were by psychological theory.

The retail trade's characterisation of women as suggestible dovetailed with its construction of them as childlike and primitive. 'Nervous and querulous' customers were described in one sales manual as 'merely spoiled children in adult form', while under the heading 'Our Ad Man Talks on the Psychology of the Woman Purchaser', the *Draper* asserted in 1922 that women had a childlike trust in advertising and were 'always ready to listen again to the fairy story of "miraculous values"'.[49] Writers with some familiarity with psychology and anthropology drew retailers' attention to women's 'primitive' instincts. Kinduno thought that the average man overlooked the fact that women spoke a particular and peculiar language of their own, a feature reminiscent of 'certain savage tribes' in which men and women had distinct vocabularies. Classical scholar Professor T.G. Tucker stated that women were always ready to defy discomfort and pneumonia in their pursuit of ornamentation, and argued that their fondness for feathered hats and jewellery was evidence of their affinity with savages.[50] One window-dressing expert reported that cultured individuals repressed the primitive, natural response to strong colour in favour of 'taste'. Women were possibly more primitive than men because they were more daring in the wearing of colour: red was women's first choice and blue their second, with the order reversed for the more 'repressed' sex.[51]

This evidence of sexual differentiation in retail-trade literature suggests that, increasingly from the first decade of the twentieth century, psychology enabled the codification and elaboration of constructions of womanhood that had influenced retailers from the nineteenth century. The general picture of female psychology that emerged from this literature was of a mind dominated by instinct, impulse and emotion. Women were portrayed as beyond control. They lacked social, moral and economic restraint in their desire for change, pleasure and possession. Just as women trapped in the net of the criminal-justice system in this period were portrayed as easily tempted into sexual misbehaviour, carnality and depravity,[52] retailers viewed female shoppers as easily seduced by beautiful goods and spectacular presentations. The female customer was constituted in retail discourse as 'other': at best unpredictable and impetuous, at worst frigid, highly-strung, and primitive. Childlike and, paradoxically, instinctively maternal, women were seen to be closer to nature than to culture. The male customer, by contrast, was civilised, economically rational, seldom swayed by impulse, conservative and predictable, technical if not intellectual, and a creature of the comfortingly familiar public world of work and politics.

The association between men and reason, women and its absence, evident in western social and political thought from the eighteenth century, is clearly reflected in these twentieth-century psychological constructions of sexual difference. The reason/passion dualism buttressed marketing psychology and made possible its authoritative statements about the female shopper. Psychology depended on other sexual knowledges—scientific, medical, religious, criminological—fundamental to the dominant ways in which retailers and advertisers made sense of the world. The emergence of marketing psychology was therefore made possible by, and superimposed on, pre-existing knowledges of the differences between men and women.

Marketing psychology emerged at a time when the increasing visibility of women in the public sphere, and feminist demands for equality with men were creating intense anxiety. By the 1920s many women were experiencing a 'new freedom' which allowed them unprecedented ease of access to public spaces such as department stores. Martin Pumphrey argues that advertisers appropriated this public freedom by promoting the female types of the 'flapper' and the 'housewife' as symbols of modernity occupying both the public and the private spheres, thus limiting the potentially radical and destabilising effects of women's political advances.[53] Psychology was a critical arm of this general advertising impulse to transform feminist social and political action into female consumer behaviour. At the same time as women were constituting themselves as rational political and economic subjects—citizens and workers—psychology was constituting *woman* as irrational and childlike. The battle between the 'new woman' and the 'old man', which Allen details in relation to crimes involving women in this period, reverberated in the pages of retail trade publications.[54]

At the same time, marketing psychology constructed new social categories, roles and identities for women in twentieth-century consumer society. Psychology actively constructed the female (and to a lesser extent, male) subject in historically specific ways. By the 1920s, psychology was beginning to enunciate new categories of woman—the 'bachelor girl', the 'young unmarried woman', the 'business girl' and the 'married professional woman' —which provided promising alternatives to the 'housewife' or the 'shopper'.[55] This construction of a range of social identities, and the systematic use of surveys designed to generate more usable consumer information, emerged more clearly with the development of the statistical, sociological and psychological forms of analysis characteristic of market research from the 1960s.[56] In this earlier period, however, psychology was concerned less with market prediction and analysis than with understanding the behaviour of the sexed individual. Psychology offered women new identities which gave them a secure place in an emerging consumer culture.

The professionalisation of selling and advertising, the new sciences of psychology and sexology, the political mobilisation and organisation necessitated by industrial legislation, and a booming economy favoured the expansion of the big drapery stores of the nineteenth century into the department stores characteristic of urban culture in the 1920s. Bound by a common masculinist and rational business culture, the men of the retail industry constructed an increasingly sexualised view of consumption. The arrangement, display and meanings given to consumer goods themselves played an important role in this sexualisation. The next chapter shows how mass-production techniques helped fix and standardise the sexual meanings of department store commodities.

4 Sexed commodities

Drapery-store goods were invested with a range of meanings. A lady's mantle, a man's hat, a parasol, a teacup, a comb or a clock promised to fulfil both material needs and the less tangible social aspirations and desires of the consumer who considered purchasing them. A man's straw boater, for example, did more than keep the sun from its wearer's head. It also functioned as a sign of youth, social position, sartorial propriety and leisure. Above all, a man's boater represented masculinity. A lady's straw sailor hat may have been almost identical in appearance except for the addition of a decorative ribbon. But those few inches of ribbon transformed a masculine hat into a clearly feminine one. Despite similarities in function, different sexual meanings attached to a man's umbrella and a lady's parasol; a man's cravat and a lady's shawl. Women bought from their chosen department store, not mere hats, coats and combs, but the accoutrements of contemporary manhood and womanhood. These sexual meanings and boundaries were fundamental to the organisation of department-store goods, sales personnel and profits. The rules governing the arrangement and sale of men's and women's commodities implicitly instructed customers in masculinity, femininity, sexuality and socially acceptable forms of relationships between the sexes.

As the industrial manufacture and design of drapery and household goods became more common in Australia from the second half of the nineteenth century, and especially in the first two decades of the twentieth, their gendered nature became more marked. Adrian Forty suggests that contemporary ideas of social difference, filtered through and supplemented by manufacturers' own ideas, transformed raw materials into desirable and profitable commodities. Design became a potent vehicle for gender ideology by providing 'enduring, visible and tangible signs' of contemporary sexual difference.[1] Not only were there clear differences between men's goods, such as collars, and women's goods, such as corsets: apparently sex-neutral articles such as pocket-knives, watches and hairbrushes also came in male and female varieties.

Ann Game and Rosemary Pringle show in their analysis of the retail industry how the department store's division of goods into male, female and gender-neutral categories organised and constructed gender.[2] Articles of manufactured men's and women's clothing and accessories were the most unambiguously gendered drapery commodities. Men's wear and women's wear was perceived in the trade to be radically different. As the *Draper of Australasia* advised window dressers in 1908, the adjectives 'ladies' or 'men's' were superfluous on show cards, as 'the article shows for itself that it is for a man or a woman'.[3] Retail managers segregated other commodities on the basis of a perceived sexual division of labour. Children's clothes (boys as well as girls) were categorised as women's goods, because women were responsible for child-care and for buying the clothes of their sons and daughters. Haberdashery, furnishings, manchester and most fancy goods were also women's commodities, because they were closely associated with the domestic sphere. Ironmongery, hardware (except for household items), workmen's tools and materials, smoking requisites, leather and sporting goods were male. Furniture occupied an ambiguous position in this gendered world of commodities: male by virtue of its bulk, but female in its household associations.

Although retailers assiduously maintained the distinction between men's and women's goods, they were keen to capitalise on changes in sexual identity where these might lead to increased sales. An early example was the *Australian Storekeepers Journal*'s prediction in 1895 that the New Woman and popularity of the bicycle would produce a 'revolution in ladies' dress'. By the 1920s retailers were exploiting a number of marketing strategies which challenged the sexual definition of some drapery goods. The *Draper* advised retailers to create a display of lingerie in the men's mercery department to persuade men to buy these articles as gifts for women, and encouraged women to buy clothing from the menswear departments when 'the mannish mode for feminine sports wear' was in vogue in 1927.[4]

There were clear limits to these temporary sexual transgressions, however. While encouraging retailers to be innovative and aggressive marketers, trade journals warned of the dangers of going too far. The New Woman's wholesale adoption of male attire 'would, in the vast majority of cases, be most unbecoming', decided the *Australian Storekeepers Journal* in 1895. In placing women's underwear in the mercery department, shopkeepers were warned to keep the display restrained and high class, and not to make it look like a 'women's store'. And the entry of women into the men's sections of the store created some anxiety. A cartoon in David Jones' house magazine *Between Ourselves*, headed 'Wartime in London', showed a female land worker dressed in riding jacket, breeches and boots asking a perplexed shopwalker to direct her to the underclothing department. 'Certainly', the shopwalker automatically replied, then hesitated. 'Er—ladies or men's?'[5]

Because commodities played a significant role in maintaining sexual cultural boundaries, retailers had to tread a fine line between tradition and innovation. On the one hand they made little distinction between the money of a male shopper and that of a female shopper, and it mattered little whether customers conformed to sexual conventions in purchasing their clothes as long as they bought them. On the other, they assumed that the majority of customers would be discouraged from shopping in a store that mixed its men's and women's goods too promiscuously. It was in retailers' interests to maintain some version of the division of commodities by sex, even if they occasionally modified or slightly rearranged the boundaries.

The same sexual tension existed in the stores' marketing of men's goods to women customers. Although retailers knew that women bought mercery and other menswear goods as often as, or even more frequently than men, their display and advertising policies for these departments had to ensure that they retained their masculine associations. The sex of the commodity, rather than the sex of the customer, thus determined the sales strategy. Retailers were aware of the commercial necessity of selling to women, perceived as the traditional guardians of sexual order, both masculinity and femininity.

It was also important for retailers to match the gender of the commodity with the sex of the salesperson. Until the early years of the twentieth century, women were usually employed to sell and manage women's clothing, millinery, accessories, haberdashery and trimmings; men to sell and manage men's clothing, dresses (that is, dress materials), hats, boots, manchester, sports goods, furniture and hardware. In most industries employing women and men from the late nineteenth century, employers rationalised the sexual division of labour in terms of differentials of skill, manual strength, dexterity, and ideologies of domesticity.[6] The rationale for the sexual division of sales labour within the big stores was somewhat different. The feminisation of the retail workforce which began in the late nineteenth century, a process that historians have explained primarily in economic terms as a response to employers' demand for cheap and docile female labour, was also a consequence of the expansion of the women's departments and retailers' need to maintain sexual propriety by employing women assistants to sell women's goods to women.

The employment records of the big stores suggest that women's goods, especially those requiring personal fittings and therefore close bodily proximity between seller and customer, demanded women sellers.[7] Farmer's began to employ a substantial proportion of women only when the millinery, mantles and costume departments began to expand in the late 1880s, and Peapes & Company stopped employing saleswomen when it changed from a general drapery to a menswear store around 1891. William Lowe told the Arbitration Court that he had not employed female assistants at his George Street store since he removed the women's departments to new premises in Oxford Street in 1906.[8]

While employers undoubtedly preferred to engage cheap and amenable female labour wherever it was proper to do so, there were clear social limits to the extent to which they could employ women in traditionally male departments and vice versa. A woman selling men's underclothing, for example, would have transgressed the strictest of sexual taboos. The head of Mark Foy's mercery department told the Arbitration Court with evident discomfort. '. . . it would be impossible to have a girl in the mercery department, for instance, with underpants, where we have to measure customers sometimes, it would be impossible to have a lady there'.[9]

Edward Bennetts, president of the Shop Assistants Union, agreed that mercery was 'hardly a fit department for a woman to serve in . . . A girl behind the counter serving those things would have to meet all classes of men'.[10] In handling underpants, especially if the sale required personal fitting, an assistant was handling an article which was almost indistinguishable from the male body of the customer. Not only would it have been the height of impropriety for a woman to be seen handling men's underwear in public, men themselves would have been so embarrassed by this female incursion into masculine culture that retailers risked irretrievably losing their custom.

The same unwritten rules applied in the sale of women's underwear. Susan Porter Benson reports that the American retailer Marshall Field first employed women in ready-to-wear and lingerie, 'departments where the merchandise needed to be fitted, and where questions of delicacy made them preferable to salesmen'.[11] Samuel Hordern, a conservative employer who still preferred male shop assistants in 1907, admitted to the Arbitration Court that he needed to employ women in the ladies showroom and underclothing departments. While men supervised the stock in the women's underclothing department, 'the girls keep it forward'.[12] Men were employed, especially in the early years of the emporium, as buyers or heads of women's departments such as underclothing, haberdashery, perfumery, gloves or hosiery. The perception that men were better than women at managing stock and finances in these cases overruled the unwritten law that goods and sellers be of the same sex, because at the higher levels of management, employees had little direct contact with either the stock or customers. Hordern's evidence suggests that, rather than a direct equation between commodity and salesperson, it was physical contact with the goods and social contact with the customer that determined the sexual division of labour in the drapery store. The commodity acted as a cultural mediator, a vessel of sexual meanings, establishing in the store strict guidelines of heterosexual conduct.

The central role played by the commodity in conveying sexual meanings and relationships helps explain the anxieties expressed by male shop assistants at the movement of women into what they perceived to be their own territory. As part of their first log of claims submitted to the New South Wales Arbitration Court, and in subsequent claims, the Shop Assistants Union asked that no female assistant be employed in the manchester, dresses, (men's) clothing, mercery, ironmongery, furniture or sporting materials departments.[13] Men's primary concern in such proceedings, as feminist historians have pointed out, was that women would deskill the profession, lower the status of shop work and depress wages.[14]

Court transcripts also suggest that men resented and feared the tendency of retail proprietors to sexually reassign staple commodities in departments such as manchester. Industrial methods of production and design had changed the sexual meanings and assignation of labour in the manchester department by the turn of the century. The nineteenth-century manchester department sold bulk goods such as sheeting, towelling, cottons and other materials which women would make up into household articles either themselves, or have made for them. Changes in the manufacture and packaging of piece goods—increasingly sold in shorter and more easily handled lengths—in the dresses and manchester departments allowed retailers to transform them from men's to women's departments. By the turn of the century, manchester departments were increasingly selling small manufactured items such as tablecloths, napkins, table centres and runners, pillowslips and doilies. In the process of manufacture and design, these goods absorbed and fixed contemporary ideas of femininity, domesticity, gentility and household aesthetics. Similarly, as industrial manufacturing methods allowed more variations in the design of crockery, enamel goods and kitchenware, the ironmongery department of the universal provider began to include kitchen sections with a notably female character.[15]

Retailers like Mark Foy's employed women in the sale of some manchester goods such as doilies, tablecovers, towels, pillow covers and 'other light things, the selling of which is really not a man's occupation'.[16] The salesmen's claim that rolls of manchester materials were too heavy for women to handle was increasingly difficult to sustain. Many manchester items were sold in smaller lengths known as 'short ends'. Employers argued that it was quite appropriate for a woman to sell small manchester articles, dresses (that is, dress material) and silks, hosiery and kitchenware. Ironmonger Herbert Evans could see no reason why women should not be employed to sell small wares, kitchen and enamel goods, because 'they know more about a teapot than I do'; and John McDowell argued that women were 'more particular than the males in getting a good [colour] match'.[17]

Retailers' objective in allowing women into sections of some male departments was to make sure that they did not lose cus-

Costume Department, David Jones, Elizabeth Street, Sydney, 1927. Bigger, lighter and more spacious than its predecessor of 1887, the new showroom encourages the shopper to select her own ready-made garment from those on display. The (still headless) female dummies appear to be standard in shape and design. (DAVID JONES (AUSTRALIA) PTY LTD)

tomers who had to go from one department to another to buy what they wanted. Customers expected to be 'served through' the shop—that is, taken from counter to counter by one assistant—and this might entail a stop at both male and female departments. The arguments put forward by retailers in defence of their employment of women suggests that they were aware that the ideological content of the goods had more marketing potential than their material or use value. Lace doilies, teapots and silks were sold by women because they were more strongly associated with feminine culture than they were with the masculine bulk goods of the traditional manchester department. In buying a lacy tablecloth or a length of delicate silk, a woman was in effect buying femininity.

The spread of industrial methods of manufacture also affected the contents and sexual meanings implicit in the men's and women's clothing departments. The dressmaking, tailoring and millinery workshops central to the success of the nineteenth-century drapery establishment continued to be profitable into the twentieth, but catered to an increasingly exclusive market. Meanwhile, the ready-made clothing departments rapidly overtook hand-made garments in importance. Once associated with the working class—particularly working-class men's clothing, or the 'slop trade'—ready-made clothing dominated both the working-class and middle-class trades by the 1920s. There was by 1909 a 'wonderful change' in Mark Foy's ready-made department, which no longer sold the 'charity garment' but clothes of the very best quality.[18] The David Jones executive, in an attempt to appeal to a wider market in 1916, decided to discontinue the making of costumes to order in the ready-made costume department, and to sell more factory-made goods throughout the store. The change in policy was sufficiently successful to secure in 1924 for the female head of the store's ready-made clothing departments a considerable salary of £1000 per year plus bonuses.[19]

The major retailers were themselves innovators in the development of clothing manufacture in Australia. After the turn of the century, most expanded their workrooms, embraced mass-production techniques, and moved into separate factory premises. Samuel Hordern's men's clothing and shirt factory, opened in 1898, was reported to be the largest of its kind in the colonies. After expanding his operations and moving into the production of dresses, millinery and underclothing after the move to the Palace Emporium premises in 1905, Hordern employed more factory operatives than any other Sydney factory.[20] By 1925, the president of the Retail Traders' Association of New South Wales proudly reported that his organisation included in its membership the largest clothing manufacturers in Sydney.[21]

Women appeared to seize on the convenience of ready-made clothing with alacrity. A survey of American women carried out in the mid-1920s, reported in the Journal of the *Retail Traders' Association of New South Wales*, found that women preferred ready-made garments because they saved the time and energy necessary for homemade items, and because they offered superior styles and designs. Jacob Segal, manager of the Palace Emporium factory, told the Royal Commission on the Shortage of Labour in 1911 that the volume of trade at the store had increased by 30 to 50 per cent over the previous two or three years. Consequently 'the demand has become so great that I cannot cope with it'. Segal attributed this demand to the general increase in prosperity and women's fondness for new clothes: 'They will have the new dress or hat whether the husband will have to wait or not'.[22]

Some retailers, such as David Jones, promoted their own lines of ready-made clothing as a form of advertising. The Orient label had been immediately identifiable as a David Jones product since the late nineteenth century. Soon after the company's Marlborough Street factory was opened in 1914, department heads were instructed to move towards more standardised stock based on Orient products. In the men's mercery department, for example, the company was:

> . . . in the practice of carrying a great many different lines of Underwear; the Customers had their likes and dislikes; these were catered for, and small stocks were ordered to suit individual needs, resulting in some serious stock losses as time went on. The endeavour of the Management now is to put in standard makes of our own name and to sell those proprietary trade mark lines that the public demand *[sic]*.[23]

Retailer-owned factories eliminated 'middleman' costs and limitations imposed by reliance on outside manufacturers and wholesalers. In-house retailing also helped retailers control the quality of the goods they sold, and consequently improve their community reputation as efficient businesses and fair dealers.[24]

The increased reliance on industrial methods of manufacture tended to standardise the style and design of the goods displayed on the shelves and racks of the department store. This standardisation limited the extent to which the consumer could choose her own version of femininity (or masculinity, if she was buying goods for her father, husband or sons). As an article from the American trade journal the *Dry Goods Economist*, reproduced in the *Retail Traders' Association of New South Wales Journal* in 1927 pointed out, the new techniques of dress manufacture meant that 'Garments could be cut by the dozen instead of by ones or twos or threes'.[25] The more mass production took hold, the more difficult it became for consumers to deviate from accepted notions of femininity and masculinity crystallised in the commodities they purchased.

Two staple drapery-store commodities with particularly strong associations with femininity played an important economic role:

women's hats (millinery) and corsets. Women (and retailers) viewed hats and underwear as essential articles of clothing that encapsulated contemporary ideas of fashion, indulgence and female desirability. Both hats and corsets bore an intimate relationship to the female body, enabling a woman to recreate her imaginary body to conform with the feminine ideal. This similarity was made explicit in a humorous article on millinery in the *Lone Hand* in 1911: 'Curious, isn't it? That a man always does what's left of his hair in the same old way, and buys a hat that fits his head; but a woman fits her head to her hat, just as she fits her body to her corsets.'[26]

The millinery and corset sections were not only core departments of drapery establishments, but often their most profitable. The businesses of nineteenth-century female milliners and staymakers such as Ann Hordern (established 1825), Mrs E. Way (1864), and Harriette McCathie (1886) were so successful that, after expanding into general drapery stores, they eventually developed into some of Sydney's major emporiums.

The ladies' corset and underclothing department literally constituted one of the foundations of the drapery store. References in drapery-trade literature to the high demand for corsets and the prominence of corset advertisements in trade and women's magazines suggests that by the 1890s retailers had recognised their importance as particularly profitable and attractive commodities. Women demanded, or were encouraged by social and sexual conventions to demand, corsets. Historians have offered a number of explanations for the extended appeal of corsets, particularly during the height of 'tight lacing' in the mid to late nineteenth century. These explanations range from feminist analyses that argue that corsets reinforced the frail, submissive and decorative nature of nineteenth-century womanhood to the suggestion that tight lacing was for many Victorian women a form of sublimated sexual expression.[27] Valerie Steele, on the other hand, argues that the corsets of the late nineteenth century helped shift the erotic focus of the female body from the waist to the bosom. The combined effects of 'silky materials gently rubbing against the skin, an intimate connection with the body, a combination of secrecy and visual effect' made corsets intimately feminine and erotic drapery commodities.[28]

Derived from the diminutive of the Old French term for body, *cors*, the corset embodied a potent material connection between the female body and femininity. More than any other female garment, the corset directly impinged on the imaginary female body to shape a specifically feminine consciousness and subjectivity.[29] The experience of being corseted came to be so internalised as women's imaginary and feminine body that by the late nineteenth century corsets represented the essence of female sexual appeal and identity. No wonder, then, that retailers paid considerable attention to their corset departments in building up mammoth stores largely patronised by women.

Importers and retailers used this sexual appeal to sell corsets with the language of grace, elegance and womanly perfection in the 1890s and 1900s.[30] The marketing of corsets changed, however, after local manufacturers such as the Unique Corset Company, later Berlei Ltd, were granted tariff protection and the Australian corset manufacturing industry expanded after 1915. Notions of 'scientific' dressing, corsetry expertise, health, hygiene and fashion made the corset a central and highly desirable female commodity by the 1920s. The corset became an item of lingerie—the term was first used in the early 1920s—associated with luxury and sensuality. A woman, asserted a male writer in the *Draper*, would never wear cotton undergarments again once she had experienced 'the silky feeling that accompanies dainty lingerie'.[31]

Aided by the development of new, lighter fabrics such as rayon and the use of pastel colours and trimmings, the corset was marketed as a fashion commodity by the 1920s. The new-style corset was advertised as a 'light, elegant and dainty article' that bore no relation to its old-fashioned predecessor. A woman could buy special corsets for sports, dancing, singing, typewriting, evening wear, or a boned model for wearing under a tailor-made costume. Trade journals suggested that retailers dress their corset windows to suggest a boudoir, and display in the department 'dainty little trifles such as ribbon bows or floral mounts to pin in front, little silk sachet bags, ribbon garters, suspenders, etc.'[32] Retailers were warned that the word 'corset' conjured up inaccurate and archaic images in the consumer's mind of the unattractive and restrictive Victorian garment. Instead, they were advised to use brand names such as Berlette or euphemistic terms such as girdle, corselette, or wrap-on.[33]

The corset was promoted by new marketing techniques featuring live modelling demonstrations, revues and mannequin parades. In collaboration with Berlei, stores such as Anthony Hordern & Sons and Hordern Brothers from 1919 staged dramatised demonstrations using 'living models' and displaying corsets for every occasion. Stores throughout the country advertised the services of visiting Berlei corsetiere-consultants and organised mannequin parades incorporating a display of the latest styles in corsets.[34]

Berlei took the lead in promoting corsets as a fashion item in Australia. Under the direction of a scientist and a doctor from the University of Sydney, Berlei conducted a much-publicised 'anthropometrical' survey of 5 000 white Australian women, arriving at the conclusion in 1928 that there were five basic Australian female figure types: the sway-back, the hip, the abdomen, the short-below-waist, and the average. Berlei built on the publicity generated by the survey by staging in the theatres of the country's major cities a series of highly successful live revues or pageants with titles such as 'Radiant Woman at Beauty's Shrine' (1926), 'Lady Be Beautiful' (1929) and 'Her Grace—the Lady of Line' (1931).[35] A common theme in these displays was woman's instinctive desire for beauty. Fairy caverns, nymphs, elves and enchantresses, magic mirrors and moonlit gardens of dreams conjured up a fantasy world of femininity, all made possible by the Berlei corset. The *Draper* described a typical scene:

> At the wave of a fairy wand and an uttered incantation, there rises from the mystic cauldron the ideal of modern beauty, the lissom figure, lightly encased in the natural fitting corset of to-day. The scene changes to a moonlit garden of dreams, where the seeker [after Beauty], still following the enchantress, learns the secret of poise, the art of being well dressed, and feels that at last she is on the threshold of the promised land . . . In the final scene at Beauty's Shrine in an enchanted cave is seen the 'Radiant Woman', the modern ideal, standing with outstretched arms receiving the homage of living jewels in gorgeous raiment.[36]

The Berlei promotions, and the department-store sales strategies on which they were modelled, captured in essence the new culture of marketing's reliance on selling the symbols of modernity and femininity.

The sale of corsets became a specialised facet of scientific salesmanship requiring specific skills and training. An ill-fitting corset was said to be the cause of a number of female ailments including cancer. David Jones engaged specialised and relatively well-paid corset fitters and demonstrators from the United States after 1910, the *Draper* ran feature articles on successful sales techniques for the corset and brassiere department from 1917, and a Farmers' mannequin parade of 1918 promoted corsets and underwear to women interested in the 'science of dress'. It also became clear to retailers and corset manufacturers that training was a good way to increase sales. Berlei promised readers of the *Shop Assistants Magazine* that they would be transformed into trained corsetieres by attending its school for corset saleswomen, opened in 1926. The school offered classes in female anatomy, the classification of Australian figure types, and selling to different categories of female customer.[37] Trained brassiere saleswomen were also in demand after retailers began to market brassieres as a separate and essential item of fashion and femininity from around 1917. The brassiere effectively fractured or deconstructed the female body into parts which could then be reassembled to construct a perfect feminine form. As a result, retailers and manufacturers were able to increase the value of women's underclothing.[38]

A major theme in the pronouncements of these corset experts, echoed in retailers' promotions, was the role of the modern corset in ensuring women's health. Special surgical and maternity models were a feature of Berlei's promotions. In an attempt to recapture the corset market after many women apparently decided to do without them in the late 1910s and early 1920s, the *Draper* noted with some satisfaction that '. . . the vogue of the unrestricted figure has been attended by unforseen ill-effects . . . The urgent need of corrective corsetry in order to check the resulting misdevelopment, and graceless carriage, is now universally admitted.'[39] Berlei fitting supervisor Mrs Alyce M. Reid grimly warned a special audience of Brisbane's medical men and their wives in 1931 that if girls failed to get into the corset-wearing habit when they were young 'they will most surely develop into most unsightly collections of flesh'.[40]

Terms suggesting the anarchy and ugliness of the uncorseted female body were common in this promotional discourse: women's bodies were subject to slackness, thickening and spreading; they suffered from excess flesh, figure faults and carelessness of figure culture urgently requiring correction and—above all—

control. Sue Best argues in her reading of Berlei advertisements in the 1920s that the female body was represented as blighted, rather like a potato. Corsets added and subtracted to produce the modern body:

> The corset was adding health, purity and beauty to the body, adding to make up for a lack, subtracting unnecessary flesh, subtracting the deleterious effects of age, subtracting unwanted sexuality and adding morality. Berlei was adding and subtracting but never balancing the body.[41]

This ubiquitous vision of women's bodies as out of control suggests a more general fear of an uncontrollable and threatening female corporeality. The department store's promotion of corsets quite literally put women in their place.

Like corsets, millinery represented a profitable combination of fashion, fantasy and femininity. Millinery referred to fashionable and, until ready-made hats became more widespread in the 1920s, individually-tailored or hand-trimmed women's and children's hats. Hats were high fashion. They were also essential to a woman's female identity and knowledge that she was well and attractively dressed. Women's hats and women's heads were closely attached in images of feminine beauty. By fitting her 'head to her hat' a woman could escape, momentarily at least, her own physiology to see reflected in the mirror an image of herself as feminine, fashionable and desirable. Retailers believed that considerable tact and skill were required on the part of the saleswoman to accommodate millinery fantasy to bodily reality. Millinery saleswomen were instructed to study the customer's features, the shape of her face and head, her colouring and figure, and to remember that 'a hat is hopelessly and entirely "wrong" when it produces the effect of having no sort of relation to the wearer'.[42]

Eugenie McNeil recalled in her reminiscences of Sydney around the turn of the century that hats were not designed to be functional, but represented 'marvellous fantasies' constructed out of aigrettes (plumes of feathers), pheasants' wings, ostrich feathers, silk roses, velvet ribbon and lace. A spring hat, speculated a writer in the *Lone Hand* in 1911, was not a hat but 'sunshine and joy, moonlight and dreams, twilight and serenades'. Using similarly romantic rhetoric, a contributor to the *Woman's News* likened a pink and grey hat to dawn breaking over the Gippsland hills.[43]

The millinery displays of the large drapery establishments were lavishly feminine. In 1921, Farmers staged a spectacular spring millinery show on a floral theme. After passing by the fourteen millinery windows, each featuring flowers of different colours arranged with bows, urns, bowls and window boxes, the customer entered the store to find an equally enticing interior:

> Handsome pergolas between the rows of counters were entwined with flowers, and adorned with hanging baskets of ferns and plants, while tables and stands of cut flowers (on sale) were dotted everywhere about the floors. Youthful mannequins in the most summery of frocking—organdi, for the most part, in gay apple-green, nasturtium, mauve and lemon—with large flowery hats, wandered through the departments and diffused pleasant flower odours with Parviola perfumes.[44]

Millinery saleswomen, imposingly dressed in the early twentieth century in black gowns with sweeping trains, were regarded with some awe by their customers. Entering a millinery showroom could be a mixed experience: 'You pass from the bleak, wintry streets into a bower of Spring blossom, a Garden of Paradise inhabited, as is fitting, by slim and graceful black snakes'.[45]

Most retailers were conscious of the need to employ skilled milliners and sales assistants and stock up-to-date millinery, if somewhat bemused by its appeal to women customers. The chairman of the Fair Profits Commission's reluctance to 'lay sacrilegious hands on the millinery departments' suggests that millinery continued to be closely associated in men's minds with female irrationality into the 1920s. Retailers could not afford, however, to dismiss lightly the millinery business. The partners of David Jones took considerable pains in 1891–92 to engage a capable milliner and showroom manageress, knowing that 'its productions are perhaps more talked about by ladies than any other goods'.[46] Because drapery proprietors had to engage buyers who could predict styles that would be popular with women, opportunities for women to be employed by the major drapery houses as millinery buyers opened up from the 1890s.

High-fashion articles such as millinery and corsets were commodities of considerable value to both buyer and seller. Millinery was frequently used as an instructive example of how to sell a commodity using ideas communicated by clever salespeople to gullible consumers. Herbert Casson suggested in his sales text *The*

Art of Customer-Finding: 'If I want to sell a trimmed hat to a lady of forty, I do not tell her what the hat is made of; certainly I do not tell her the price at first. NO! I tell her: "Well, madam, one thing is certain—that hat makes you look ten years younger".'[47]

Casson's millinery sales lesson constructed women as particularly susceptible to the fantasy of youth. A woman buying a hat, asserted a sales writer in 1929, was really buying 'beauty—admiring glances—youth'; women, said another in 1930, bought hats for sentimental rather than practical reasons.[48] Marketing goods not for their utility but as promises or illusions of use value—sexual attractiveness, youth, physical perfection, individuality, femininity—allowed retailers to extract the maximum exchange value from the transaction.

In the sales language of the 1920s, sellers and advertisers talked about selling ideas. Berlei's publicity director Phil Warner told his colleagues in the advertising industry in 1929 to 'SELL IDEAS. Never mind about the commodity. SELL IDEAS. Show the commodity in the idea . . . ' The director of Adshead Rose Publicity employed a literary allusion to make the same point: 'The idea—as Hamlet should have said—is the thing'. Translated into more practical sales advice, sales expert Herbert Casson told retailers to sell cleanliness not soap, fashion not gowns, social prestige not pianos. Alex Whyte, advertising merchandising counsel, told *Rydge's Business Journal* that a car could be sold to a prospective customer by encouraging him to see himself 'in his mental picture palace, rolling down the highway in a glittering limousine'.[49] All these experts urged retailers to sell the intangible and ethereal aspects of commodities; to sell dreams and fantasies as well as material objects, and to construct those fantasies differently for men and women.

The combination of fashion and femininity in commodities like corsets and hats was an extremely profitable one. Millinery was viewed within the trade as fashion exemplified, and retailers were able to extract a greater rate of gross profit (gross profit referred to the difference between cost price and selling price, and rate of gross profit to the gross profit expressed as a proportion of the total volume of sales) from millinery than from most other lines of drapery merchandise. According to Hugh Macken, representing Mark Foy's at the Necessary Commodities Control Commission in 1920, at the beginning of the season millinery frequently attracted double the average rate of gross profit. The lingerie and corset departments were also reported by the *Draper* in 1929 to be the most profitable sections of the drapery store. David Jones' departmental trading results reveal that in 1921 the corset department yielded a rate of gross profit of 33.3 per cent, 7.8 per cent above the average for all departments. By 1930, the rate of gross profit had increased to 46.7 per cent, 18.3 per cent above the average.[50]

The economic success of the millinery and corset departments reflected the profitable nature of women's goods in general. The profitability of a particular department depended on a combination of factors: stock turnover; departmental expenses, including labour costs; the price of individual items; the fashion content of the goods; the judgement of buyers and department heads; advertising expenditure; seasonal shifts in demand; and the unpredictable preferences of shoppers. Stock turnover was generally greater in women's goods, for example. Noting the striking difference between 'the lavish adornments of our sisters in silks and furs and the threadworn clothing of the sterner sex', the *Draper* reported in 1917 that struggling menswear stores which added women's departments markedly improved their economic performance.[51]

The prices at which goods were sold were flexible and somewhat arbitrary. As Harry Lassetter told the New South Wales Arbitration Court in 1907, 'there is no fixed rule. We arrive at the value by what we think it will fetch'. However, it was accepted retail wisdom that women's commodities fetched more than men's, and drapery proprietors consistently charged higher prices for women's clothing. A comparison of the average prices of men's and women's clothes sold by Anthony Hordern & Sons, compiled for the New South Wales Board of Trade enquiry into the cost of living in 1920, reveals that articles of clothing that served essentially similar functions and contained a comparable quantity and quality of material generally cost the female consumer more. Women's tweed costumes cost 75s and men's tweed suits 57s 6d; women's serge skirts 55s and men's serge trousers 25s 6d; women's collars 5s 11d and men's collars 1s each. Retailers were allowed by the Queensland Board of Trade in 1927 to mark-up their women's shoes by 42.5 per cent on the landed cost, compared with 35 per cent on that for men's boots and shoes. The 1920 enquiry into the basic wage confirmed the higher annual cost of clothing for women: £30 4s 6d, compared with £23 18s for men.[52]

A major reason for the higher costs and turnover of women's clothes was that women's clothes were more susceptible to fashion and hence more profitable. Retailers defended their profit levels to the arbitration court and to various state and federal government enquiries into the cost of living in the years immediately following World War I. They stressed that 'high grade' or fashion goods carried considerably higher rates of gross profit than 'necessary' commodities or goods such as men's boots or men's ready-made clothing aimed at a working class or 'bread-and-butter' trade. Whereas necessary commodities attracted rates of gross profit generally lower than the 33.3 per cent fixed rate recommended by the Interstate Commission in 1919, fashionable lines brought in gross profits up to 80 or 100 per cent on cost price.[53]

Women's goods such as millinery, mantles, costumes and shoes embodied this profitable fashion component far more extensively than men's. George Wright, managing director of Farmer's, told the Necessary Commodities Control Commission that whereas men's boots yielded a rate of gross profit of 20.1 per cent, women's shoes produced a rate of 26.4 per cent. Merely adding a smart buckle to a ladies' shoe, he argued in defence of his profits, transformed it from a necessary commodity into a fashion article. A length of blue serge material that could be sold by wholesalers in either the men's or women's sections was more expensive in the latter, because serge was transformed into a fashionable commodity once it appeared in the mantle department.[54]

The most successful departments were likely to be those that employed cheap labour (that is, junior or female staff) and sold popular, high-cost fashion articles at a consistently high rate of turnover. The men's and women's clothing departments were at the top, and departments selling small items such as haberdashery, trimmings, lace, ribbons and fancy goods came towards the bottom of the departmental profits hierarchy. Witnesses for both the employers and the union giving evidence at the 1907 New South Wales Arbitration Court shop assistants case agreed that the men's clothing, women's mantles, millinery and costume departments were the most profitable. Margaret Ryan, for example, spent fourteen years working in Mark Foy's haberdashery department before being 'promoted' to lace. She then asked to be placed in the ladies showroom, 'as I understood it was the best experience a girl could get'.[55]

The women's departments, particularly the ladies showroom, consistently sold more goods and made more profits than the men's. New South Wales government enquiries into the retail trade in 1907 and 1911 revealed that the women's departments of the major drapery establishments had since the turn of the century expanded noticeably and were doing bigger business than others.[56] In a lecture on turnover (the movement of stock in and out of the store) and profit, delivered to his colleagues in the Retail Traders' Association of New South Wales, Joseph Neal Grace provided figures that suggested that whereas most goods were expected to turn over four times a year, those in the women's fashion departments were expected to turn over five, six or even eight times a year.[57]

The development of the ready-made clothing trade ensured that the costume, mantles (by 1930 covering not just outer garments but frocks, blouses and skirts) and millinery departments maintained their privileged place at the top of the profit lists into the 1920s. David Jones' departmental trading figures reveal the expansion and increasing specialisation of the women's, boys' and girls' ready-made clothing departments during the 1920s. They also show that the women's departments frequently achieved a higher rate of gross profit than comparable men's sections. In 1921, the ladies' blouse department made 29.9 per cent gross profit, compared with 25.7 per cent for men's shirts; ladies' boots made 24.5 per cent and men's boots 21.9 per cent; millinery made 26.7 per cent and men's hats 25.9 per cent. Corsets, millinery, perfumery and beauty products, furs, paper patterns and jewellery, men's tailoring, regalia, stationery, blankets and woollens had the best economic performances. The majority of these profitable articles were clearly marked as either feminine or masculine commodities.[58]

Those departments which consistently showed comparatively high rates of gross profit—millinery, corsets, mantles, costumes and women's ready-made clothing—were unambiguously feminine and, by the 1920s, largely manufactured commodities. The expansion of the women's ready-made clothing trade strengthened what was already a commanding economic lead by creating a profitable relationship between femininity, fashion and manufacturing. The incorporation of design into clothing production made manufactured fashion goods more definitively sexed, more desirable and hence more marketable than unmanufactured dress materials. The expansion of drapery shops into department stores was largely built upon the successful incorporation of perceived feminine fantasies into women's fashion goods.

The department store was an object lesson in sexual relations. Its departments and windows and the commodities within them contained spectacular messages and material embodiments of current notions of masculinity and femininity. Retailers and sales experts partly followed and partly led sexual conventions. Within certain social constraints, they actively shaped new definitions of womanhood and subtly shifted sexual boundaries. Consumers and viewers were shown which goods were appropriate to which sex, how female bodies should present themselves, and appropriate rules for physical contact between the sexes. Space, spatial arrangement, and display, as the next chapter shows, were as significant in this educational process as the meanings encapsulated in commodities.

5 Windows and interior displays

Customers found in the different departments and windows of the big stores, as they did in the commodities sold and displayed within them, plentiful ideas about contemporary masculinity and femininity. The decoration and arrangement of these spaces enhanced the desirability of commodities and created potent codes of sexual conduct. It would have been unthinkable and financially counter-productive, for example, for men's hats to be sold in the typically carpeted, mirrored and floral environment of the millinery department. The unspoken rule of retailing was that women's goods were sold in feminine spaces, and men's in masculine spaces. During the first three decades of the twentieth century, selling spaces became more separate and more distinctly sexed. Retailers tempted women into buying by offering them the experience of participating in an ideal and carefully managed feminine environment. A woman shopping for underclothing enjoyed not only the delicacy and sensuality embodied in the particular camisole or nightdress that she bought, but the sights, sounds, smells and sensory pleasures of the space in which they were displayed. Encoded in those pleasurable sensual and visual experiences were contemporary messages of female desirability.

Retailers, as they expanded their stock and extended their premises, had to allocate merchandise and personnel to separate departments if they were to retain control over all aspects of the business. This departmentalisation was primarily an accounting procedure designed to help the retailer analyse and compare rates of profit and quickly identify problem sales areas. Departmentalisation also helped the retailer manage his growing workforce by delegating responsibility to section heads, and by encouraging a productive loyalty and rivalry between departmental staff. Not least, departmental organisation made shopping more convenient for the customer, and might encourage her to buy an article she had not planned or budgeted for.[1]

The segregation of men's and women's departments, a feature of even the earliest drapery stores, became more pronounced with the expansion of major drapery businesses in Sydney's retail building boom of the first decade of the twentieth century. Men's and women's commodities were separated, not only horizontally into discrete departments, but vertically on different floors of the building. Farmer's (in 1902) and Buckinghams (in 1903) both devoted their first floor to women's showrooms, while Anthony Hordern & Sons' New Palace Emporium (1907) reserved the ground floor for menswear, the first floor for manchester and the second for the women's fashion showroom. Marcus Clark's Railway Square building (1906) placed the men's, drapery and floor covering departments on the lower three floors, the millinery showroom on the third, and furniture and furnishings on the fourth and fifth. David Jones sold dress materials and trimmings and men's clothing on the ground floor; millinery, costumes and mantles, carpets and curtains on the first; and furniture on the second. Lassetters in 1908 had one lower floor 'devoted to the needs of merely men' and the first floor to women's goods. McDowell and Hughes followed the same spatial arrangement in its new 1915 store and David Jones in its 1927 Elizabeth Street store. The showroom spaces of wholesale houses such as Robert Reid were also organised by sex.[2]

The men's departments were usually located on the ground floor because, according to retail trade experts, a man preferred to do his shopping 'in the few minutes he has to spare on his way back to the office from lunch'. Male departments—and ladies' gloves, reportedly bought by men as gifts for women—were therefore located separately from drapery, and made easily accessible from the street. Men apparently disliked having to walk through the women's departments and found it an ordeal to 'pass under the gaze of rows of lady assistants through departments where are displayed women's garments, very often of an intimate nature'.[3] The department store was one of the few public spaces not only open to women, but dominated by them. Men clearly felt out of place in what Susan Porter Benson has called an 'Adamless Eden'. Many also felt extremely uncomfortable in the presence of goods so clearly associated with the female body. This male aversion to the accessories and spaces of femininity led the *Draper of Australasia* to suggest in 1915 that proprietors consider having separate men's and women's entrances to their store. The physical segregation of men's departments reached its culmination in the creation of separate stores such as Mark Foy's men's store opened in 1929 and Lowes' removal of its women's section to different premises in 1906, allowing its main George Street Store to trade exclusively in menswear.[4]

Why were retailers so concerned to separate men's and women's departments? Apart from men's aversion to female space, sales experts stressed that effective marketing and display needed to be sexually-differentiated. Retail trade journals advised proprietors that they could not expect to operate men's departments in the same way as women's: they should be run separately and on different principles. The *Draper* reported with approval the experiences of a large American retailer whose managers had rescued an ailing men's department by substituting salesmen for saleswomen, securing a window-dresser specially skilled in the display of men's goods, advertising its menswear separately from other items, and employing two additional cashiers so that male customers would not have to wait around for their change.[5] Such strategies suggested that retailers believed the presence of women and the feminine inhibited male customers from spending their money.

Retailers faced a marketing dilemma: how were they to encourage the shy male customer into the men's department while making sure that they did not lose 'the women's business' in menswear? In 1925, the *Draper* ran an essay competition on the subject 'How to Attract Women to a Men's Wear Store'. In response, William Allen suggested that the store should be split down the middle:

> . . . [with] the entrance on one side, 'Lady buyers this side', and on the other 'Gentleman buyers this side', thus showing there are two distinct, individual and separate sides to the shop for a settled and specific purpose, which plainly shows itself to be 'Separate sides for the sexes' . . . Then the women could shop with women, and a lady assistant if necessary to serve them, and the men could gather with men on their own side without qualms of conscience or fear of women's interruption.

Farmer's Tea Garden, Sydney, 1919. The restaurant and cafes of the big stores proved extremely popular female spaces.

Farmer's famous roof garden restaurant featured a goldfish pond with a fountain—obviously popular with children—and tables placed in greenery-covered caverns. (BICENTENNIAL COPYING PROJECT, STATE LIBRARY OF NEW SOUTH WALES)

Commenting that some women felt as uncomfortable in the men's underwear department as a man in a corset department, Allen proposed counter notices stating 'This portion for lady buyers only'. As Australian men and women of the 1920s were used to 'ladies only' sections of other public spaces such as baths, sporting venues and public bars, this suggestion probably made some sense to Allen's readers. He simply reiterated conventional retailing wisdom when he concluded that: 'There are the two sexes and that both buy in a men's shop. That some men feel awkward buying beside women and vice versa. That both are valuable to the mercer and neither must be lost.'[6] Allen's proposal for a sexually-segregated menswear store was not as absurd as it seemed. His essay suggests how deeply ingrained in masculine retail culture was the conviction that sexual order must be maintained.

That order was just as evident in spaces devoted to customer service. Store telephone bureaus, ladies' writing and rest rooms, information bureaus, theatre-booking desks, post offices, bank branches and tourist bureaus were populated and staffed predominantly by women.[7] Store restaurants, such as David Jones' Great Restaurant and Farmer's Roof Garden (featuring caverns, goldfish pool and a fountain), were women's and children's worlds. Those brave men who wished to eat in David Jones could do so in the sanctuary of the Men's Grill, a place where 'mere man can eat alone, undisturbed by the presence of the more attractive sex'.[8] Men had their barber's shop, and boys their dragon dens; women had their beauty parlour, and girls their fairy dell. Some female customers' resentment of the presence of male shopwalkers in the women's showroom suggested that customers' aversion to members of the opposite sex occupying their territory was mutual.[9]

Changes in retail display techniques after 1910 made unambiguous their assignment as male or female space. In Australia, as in the United States, retail managers realised that traditional stock storage, management and display resulted in assistants spending too much time locating, retrieving and returning the goods to their shelves or drawers. To make the sales procedure more efficient, managers paid systematic attention to the organisation of selling space and the arrangement of stock.[10] Although glass display cases and shopfronts manufactured by companies such as Beecham and Company were being used by storekeepers in 1900, display fixtures were not aggressively promoted as essential to the modern

Australian store until around 1911 when Bray and Holliday opened their Sydney factory. The firm claimed in 1924 to be the largest shop and office fitters in the southern hemisphere. The principle behind the move to glass display fixtures was that it was 'easier to sell to a customer who says "I'll take one of those" than it was to the customer who asks "Have you got so-and-so?" '.[11]

By the 1920s the main effort associated with store design had shifted from external cathedral-type architecture to the professional planning of interior shop display and decoration. The modern department store, according to one Sydney architect, should 'harmonize with the spirit of progress and mass production', conjuring up the promise of fine goods and encouraging customers to pass by as many displays as possible on their way to the lifts or restaurant.[12] The new emphasis on interior-store design occurred simultaneously with the development of interior decorating as a modern area of expertise. Home interiors became lighter, with more open spaces, featuring an informal living room in place of the formal Victorian parlour. This living room was seen as the heart of the home and of family living, expressing the personality of its residents.[13] Department store interiors similarly became relatively informal spaces which encouraged the consumer to express her personality and sexual identity.

One of the central principles of the new store design was that goods would be made more attractive to customers by opening up each floor, removing internal walls, pillars and columns, raising ceilings, and generally increasing the amount of light and space.[14] This conscious attention to the display of goods had been pioneered in the ladies' showrooms of the late nineteenth-century drapery store. The showroom characteristically displayed made-up gowns, blouses, skirts, costumes and mantles in a manner which invited the customer to walk around and closely inspect the garments in a spacious, uncluttered atmosphere. The showroom became bigger, lighter and more colourful after the turn of the century. One American historian argues that in this period the concept of show—whether in the form of a theatre show, a baby show, a show-girl, a showplace or a showroom—invaded the domain of culture. American retailers began to enthusiastically employ natural and artificial lighting and mirrors to create illusions of space, spectacle and abundance. Display managers exploited new technologies and theories of colour to create enticing interiors that turned department stores into theatrical stage sets.[15] Sydney's shops, with their brocade chairs, gilded Napoleonic furniture, Venetian framed mirrors, lead-lighted doors and 'gorgeous electric cage and attendant' were described in 1919 as 'Eastern bazaars—rich in colouring and designs, and wonderful in display'.[16]

These 'chaotic-exotic' displays encouraged the customer to indulge in fantasies of wealth by entering the dreamworld of commodities.[17] A central feature of Buckinghams' new showroom, opened in 1902, was the large number of windows, one of which was made of stained glass and lent colour and a 'soft and rich' appearance to the room. Marcus Clark's millinery showroom, opened in its new Railway Square building in 1906, was decorated in Morris green and included many mirrors and a 'moonlight' carpet that changed colour under artificial light. Farmer's decorated its showroom in 1918 with large bowls of arum lilies and Iceland poppies, green carpets, rich mahogany fittings and walls lined with mirrors and glass cases. The 'richness' of the interior decoration, especially the quality of the carpet, was clearly considered a strong selling point. Retailers assumed that women, probably accustomed in their own homes to linoleum and other practical floor surfaces, would be attracted into their showrooms by the luxury of an extensive, richly patterned and colourful carpet. All the floors of David Jones' Elizabeth Street store were covered in thick, pale grey carpets 'in which the feet sink in as in wild-couched lawns'.[18]

The attention paid to light and mirrors in these descriptions suggests that female retail spaces were designed to produce, illuminate, reflect and direct images of femininity to the women who shopped there. Mirrors and the skilfully-managed reflections they created were seen by interior-decoration experts of the 1910s as indispensable to modern spaces. Mirrors not only heightened the desirability of the goods on show and created an effect of glittering abundance, but reflected the good taste and feminine personality of the consumer who stood before them. As Karen Halttunen remarks, a key feature of twentieth-century consumer culture is 'the conviction that the things around us are reflections of our essential, idiosyncratic selves'.[19] Mirrors displayed and offered for purchase images of desirable womanhood.

Women's underwear and corset departments, in particular, communicated unambiguously feminine meanings by the 1920s. Corsets and brassieres, an article in the *Shop Assistants Magazine* advised, should be sold in a space that was intimate and refined, because women were 'peculiarly susceptible to environment'. Experts recommended that soft colours, pretty furnishings, restful backgrounds and dainty accessories would counteract the more commercial (meaning, perhaps, more masculine) atmosphere of the rest of the store. The management of David Jones appears to have followed these principles in decorating the beauty parlour of its Elizabeth Street store in 1927. Walls were pale pink, patrons were supplied with pink lambswool blankets, and the parlour featured floral designs by well-known artist Thea Proctor.[20]

The men's departments of the same stores looked dramatically different. They epitomised a masculinity characterised by sobriety, utility and restraint. One of the motives behind the clear distinction between men's and women's spaces, as Leach argues, was to 'give men psychological peace of mind'.[21] As many women also bought goods from the men's departments, however, masculine spaces were also designed to reassure women that they were buying unambiguously male commodities and to confirm their own femininity. Farmer's menswear department, opened in 1902, was furnished with cedar-wood counters and a linoleum floor. Peapes' menswear store modernized its premises in 1905 by removing interior department walls to create more space and light. Nevertheless, observers hastened to reassure male patrons that 'conservatism reigns supreme'. A newspaper article describing the new premises used masculine adjectives: the design was bold, simple and geometric. The new interior was painted in a restrained parchment white and Wedgwood blue, and was emphatically 'handsome' in appearance. When the same firm opened the 'Pepys Room' for male customers in its new building in 1923, it ensured that no man would be deterred by any hint of modernity or femininity. Complete with antique furniture and painted portraits on the walls, the room was 'an elegant chamber of the style of so long ago' The Pepys Room appeared to be modelled on those other male sanctuaries from bustling womanhood: the men's club. This parallel between the men's department and the men's club is explicit in a description of Lowes' hat store, opened in 1928. The store interior was decorated with wood panelling which created a 'clubroom effect, with handsome swing mirrors, carved service tables, comfortable chairs and smoking stands'. Floor coverings were also sexually-specific. The only department in David Jones' Elizabeth

Street store which was not graced with the thick grey carpet was the men's department. There it was marble.[22]

Enticing window displays were the aesthetic and sensual bait with which retail managers and a growing band of display experts attempted to lure consumers into these interiors. Increasingly after the turn of the century, brightly lit, colourful and carefully designed store windows were seen to play a critical role in persuading the potential customer physically to cross the threshold.By creating pictorial representations of the sexed commodities sold within the store, display windows presented immediate and visually arresting tableaus of masculinity, femininity and heterosexuality. Window decorations were free public spectacles without rival as a mass form of visual entertainment in the years before cinema and television began to take their place in the fantasy worlds of consumers.

Window-dressing became professionalised during the 1910s and 1920s. David Jones, for example, ran window-dressing classes from 1912, and by 1919 budgeted £1800 for ticket marking, windows and display fittings. The Sydney Technical College offered a ticket-writing course and, from 1916, a full window-dressing course which taught students about backgrounds, draping, the use of stands, fabrics, colours, lighting, layout and the creation of special effects.[23] Window-dressing remained an exclusively male profession in Australia until the 1930s.[24] Men were considered to be the more artistic and professional sex, and it would have been thought improper for women to be seen displaying themselves and dressing naked dummies in full view of the public. Male window-dressers often felt self-conscious arranging articles of feminine attire, especially underwear. The embarrassment of some men in dealing with 'dainty pretties of lace and frills in front of passers-by' testifies to the implicitly sexual meanings attached to publicly-displayed drapery commodities.[25]

Changing forms of window displays after 1900 intensified the appeal of the goods on show. American display strategists, using a new technological repertoire of glass, colour and light, created a 'visual vocabulary of desire' that self-consciously drew on the fantastic, the theatrical and the carnivalesque.[26] Windows which, throughout the nineteenth century, had revealed a confusing and cluttered array of goods using every inch of space were, by the early twentieth century, more restrained and consciously designed to cultivate certain effects. The *Draper* told retailers that attractive settings and 'suggestive presentations' were not only more effective than the old-style clutter, but signified a superior class of trade. By 1914 the object in window design was to 'concentrate the eye on a few articles, and to attract the women into the store to see more'.[27]

The modern store window created an 'atmosphere'. The general objective in creating atmospheric windows was to promote sales by suggesting and selling through dramatic presentation certain values associated with the material goods on show. The *Draper* praised Farmer's windows in 1930 for displaying light spring fabrics in a tableau that included geese in flight, deer leaping from rock to rock, and dolphins playing in the sea. This display naturalised the idea of 'lightness' and suggested an association between buying the new seasons's drapery and the natural energy of spring. A similar attempt to naturalise consumption may have shaped Hordern Brothers' 'rustic' window displays of 1928 which incorporated fountains, rock grottos and miniature trees in shades of gold and green.[28]

Window displays of menswear were generally less appealing. Well into the 1920s, writers in the *Draper* complained that the design of menswear windows lagged behind women's fashion displays. Men's goods were often crowded into the window with little attention to display or the use of space.[29] Photographs of drapery-shop windows reproduced in the *Draper*, which ran an annual window-dressing competition to encourage higher standards of drapery display, confirm that women's windows were more aesthetically arranged than men's. As in interior sales areas, women's fashion goods allowed modern marketing techniques to be implemented in window design more successfully than men's goods.

Leach argues that the new window displays blurred the lines between male and female. A feminist reading of the Australian literature suggests the opposite. While displays may have become more sensual, sexual difference in fact became more marked, and the heterosexual messages implicit in window texts became more explicit as retailers paid more artistic, technological and professional attention to their displays after 1900. Experts assumed that, as windows became less cramped and more deliberately alluring, men's and women's goods would be displayed separately and according to different principles. Following the rules of sexual segregation in departmental display, men's and women's goods rarely appeared in the same window. *Rydge's Business Journal* advised that windows would 'pull better if they appeal to only one sex'. In the case of drapery stores, store windows needed to appeal predominantly to women. In September 1918, for example, all of Mark Foy's eleven fashion windows displayed women's clothes or accessories.[30]

Men's and women's windows created sexually-specific associations and had to be dressed according to sexually-specific principles. The Window Dressing column of the *Draper* drew readers' attention in 1904, for example, to two displays. One featured millinery in a window decorated with a giant butterfly made out of feather tips; the other, for men's hats, showed how they were manufactured. The butterfly symbolised fashion, delicacy and a softly fluttering femininity. The men's hat display, on the other hand, stressed the association between practicality, production and masculinity. Farmer's windows in 1920 showed a similar contrast between masculine and feminine display. The women's fashion windows used graceful Australian flowers and birds arranged so that the light 'fell softly on the feathered occupants'. Birds 'of more sober plumage'—wood pigeons, kookaburras and savage hawks—were used in the menswear windows.[31]

Window-dressers were explicitly instructed to dress their windows differently for men and women. Menswear windows had to appeal to a man's mind rather than his eye. They had to have character and strength so that the man in a hurry would grasp the message quickly. A textbook on window-dressing and display written in 1922 advised retailers to use the new season's 'vogues and vanities' to make women's fashion displays redolent of spring and autumn. Men's mercery, on the other hand, was 'prosaic' merchandise calling for 'utilitarian treatment', and men's tailoring required a dignified, simple and practical display. Research cited in the *Retail Traders' Association of New South Wales Journal* found that women, the more 'primitive sex', were strongly attracted to the colour red and men, the repressed sex, to blue.[32]

A few window displays featuring male and female figures, and a mixture of men's and women's goods began to appear in the 1920s. These displays tended to be in the form of tableaus of heterosocial activity. A drawing-room scene, for example, presented a man dressed for dinner and a woman playing the piano,

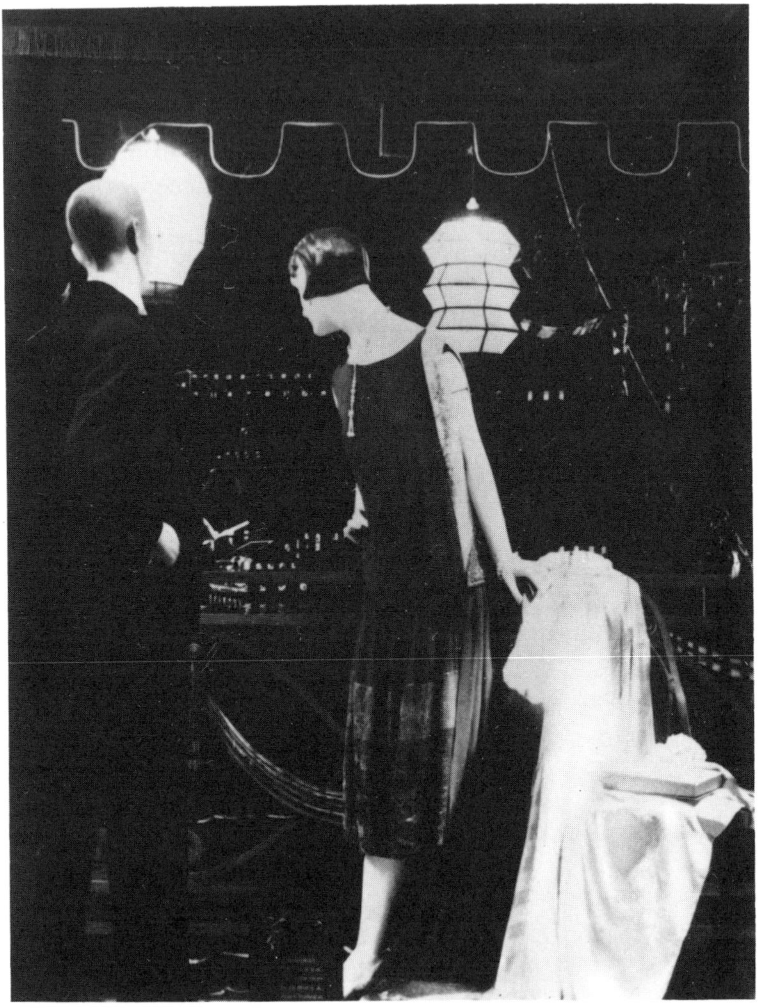

Evening wear window display, David Jones, c. 1920s. A young, fashionable and attractive couple enjoy a night in the city. The window suggests that a man's purchase of an elegant suit and a gift for his partner, and a woman's selection of an elegant frock and jewellery, were necessary for successful heterosexual dating in the 1920s. The man's body indicates his casual command of the situation, hips thrust forward; her body bends in compliance and requires the balcony and chair for balance. They do not appear to be communicating. (DAVID JONES (AUSTRALIA) PTY LTD)

Bridal clothing window display, David Jones, 1927. From the 1920s and 1930s, display experts created representations of courtship, marriage and romance. This tableau of a bride, bridesmaids and pageboy in an ecclesiastical but theatrical setting evoked the romance and glamour of the wedding ceremony. (DAVID JONES (AUSTRALIA) PTY LTD)

and a balcony scene showed a cameo of a young woman and man enjoying a romantic evening together.[33] One writer told retailers that a display atmosphere could be created by showing a bride's trousseau in a cathedral-like setting. He might have been referring to a cathedral scene created by David Jones' window dresser in 1927. The combined effects of bride, bridesmaids, flower girl, pageboy, floral bouquets and stained glass window evoked the pleasures of romance. Drawing-room, courting and wedding windows also visually reinforced and gave concrete expression to a romantic ideal of heterosexual love common in movies, novels, magazine stories and other forms of cultural production.

Windows provided the women and men who viewed them with information about their sexual identity. The window, as it did in a peep show, created a safe transparent barrier between buyer and seller, allowing those on the outside to construct their own, private, fantasy relationships with the goods and figures exhibited on the other side. Rachel Bowlby likens the female consumer to

…ssus gazing at her own reflection in the pool, wanting to …ssess an image which she does not recognise as a reflection of her own body. 'Seducer and seduced, possessor and possessed of one another, women and commodities flaunt their images at one another in an amorous regard'. The shop window represented both barrier and transparent substance, distance and desire. It destroyed the illusion that there was a meaningful distinction between reality and fantasy.[34]

Implicit heterosexual codes heightened the seductiveness of the modern window display. As a desire-enhancing transparent barrier, the shop window encouraged a voyeuristic relationship between retailer and customer. The window separated and protected the voyeur, the subject, from the object of desire. The voyeur remained safely hidden behind a transparent barrier which allowed unrestricted vision, control over the fantasy behind the window, and visual pleasure. The consumer played the role of voyeur, while the commodities on display constituted the sexual fantasy objects owned, controlled and manipulated by the retailer. Retailers, like pimps and peep-show owners, used the window to titillate. The window provided sexual pleasures and knowledges in its own right, as well as advertising the sensual delights for sale within. While the overwhelming majority of consumers of sexual services have been men, department-store window voyeurs of the early twentieth century were female as well as male. Retailers and advertising men drew on and effectively imposed a masculinist model of heterosexual relations on their predominantly female clientele. The men behind the screen/window were those in control of the sex being sold, the women on the footpath the often unwilling recipients.

Some women resisted being placed in the position of passive voyeur. American retailers faced vocal opposition from feminists and other reform groups around the turn of the century to the display of undergarments and scantily clad mannequins.[35] Australian fashion columnists sometimes implied that women were irresistably and perhaps dangerously attracted by the well-dressed window. Despite the customer's resolutions not to spend more than she could afford, she was drawn into the shop convinced that 'she will look as graceful as that figure in the window draped by a master hand'. Jocelyn Perkins, writing in *Helen's Weekly*, asserted that women were often lured into shops by bargains displayed in windows, only to meet inside assistants determined to sell them more expensive items. This, Perkins claimed, was selling on false pretences.[36] M. Barnard Eldershaw commented on the often tawdry seductions of Sydney's big stores of the 1920s in their book *Tomorrow and tomorrow and tomorrow*:

> Bright shop windows, endless with fulfilment, emblems of paradisaical, unattainable living—model rooms in machine-made taste; eternal sylphs of papier mache arrayed in Fashion's dictates for spring, brides who will never go to bed with their waxen bridegrooms; wooden legs that will never lose their line in stockings that will never ladder, lingerie for a harem with no afterthought of the washtub; food voluptuous and ornate beyond the compass of any stomach; mumbo-jumbo of perfumery; secrets of eternal youth and fadeless beauty at bargain prices; no promise too large or improbable, the constant titillation of every gambling impulse . . . humanity feeding on this display as on a new pasture, satisfying eye and imagination for nothing, taking the bait and leaving the hook.[37]

Late-night window shopping is represented in the novel as an indecent display of shoddy manufactured goods creating the illusion of 'Plenty, plenty, plenty'.

As these authors suggested, men and women engaging in window shopping derived their own pleasures from the ritual without necessarily swallowing the hook. Many women enjoyed assuming the unaccustomed position of voyeur. A survey carried out in the United States in 1923 and subsequently reported in the *Draper* found that city women were more often influenced by window displays than any other form of advertising.[38] Australian women, on the whole, also reacted enthusiastically to the big stores' displays. Women's journals devoted regular column space to descriptions of new fashions as they were revealed in store windows for the information of female readers. The *Commonwealth Home*'s female 'Shop Window' columnist passed consistently favourable judgement on the relative merits of different store windows. Women columnists' approving comments on the displays of highly feminine clothing, especially underwear and evening dress, suggests that women derived a private, barely legitimate, sensual pleasure from looking at some store windows. A contributor to the *Shop Assistants Magazine* in 1926, for example, expressed relief that flannelette underwear had been replaced

Underclothing window display, McCathies Ltd, Sydney, 1917. The Draper of Australasia *(May 1917, p. 131) nominated this as one of its prize windows in the general drapery class. The pastel colours, flowers, birds and generally delicate and dainty appearance of the window mark it as female. Because the goods displayed were closely associated with the bedroom or boudoir, and worn next to the female body, the window shows how in the 1910s the selling of women's underwear began to construct and display a sexualised femininity.* (STATE LIBRARY OF NEW SOUTH WALES)

by the 'giddiness of georgette and alluring mystery of crepe-de-chine'. There was, she pointed out, no such allure in windows dedicated to men's wear.[39] The drawing-room scene depicted in

Mark Foy's window in 1928 prompted another woman to describe the attractions of feminine consumer goods:

> . . . the thought struck one that the shop windows would no longer have any attractions if women's fashions changed as infrequently as men's. This man in his dinner suit was quite correct but not a bit different from every other man. The lady at the piano was wearing a scrumptious dress of pale pink georgette with sprays of autumn leaves scattered over, bordered with diamente.[40]

Perhaps women found McCathies' 1917 window display of underwear equally alluring. The window displayed a selection of silky nightdresses, lacy camisoles, embroidered boudoir caps, knickers and garters. The background screens were covered in grey calico, trimmed in black, white and pink, and decorated with blue swallows and paintings of arcadian scenes. Pink lingerie ribbon hung from the ceiling in sensual disarray. The centrepiece was a large jardinière of pink roses, lit by three red lights.[41] The window presented an intimate, delicate femininity that coyly revealed contemporary notions of female sexuality.

Modern store displays were premised on the assumption that women would be seduced by the revelation of (sexed) commodities, sexual display and exhibition. Feminists have argued that exhibitionism is a demonstration of male power designed to effect women's submission. Exhibitionism restricts women's capacity to act autonomously in public places and reminds them to whom these public spaces belong—to men.[42] The exhibitionist/retailer similarly attempted to provoke awe and submission in the women to whom he exposed his goods. Just as exhibitionism is motivated by men's desire to manipulate and seek gratification from evidence of women's submission, store displays were a visible expression of masculinist marketing techniques designed to persuade women to abandon themselves to the culture of consumption for the pleasure and profit of men. Once achieved, however, that female submission had to be carefully managed. As the next chapter shows, women consumers' translation of desire into action frequently evaded retailers' control.

Part III: 1915–1930

6 Managing women's desires

The difficult customer was frequently portrayed in celebratory store histories as an obstacle in the path of the master retailer's success. She was the ubiquitous subject of anecdotes which sought to show to best advantage the founder's firmness and refusal to be intimidated. Francis Foy instructed one difficult customer to tell her husband to give her a good hiding, and personally took the measurements of another, who had dared to criticise the dress-maker, declaring that they were 'for the wooden box you should be in'. David Jones lost his temper with an assistant who failed to deal properly with a customer who was unimpressed with the latest styles from Paris and demanded 'the best the Store can show me'. Charles Lloyd Jones gallantly stressed in his autobiography 'Customers are Human' that the customer was always right, 'even when she is being unreasonable, cantankerous and perhaps a little dishonest, as customers sometimes are'.[1] The title of his manuscript suggests the reader could be forgiven for assuming that sometimes the customer was less than human.

The character traits that retailers and sales experts believed made women ideal consumers, particularly their presumed susceptibility to temptation, rendered customers potentially recalcitrant. Customers who failed to act in the manner expected of them were constructed as 'difficult'; that is, uncooperative, demanding and aggressive. At the extreme end of the range of difficult customer behaviours was the shopper who conformed to the sexual stereotype of impulsive and instinctive woman but who failed to pay for the desirable articles with which retailers tempted her: the shoplifter. Common to the figures of the difficult customer and the shoplifter was their tendency to overstep the bounds of what retailers deemed acceptable feminine behaviour. Recognising the need to channel women's desires, manage the difficult customer and stem the tide of shoplifting, retail managers and their professional helpers devised a number of strategies to regulate female consumer behaviour in the late 1910s and 1920s.

In their attempts to manipulate and derive pleasure from making visible female desire, retail men participated in and encouraged a wider heterosexual culture which eroticised female submission. The language of female desire, temptation and abandonment to irresistable pleasures had permeated descriptions of the big stores since the 1880s. Strengthened by psychological knowledge after the turn of the century, retailers believed that women's desires could be effectively managed, if not actively stimulated. There was clearly strong popular appeal in the image of passive, desiring womanhood passionately awaiting the temptations carefully placed in her way by the smart retailer.

Major retailers consolidated and made more explicit their attempts to seduce women by articulating a formal theory of consumer desire in the 1920s. Sales writers explained, for example, that women's motives for buying were essentially narcissistic and typically expressed in their innate if inexplicable desire for personal adornment. If women were perceived to be suggestible and easily led, then it is not surprising to find that women were constructed as peculiarly inclined to fashion. One writer in the *Home* magazine argued that 'In dress, men are classical, women are romantic'. The rational man with little time to waste on fashion had banished emotion and feeling from his clothes and reduced the art of dress to 'a matter of rules and regulations'. Retail-trade associations and journals acknowledged that women played an economically significant role in determining the relative success of a particular fashionable line of merchandise, and businessmen typically attributed their fashion failures to female fickleness and the unpredictability of women's fashion preferences.[2] Hence fashion constituted a persistent point of tension between female customers and male retail managers.

Women's apparent addiction to fashion reinforced perceptions of them as irrational. The *Draper* carried a series of articles in the early 1920s on the subject of women's taste for adornment, one written by Melbourne University Professor T. Tucker. Tucker suggested that women's desire to adorn themselves was similar to that of savages who wore ornamental rather than functional clothing. With characteristic male disdain for women's clothing preferences, he asked his readers: 'for what else are feathered hats and jewellery intended?' Another male academic, Professor J. Flugel, was equally patronising in a paper presented to the London Sex Congress in 1929 and reported in the *Sydney Morning Herald*, in which he stated that men's dress may have lacked romance, but it also lacked the 'envy, jealousy, petty triumphs, defeats and spitefulness engendered in women over dress'. Women often agreed with these masculine pronouncements: 'When it comes to the question of personal adornment, a woman employs no reason; she knows no logic . . . that is the feminine nature.'[3]

Sales literature of the 1920s drew openly on sexual imagery which reinforced perceptions that women were ripe for sensual abandonment. Lustre Hosiery instructed shop assistants that women's unconscious motivations for buying included 'self-gratification' and 'yielding to weakness'. Shopping was, for women, a 'pleasurable excitement' that should be indulged. Members of the New South Wales Retail Traders' Association were urged in 1922 to deliberately promote these sensual pleasures: 'Keep in mind that 65 to 80 per cent of the impulse to buy a given article comes when the customer is where she can touch, feel or smell ... the goods.' Understanding that the buying process was a 'chain of mental processes'—attention, interest, desire, confidence, decision, action and satisfaction—could help the progressive retailer of the 1930s make selling a scientifically-controlled adventure in which desire itself could be manufactured.[4]

By the late 1920s, sales experts were attempting to convince retailers that women's natural desire for beautiful goods could be actively created through the use of such devices as sale points. Goods were deliberately arranged in order to tempt women into what would today be called impulse buys. Tables displaying inexpensive items designed to meet everyday requirements, such as slippers, manicure sets and handkerchiefs, were placed on the ground floor, and counters of other convenience goods were placed near entrances. Retailers tried to persuade women to buy more than one garment at a time by displaying together certain combinations of clothes so that customers would be tempted into purchasing a blouse and matching skirt.[5] The term 'accessories', also indicating the need for a coordinated outfit or ensemble, began to appear in trade literature in the 1920s.

Creating desire went hand-in-hand with creating demand, a phrase which began to be used by retail managers around 1920. A department store had to actively shape demand and take the lead in showing women the cultural standards to which they should aspire. Charles Lloyd Jones decided to make shopping in his new Elizabeth Street store, opened in 1927, 'a journey of discovery in which the lady of the future would be beguiled by colour, bright lights, new fabrics, new shapes and designs, new smells, sweet and spicy'. His store 'would not only have to sell things, but also create public taste and help cultivate it . . . be a guide to gracious living'. The *Draper* in 1928 praised those retailers who had successfully educated the consumer into believing that she needed more commodities than she initially planned to purchase by teaching her to 'wear a tennis frock for tennis and a golf suit for golf, and to eschew both for afternoon wear'. This theory of consumer education was formalised by Alex T. Whyte, who pointed out in an article in *Rydge's Business Journal* that a bewildering range of choices faced the modern consumer. He advocated a policy, based on the principles of beauty, science and efficiency, of Educational Development of the Consumer.[6] Whyte's inclusion of beauty as one of the principles of consumer progress reveals the sex identity of the consumer to be educated.

The vocabulary of sales experts included by the late 1920s such concepts as market analysis, believed to be the scientific study of the desires and habits of the female consumer, and market promotion. The big-city stores cooperated in devising a number of special promotions such as Empire Shopping Week, Australia-Made Preference League displays, an 'Official Opening of Spring' campaign (1925), Mother's Day (from 1925) and Father's Day (1929). Other promotions drawing on family sentiments encouraged women into the stores. Nock and Kirby organised a demonstration of 'labor-saving devices for the home', with afternoon tea, in 1929. Sydney's department stores staged increasingly spectacular Christmas displays and entertainments. In December 1929, Sydney mothers and their children could choose to see Santa Claus arrive in Sydney by flying boat from Iceland, courtesy of Anthony Hordern & Sons; a smugglers' cave at Mark Foy's; Punch and Judy at McDowells; a Ginger Meggs tableau at Grace Brothers; and circus acts at David Jones.[7]

A range of customer services, most of them designed to make

the store particularly attractive to women, were established as a marketing strategy in the 1920s. Stores such as David Jones, Farmer's and Anthony Hordern & Sons offered delivery, customer credit and removal services, restaurants, telephone bureaus (where an attendant dialled the number while the weary customer rested), ladies' writing and rest rooms, post offices, banking facilities, and information on public transport, entertainment and sightseeing. Stores' provision of meeting rooms, and moral and financial support to selected women's organisations also captured a loyal corner of the female market. David Jones, Farmer's and Marcus Clark were among those stores which cooperated in the Women's Commonwealth Patriotic Association's National Economy Exhibition in 1917. The Young Women's Christian Association was on good terms with the managements of several city stores through its involvement in welfare work and sporting activities for working women. Stores contributed financially to, and Charles Lloyd Jones was chairman of the Publicity Committee for the YWCA's 1919 fund-raising campaign, and Farmers loaned its Welfare Hall to the YWCA for its Girls' Meetings. David Jones offered the Country Women's Association—many of its members regular department store patrons—space for its head office and rest rooms at a nominal rent in 1931.[8]

Despite these concerted efforts to cultivate a loyal female clientele, retailers frequently encountered opposition and resistance from women customers. The same desires and demands for satisfaction that were publicly legitimated by the new culture of consumption were often expressed in ways that retailers and their sales assistants found inappropriate or unmanageable. The 'difficult customer' became a stock figure in trade literature. The amount of attention she received, and the intensity of the hostility she provoked, indicates a strong antipathy, largely but not exclusively based on class differences between sales workers and shoppers of the same sex. Saleswomen bitterly resented, and often successfully resisted, customers' apparently thoughtless demands, complaints, ignorance and lack of consideration.[9] Whether or not female shoppers actually behaved in this way, retail managers turned the stereotype of the difficult shopper to their best advantage. By invoking the spectre of the recalcitrant shopper, retailers deflected potential employee unrest, which may otherwise have been aimed at themselves, towards a common female enemy on the other side of the counter. Manufacturing the difficult customer as a distinctively female personality type, one which most women would try hard to avoid, was an attempt to police women's activities within the store.

Representations of the thoughtless and unethical woman shopper of the wealthy classes, standard within a variety of texts at the end of the nineteenth century, assumed a less class-specific and more distinctly female form after 1910. Women were represented within trade literature by the 1920s as ignorant of their own needs and desires, unfortunate individuals incapable of knowing their own mind or, if they did know what they wanted, possessing deplorable judgement and poor taste. The *Shop Assistants Magazine* warned millinery saleswomen that if they presented too many hats at once, the customer would become confused and therefore fail to make a purchase. Women's characteristic indecisiveness was attributed to their traditional dependence on men to do all the thinking. The magazine urged retailers to train sales assistants to appreciate 'the real joy of helping those who are ignorant of what suits them'. The *Draper* advised its readers that 99 per cent of women lied about their size and therefore needed strong guidance from the skilled sales assistant. Women had to be educated so that they would know which commodities were economical or necessary for happiness. Any woman who presumed to know her own size or know precisely what she wanted was instantly characterised by trade writers as determined and difficult.[10]

These characterisations of women as poor consumers desperately in need of training and guidance from retailers and their assistants was somewhat at odds with the view of women as natural and instinctive shoppers. These contradictory representations are not as incompatible as they appear at first glance. Marketing experts did not, after all, suggest that men needed consumer education. They firmly believed that their superior abilities and experience in the retail field enabled them to develop and mould women's natural predisposition to shop into the kind of buying activity they preferred. The men of the marketing industry wanted to turn a biologically-determined attribute into a scientific and controllable activity.

Retailers enlisted the support of shop assistants in their campaign to educate and change the behaviour of difficult shoppers. A shared antagonism towards the customer was a central feature of female shop assistants' work culture. Shoppers were represented in retail organisation house organs such as David Jones' *Between Ourselves* and the *Dajonian* as callous and inconsiderate. One story told of the shopper who 'hadn't anything to do', so sauntered around about a store, trying on everything, asking prices, demanding demonstrations and making objections.

> That night this dame, with pleasant smile, told hubby how the live-long day her empty hours she did beguile by viewing fashion's fine array. The sale girl hung those dresses up, and then some twenty minutes late, dragged homeward wearily, to sup, and thought most bitterly of fate.[11]

Staff journals were also full of jokes, cartoons and anecdotes poking fun at customers.

> Customer: Are those flowers real?
> Polite assistant: Yes, Madam, we have opened a Cut Flower Department.
> Customer: Oh, they are so very beautiful, I thought they were artificial.[12]

A customer complained that the gloves she was shown could not be the latest style because black kid gloves should have tan stitches and vice versa. 'Ah, madam', said the tactful girl, gently, 'you haven't quite understood. Vice versa is French for one button.'[13] Assistants weren't always so gentle. Journalist Betty Riddell, recounting her experiences 'Behind a Sale Counter' in 1934, reported that 'Girls walked past whispering "Old hag" out of the side of their mouths.'[14]

Retail managers tried to harness shop assistants' antipathy to difficult shoppers by bringing this tension directly into discourse. In-house organs and staff-training courses educated salespeople in the best way to deal with difficult customers. *Between Ourselves*, established in 1919 to induct junior staff into David Jones' ideals of service and foster store loyalty, contained numerous lessons on the need to be cheerful, courteous, tactful and patient. Female assistants in particular were urged to feel a feminine sympathy for the woman on the other side of the counter, and to understand that female nature was a mixture of 'Vanity and Humility, Selfishness and Self-Sacrifice'. David Jones' Improvement Class was instructed in 1925 that the customer must be given the strictest courtesy and attention 'under all circumstances and on all occasions—no matter how trying the occasions may be'.[15]

Trade magazines reinforced the message that retailers were on the side of their assistants. The *Draper* published in 1920 a series of sketches by a woman shopper which showed a number of counter-conflict scenarios in which assistants were inattentive or shoppers inconsiderate. An article in the *Shop Assistants Magazine* was critical of shoppers who looked at and handled the merchandise, deploring in particular the habit of flappers who tried on numerous hats with no intention of buying. The magazine advocated teaching shoppers 'what the person behind the counter has a right to expect' and described with misogynist humour the difficult customer as having 'protruding eyes and bulbous, battered features, which would only look well if closely covered with a bag that was not transparent'.[16]

These hostile representations of shoppers, as Susan Porter Benson suggests, may be evidence of a resilient work culture among female shop assistants which was resistant to managerial control. They also served a useful function for retail managers in their constant struggle to make women's behaviour within their stores amenable to their will. Managers were acute observers of assistant–customer interactions and sought to exploit the tensions between the two groups of women to their own advantage. They openly agreed with their workers that shoppers were difficult and demanding. The Retail Traders' Association of New South Wales, opposing a 1923 Shop Assistants Union attempt to abolish late-night shopping, argued that the shop assistant's duties were not arduous, 'though perhaps irksome at times, in trying to please a thoughtless or irritable customer . . .' Berlei Limited intimated its solidarity with its sales staff against a common enemy in a series of sales manuals published in 1926. Female customers, the manuals asserted, were more 'touchy' than men. Using a military metaphor that became popular in sales and industrial relations texts after World War I, the company commiserated with sales assistants that 'many a soldier has had to salute an unworthy officer'.[17]

By sympathising with their employees, retailers solicited sales assistants' support in persuading female customers to submit to their irrational desires. The *Draper* remarked on the delight of millinery saleswomen, for example, when they succeeded in selling a particularly ugly hat to an unpopular customer: 'I sold that awful old model so-and-so to Mrs so-and-so today—she did look a fright.' These demonstrations of shop-floor culture could be turned into a useful object lesson by impressing on the saleswoman that, as she knew more about hats than did her customer, it was her duty to sell her a flattering model so that she did not become a laughing-stock amongst her friends and as a result shop elsewhere in future. Observing sales assistants engaged in the popular game of re-enacting sales transactions and mimicking disliked customers behind their backs provided retailers with the opportunity to construct didactic playlets with similar scripts.[18]

Retailers' mechanisms of customer management could be more coercive. Their attempts to curb customer and employee theft were the physical and judicial arms of a more general ideological project designed to stimulate and manage women's desires. More 'difficult' than the shopper who wasted the assistant's time or walked out without purchasing the proffered article, was the shopper who yielded to the store's exhortation to possess, but failed to pay for the goods she took. Retailers might induce in consumers the need to possess and successfully manage the act of possession, but they could not always force them to buy. The impulse behind the theft of department-store goods was essentially similar to that behind their purchase; shoplifters and legitimate customers responded almost identically to retailers' and advertisers' efforts to stimulate consumer desire. Consequently, theft rates, as Wolfgang Haug has argued, are as suggestive as sales figures in indicating the success of mass-marketing techniques.[19] The publicity surrounding shoplifting and the apprehension of offenders suggests retailers' constant struggle to establish effective mechanisms of customer surveillance.

Shoplifting had worried retailers from at least the late nineteenth century. However, the first concerted and cooperative campaign to control shoplifting was instituted in 1915, when the Master Retailers' Association of New South Wales requested the Attorney-General to collect statistics on the number of shoplifting convictions in the Sydney area over the previous three years. These and further statistics collected in 1919 suggested that the policing of shoplifting centred primarily on the big stores. Suburban courts recorded either no convictions or very small numbers, but the Central Court convicted a total of 264 persons, and Glebe Court 35, over the three-year period. By 1926 the number of shoplifting charges brought before the Central Police Court had risen to 60 in six months, with an average 'daily catch' of four shoplifters at one city store. At sale time the rate of conviction rose dramatically, with the Central Police Court recording over 150 in one ten-week period.[20] Such statistical forms of knowledge were critical in retailers' efforts to exert political pressure on legislators to impose severer penalties on shoplifters after 1915.

These figures suggest that by the 1920s, female department-store shoppers were policed more intensively than men. A deputation from the Master Retailers' Association cited only male offenders when it urged the Minister of Justice to enforce harsher penalties for store theft in 1913, and almost one-half of the 264 shoplifters convicted at the Central Police Court in 1915 were male. By the first six months of 1926, however, 97 per cent of convicted shoplifters were female; and in June to August 1928, 121 women were convicted compared with 32 men. Shoplifting was perceived within the judiciary as 'an offence to which females are peculiarly addicted'.[21] Crime statistics analysed by Judith Allen indicate that, by the 1920s, shoplifting was a female offence: simple larceny accounted for 75 per cent of all female arrests, compared with 50 per cent of male arrests.[22]

The First Offenders (Women) Act of 1919 may have encouraged stores to prosecute apparently respectable members of the 'gentler sex'. The Act was the result of pressure placed on legal institutions by various women's groups to cater for the special needs of women offenders, particularly shoplifters. It allowed first-time female offenders the right to have their cases heard *in camera* (and therefore not published in newspapers), and stipulated more lenient punishments such as fingerprinting and regular reports to the police.[23] Such provisions were deemed more appropriate to the perceived middle-class status of many shoplifting women. Magistrates believed that a significant proportion of shoplifters were 'in comfortable circumstances, of good social standing, and some of them wealthy'. Retailers shared the same perception. The Retail Traders' Association impressed on the Attorney-General that shoplifters were frequently the 'wives and daughters of reputable citizens, and are not driven by necessity to steal'.[24]

Despite this common perception, both working-and middle-class women were prosecuted. In her sample of women imprisoned for property offences in this period, Allen found that

60 per cent were married and involved in home duties, and 31 per cent were in domestic service.[25] Female domestics, waitresses and shop assistants were mentioned in press reports of shoplifting after 1929. Whether working class or middle class, court proceedings placed particular emphasis on the breadwinning capacities of their husbands and an assumed lack of material need. Annie Jones, a 41-year-old domestic, had a husband in constant work, a good home and no children.[26] Gertrude Holbrow was described as a wealthy woman with an account at David Jones; Mary Dain was married to an optician, lived in a 'fashionable residential' in Neutral Bay, received an income from her father, and owned over £1000 in shares and bonds.[27] Men accused of shoplifting were reported much less frequently, and were typically working men like printer Harry Savage.[28]

A range of criminological, sociological and psychological discourses, as Elaine Abelson demonstrates in her study of American shoplifters, constructed the female shoplifter as selfish, weak-willed, childlike, illogical and incapable of controlling or accounting for her desires.[29] A tone of moral outrage pervaded press reports of female shoplifters who were apparently well-provided for by male breadwinners. Their unjustifiable behaviour was seen to be irrational and objectionable in a typically-female way. The goods that women were reported to have stolen were those that confirmed men's impressions that women were easily tempted by beautiful and fashionable goods designed for their own pleasure. Women typically stole clothes, watches, jewellery, and articles of personal or home adornment.[30] The *Sydney Morning Herald* suggested that the display of new spring dresses filling shop windows in September 1929 had led to an 'astounding' increase in female shoplifting. Women had stolen beads, broches, hats, dress lengths and alarm clocks.[31] Observers found such theft reprehensible. As the *Truth* moralised in its report of Mary Dain's case:

> When the poverty stricken mother steals to cover the shivering bodies of her babies, or some food to quieten their starving cries, society is not too hard on her. But what can be said in amelioration of the women who, living in the lap of comparative luxury, calmly walk into our department stores and deliberately steal articles of clothing and jewellery, merely to satisfy their vanity?[32]

Mary Dain's crime was not so much the theft itself, as her feminine inability to resist the temptation of pretty things.

This submission was precisely the aim of mass-marketing policies. As members of the Retail Traders' Association themselves acknowledged, the shoplifter 'acts impulsively and yields to sudden temptation'. Business journals continued at least into the 1960s to attribute shoplifting to displays which 'put temptation in the way of people of weak moral calibre'. Reports of women shoplifters' activities suggested that their personalities were dominated and disordered by an uncontrollable sexual imperative. Shoplifters were described in the *Sydney Morning Herald*, for example, as women driven by an immoral and insatiable lust for expensive clothes. Police and magistrates stressed that only 'weak-willed' people were tempted by retailers' display methods and advertising techniques.[33] Other reports referring to women's vanity and 'love of finery' constructed them as narcissistic and self-indulgent.[34] Men, presumably, had the iron will, moral constitution and habits of sexual continence that enabled them to withstand the temptation to steal—and to buy.

Kleptomania, perceived as a manifestation of women's child-like behaviour, became the preferred explanation for this form of behaviour. The focus of medical, psychological and legal debate in America and Europe since the 1870s, kleptomania was, by the 1920s, a well-institutionalised and popular term implying women's psychological and biological inferiority, and vulnerability to temporary mental aberrations. Medical experts represented kleptomania—like homicidal mania, pyromania and nymphomania—as perversions of moral sensibility to which women were particularly susceptible as a result of physiological weaknesses inherent in their sexuality and reproductive systems. In some cases, experts made explicit the connections between kleptomania and consumer desire. Elaine Abelson cites an 1887 medical superintendent's report on a woman who was said to be suffering from a womb disease described as 'larceny and eroticism with hysteria'. These manias, according to medical opinion, were the result of 'a natural desire to accumulate exaggerated by disease'.[35] Kleptomania represented the pathological end of a normal spectrum of female consumer behaviour.

The term 'kleptomania' appears to have attracted less professional attention in Australia in the period to 1930 than it did in

America.[36] The influence of medical discourses on representations of female nature can be detected, nevertheless, in the *Draper's* observation in 1915 that two shoplifters demonstrated 'kleptomaniacal tendencies'. McCathies' refusal to prosecute one of these women because a director knew her husband demonstrates the dilemma faced by retailers who wanted to stop shoplifting, but were reluctant to prosecute members of that group of middle-class women whose custom they assiduously courted. The *Evening News* described kleptomaniacs as people with the primitive lack of moral control and selfishness of spoiled children—possibly the 'nervous, querulous' type of customer in pathological form—who 'spot something, desire it, and take it'.[37]

Whether assumed to be suffering from a female disorder, or simply characterised as unable to withstand the impulse to take beautiful objects, women shoplifters were inevitably tagged with a sexual label that trivialised and infantilised their actions. Shoplifters, like other women caught in the web of the criminal-justice system as victims of crimes such as rape and carnal knowledge, were increasingly sexualised. Allen argues that during the inter-war years new psychiatric practices and sexological discourses constructed women as openly and actively sexual beings quite capable of giving their willing consent to sexual encounters. Drawing on pre-existing knowledges of woman as a creature imbued with strong and predatory sexual desires, and buttressed by psychoanalytic theories of hysteria and sexual repression, 'sexological discourse promoted joyful, reciprocal, even rapturous heterosexuality' as the norm.[38] Shoplifters and their close cousins, shoppers, were not immune to these new discourses of sex.

How did retailers attempt to prevent women from taking consumerism too far? At the shop-floor level, women were increasingly subjected to the surveillance of shop assistants and specially trained staff. Detective schemes had, by the 1920s, largely replaced the earlier, more informal forms of customer surveillance dependent on the eagle eye of the assistant, shopwalker or cashier. Some stores employed as many as six detectives by 1928.[39] These employees often had direct links to the police force. The full title of Farmer's chief detective was House Inspector and Special Constable, and a former chief of the Criminal Investigation Branch of New South Wales was appointed to an executive position on the store's staff in 1928.[40]

The techniques used to secure convictions or prevent repeat offences also drew on methods characteristic of the criminal-justice system. One store kept a 'confession book' which offenders were required to sign if they were 'in poor circumstances, or in an advanced state of pregnancy' before being allowed to go home uncharged. Police officers investigating the case of Emily Austin, a detective instrumental in charging 97 women and ten men with shoplifting at Mark Foy's between 1926 and 1928, suggested she may have fabricated evidence in order to lay charges. It was alleged that Austin followed customers around the store, waited for them to throw away their dockets, then accused them of stealing, and pressured them into signing the confession book.[41] The charges against the zealous Emily Austin were never proven, but it is not unlikely that shoppers were occasionally harassed or provoked without cause.

This was almost certainly the case with a cooperative detective scheme organised by the major retailers in 1929 to stop theft by employees. Employers frequently complained in the same breath of dishonesty among both employees and customers, and used similar means of surveillance and coercion to deal with female misbehaviour on both sides of the counter.[42] Shop assistants, who were also consumers, were placed perilously close to the temptations of the store. Early in 1928 the Retail Traders' Association recommended the services of two inquiry agencies to members who wanted to investigate suspected staff theft and 'keep a check on efficiency'. As female department store employees outnumbered men by four to one by the 1920s, women were the main target of this campaign. These private detectives masqueraded as customers, keeping an eye out for assistants seen to be spending money regularly on sweets or engaged in similarly suspicious activities.[43]

One seventeen-year-old woman employed on the handkerchief counter of one big store was questioned by detectives after making a mistake in ringing-up a sale. She was closely interrogated about her clothes, her parents and her private life, and was accused of stealing a total of £150 over previous months. The detectives threatened that if she refused to sign a confession she would be sent to a reformatory until she was 21. The Shop Assistants Union insisted that this case was not unusual, and that many innocent assistants, most of them young women, were being unnecessarily intimidated and unfairly dismissed. Deaf to objections from the union and the Australian Labor Party—even the threat of a strike—retailers responded that honest workers had nothing to fear, and that the purity gang was a 'godsend' to beleaguered proprietors. The press, hostile to what it described as American business practices which smacked of the 'methods of the *agent provocateur*', supported the union in its outrage at 'Sydney Shop Girls Being Terrorised by Yankee "Purity Gang" '.[44]

Retailers were in the meantime attempting to legislate against inappropriate consumer behaviour. As they estimated that only one shoplifter in ten was caught, deterrence was held to be the best way of stopping those women tempted to steal. The Master Retailers' Association initiated a campaign in 1909 to persuade the Minister for Justice that offenders should be punished by imprisonment rather than fines.[45] Retailers vociferously opposed special protections for women, especially the embargo on newspaper reporting, enshrined in the First Offenders (Women) Act, and impressed upon the Minister in 1926 their belief that most shoplifters feared publicity more than any other form of punishment. They assumed, perhaps, that women 'naturally' experienced intense humiliation and shame at the public exposure of their desires. Detective Keogh's assertion that, before the Act, some women caught shoplifting at Farmer's were prepared to 'sacrifice their bodies' to him to prevent their husbands and families finding out, is as revealing of men's power and sexual fantasies as it is of women's desperation. Other women implored store managers not to inform their families, or offered to plead guilty if their husbands were not told of their offence. Mary Dain cried when the judge threatened her with gaol. 'Oh, please don't sir. I'd rather commit suicide than go to gaol. It will give me the lesson of my life if you will give me a chance this time.'[46]

Retailers fully realised that they had a potent sexual–psychological weapon in the threat of public humiliation, and placed continual pressure on the Attorney-General throughout the 1920s to allow cases to be heard in open court. They succeeded in 1929 in having the First Offenders (Women) Act amended to exempt shoplifters from its protective provisions, require shoplifting cases to be heard in public, and permit full details to be published in newspapers. Newspaper clippings from this period which survive in the archives of David Jones and Grace Brothers are testimony to the relief and satisfaction with which retailers greeted the amendment.[47]

Although publicity given to cases after 1929 tended to emphasise the remorse and penitence of women who could offer no explanation for their actions, many women had no moral qualms in deliberately cheating retailers of payment for the goods they so temptingly offered. One member of a female shoplifting gang, for example, would buy a cheap attaché case, have it wrapped, cut the paper from around the lid so that it could be opened, and fill it with silks. If she was likely to be detected, the case would be dumped and female accomplices would support the woman in her denial of ownership. In a dramatic chase through Pitt Street in March 1929, one woman felled a shopwalker and struggled with a detective before escaping, while her partner was caught, escaped and was recaptured.[48] For three years, shop assistant Jessie Powell stole dresses while her partner Minnie Munro stole shoes from David Jones, which they would then exchange.[49]

As the Chairman of the Metropolitan Branch of Stipendiary Magistrates astutely commented to the Under Secretary for Justice in 1934, increased deterrents manifestly failed to counteract the effects of the stores' attractive advertising and display methods.[50] Because shoplifting was to some extent a logical response to mass-marketing policies, legislative measures were unlikely to have much effect while retailers continued their efforts to emancipate women's desires for consumer goods. Chief Stipendiary Magistrate Mr Gates clearly blamed retailers:

> There is not the slightest doubt in my mind that the manner in which goods are strewn about nowadays is a distinct temptation to weak-minded people. In the old days we had to ask for anything we wanted; under modern conditions it is scarcely possible to walk through a shop without dragging something off a table.[51]

Many paying customers strongly disapproved of shoplifting, some agreeing with magistrates that retailers should stop the display of small items on tables which placed temptation in people's way.[52] Retailers had, according to many contemporaries, only themselves to blame.

Retailers were therefore in something of a quandary. A fundamental principle of the new techniques of mass marketing was the careful cultivation of consumer desire. Retailers and sales experts held that women were 'by nature' or, more typically by the 1920s, by psychological inclination, irrational and suggestible and therefore ideal collaborators in the new consumer venture. These same feminine qualities, however, could make women's behaviour in the department store frustratingly difficult to manage. It must have seemed to retailers that, once unleashed, women's desires were uncontrollable. Other evidence of women's agency as consumers in the first two decades of the twentieth century made progress towards a consumer society neither easy nor inevitable.

7 Madam intervenes: women and consumer politics

Although retailers appeared to have the upper hand in the shaping of consumer culture by the 1920s, women were not uncritical consumers. Retailers listened closely to these female critiques and conversations because their livelihoods and profits depended on them. Trade journals such as the *Draper* regularly included articles by shoppers on their experiences 'on the other side of the counter' or words of advice from customers to shop assistants, and reminded proprietors to listen to the opinions of their customers and even those of their own wives and daughters. One female shopper, who came out of a shop 'nursing an ugly suspicion' that its women employees did not get a fair deal, admonished retailers in 1921 that 'the customer is not necessarily blind or deaf, just because good manners generally require her to be dumb'.[1]

Members of the new breed of professional sales writers, such as Herbert Casson, and business publications such as *Rydge's Business Journal* urged retailers to systematically study women's desires and seek their opinion on the value of goods. Professional associations such as the Sydney Publicity Club made determined efforts in 1930 to educate their members on topics such as 'A Woman's View of Advertising' and 'What Housewives Expect from Advertising'. Statistical surveys, usually conducted in the United States or Britain but quoted authoritatively by Australasian trade writers, promised a more scientific approach to monitoring the behaviours and reactions of shoppers. A *Draper* editorial referred to a survey carried out on a sample group of English shoppers in 1926, 27 per cent of whom complained of slow service, short change, unsatisfactory goods, high prices, or assistants pushing the goods. Ultimately, however, these new knowledges concurred with traditional business wisdom that 'if [the wife of the wage-earner] is happy then she will make you, if she finds the atmosphere uncongenial she will break you'.[2]

What *did* women think of the new consumer culture? Some histories of the department store and of the fashion industry suggest that women responded positively to the possibilities of 'a more exciting, more appealing life, freedom remade within a consumer matrix'.[3] While women certainly derived considerable satisfactions from the activities, ambiences and meanings of consumerism, they were not necessarily passive recipients of the messages directed at them by the managers of consumption. They were active, creative and sometimes political shoppers; or, at least, as critical as the prescriptions of their class, sex and times allowed. This chapter assesses the political and discursive significance of feminist interventions into retail practices, fashion and consumer culture in the years between World War I and 1930.

This period is not normally associated with militant feminist activity, and has been seen by some historians as a dark age for the women's movement. According to Carmel Shute, conservative wartime mythologies of women's place, followed by the traditional celebration of motherhood and new efforts to protect and stabilise family life, led to the 'demise' of the women's movement in the post-war era.[4] Recent research has shown, however, that women were by no means politically inactive in this period. On the contrary, women continued many old struggles and initiated numerous new campaigns in women's interests in a wide range of areas including female wages, working conditions and employment opportunities, the welfare of women and children, female political representation, peace, prohibition, racial purity, the moral protection of young women and the prevention of venereal disease. The formation of a number of significant women's organisations—the Housewives Association in 1917, the Country Women's Association in 1922, and the Business and Professional Women's Association in 1925—suggests that the 1920s were relatively productive times for female association.[5] Although few organisations pursued what contemporary feminists might define as radical objectives, women nevertheless attempted to effect social change by creatively appropriating roles such as wife, housewife, mother, peacemaker and moral and spiritual guardian.

Women also redefined the role of consumer in the post-World War I period to embrace political meanings. Explaining that the

Housewives Association's aim was to protect the home and 'fight the consumer's battle', the president of the South Australian association added emphatically: 'And we are all consumers'.[6] Women's promotion of consumer-oriented concepts such as the professional housewife, scientific shopping, domestic science, domestic arts education, and home administration created a political environment which not only validated women's daily consumer activities but constructed strong rhetorical platforms from which a feminist critique of consumer culture might be publicly voiced. The scientific language underlying much of this consumer politics effectively challenged the dominant discourse of women as essentially irrational and unpredictable.

Middle-class women continued in the twentieth century to exercise their established right to criticise retailers for underpaying and overworking their female employees. Although state legislation to some extent forced retailers to improve wages and working conditions after the 1890s, women's organisations continued to attempt to improve conditions for women working in retail establishments into the 1920s and beyond. The Militant Women's Group argued, in terms similar to feminist objections voiced thirty years earlier, that: 'No one who has been into a big store at the busy hours can cherish any illusion as to working under such conditions—badly-ventilated rooms, insufficient accommodation and the harrowing supervision of the "floorwalker".'[7]

The National Council of Women and Labor Women were among other women's organisations who joined the Militant Women's Group in demanding the abolition of late-night shopping in the 1920s. The Young Women's Christian Association's industrial welfare work demonstrated a particular concern for health of female shop assistants, and secured the cooperation of store managements in providing facilities designed to meet young women's welfare, physical education and recreational needs.[8]

Women reformers also attempted to improve training provisions and thereby increase opportunities for young women in retail employment. The Housewives Association of New South Wales and the National Council of Women initiated a campaign in 1919 to establish training schemes and vocational guidance for shop assistants who, reported May Matthews of the Council's Standing Committee for Professions and Trades of Women, were exploited as juniors by many retail houses. The National Council of Women was subsequently represented on the enquiry into apprenticeship for junior shop assistants set up in 1925 by the New South Wales Board of Trade. The National Council of Women and the Housewives Association, with the support of the Retail Traders' Association, advocated the establishment of a Vocational Guidance Bureau. Vocational training, they argued, was essential for the career development of women working in shops and could result in more women advancing within the retail industry into positions such as buyer or even member of the Board.[9] Whether or not these aims were achievable, their articulation provides evidence that women were not afraid to take issue with and attempt to change retailers' employment policies.

Australian women seemed to have preferred negotiation to the more radical methods adopted by American feminists in their disputes with the big stores over the exploitation of female labour. The consumer's equivalent to the strike was a boycott of stores seen to be engaging in unfair labour practices. Unlike women in the United States, Europe and New Zealand—and unlike Melbourne women who led street protests against the high cost of living in 1917—Sydney women do not appear to have employed demonstrations or boycotts (either of goods sold by employers of sweated female labour, or of high-priced fashion goods) as a means of exerting consumer power.[10]

Although no formal association of consumers seems to have got off the ground in Sydney in this period, some women made preliminary moves towards organising consumer pressure groups. Feminist consumer initiatives in Australia were influenced by similar developments overseas and supported by the shared ideals of a growing international women's movement. The Civic League considered forming a consumer's association in cooperation with other women's groups in 1909, after hearing a paper given by Miss E. Fry on the Consumers Leagues of the United States, France and Switzerland. The Civic League appears to have run into organisational difficulties thereafter, and there was no further reference to the proposal. It may in any case have been too difficult to secure the widespread cooperation of women of widely differing political allegiances. A boycott of gloves aimed at forcing retailers to lower their price, proposed by the Housewives Association in 1920, was dismissed by the Australian Women's National League as an unpatriotic, crude and ineffective method of combating the high cost of living.[11]

Women did actively participate, however, in consumer co-operatives. A Women's Co-operative Society, with membership restricted to women only, was established in 1911 to carry on wholesale and retail business, and cover 'all matters of benefit or interest to women'. A Balmain Consumers' Cooperative (perhaps the same) included women among its membership, one of whom argued strongly for the involvement of women in the cooperative movement at the Australian Congress of Consumers' Co-operative Societies in 1920. Women shareholders actively criticised the mis-management of the Civil Service Co-operative Society Stores when it ran into financial difficulties in the late 1920s. Established in 1871 for the benefit of public-service employees, by the 1920s the Civil Service Stores would have catered to a significant number of women employed in the New South Wales public service, and presumably the wives of male public servants. Women criticised the management 'from the housewife's viewpoint' at a 'stormy' shareholders' meeting in 1929 and, at a subsequent meeting of 60 female shareholders, agreed to support two candidates for the board of directors and offered suggestions for improving the store's performance. The housewives' intervention was to no avail, however, as the business failed shortly after.[12]

Such direct intervention by women into store management was rare. More commonly women demonstrated their expertise as shoppers in popular print. Shopping columns for women such as the *Commonwealth Home*'s 'Shop Window' and the *Australian Worker*'s 'Purely Business' column began to appear after the turn of the century in newspapers, women's periodicals and the journals of women's organisations, and from 1914 in the *Draper*. Typically containing shopping hints, fashion information, details of goods being sold in the major stores, and sometimes offering the services of a shopping expert who would buy specified articles for readers at the lowest possible price, these columns were written by 'Housewife', 'Shopper' or 'A Woman Shopper'.[13] Shopping columns and shopping services did more than provide employment and publication avenues for individual female consumers. They legitimated shopping as a socially useful activity from which women could derive considerable self-esteem as the undisputed experts on fashion, style and bargain-hunting. Shopping advice could serve more political purposes. A Bargain-Hunter's hint to readers of *Everylady's Journal* to 'know what you want, and try to get it; if you can't get it today, wait and try again', helped women resist retailers' attempts to get them to spend impulsively and indiscriminately.[14]

The high prices, shortages and presence in shops of German-made articles during World War I gave women's organisations a stronger voice in consumer politics. Women urged shoppers to buy Australian and British-made goods and to boycott those manufactured in Germany. In a demonstration of female solidarity that transcended class-based ideological divisions, the YWCA, the Feminist Club, the Professional Women's Association, Labor Women and the Women Workers Association joined with the Retail Traders' Association to promote the consumption of Australian-made goods and institute Empire Shopping Weeks from the late 1920s. The interests of retailers and the women's movement did not always coincide, however. Women who supported the ideal of household economy were especially critical of unrestrained spending on consumer goods, and urged women to reduce household expenditure and more effectively manage the domestic budget by exercising thrift.[15]

The increased cost of commodities during the war and the desire of some women to impress on government that it was the wage-earner's wife who bore the brunt of the high cost of living led to the formation in 1917 of the Housewives Association of New South Wales. E. Marie Irvine explained in an article entitled 'Madam Intervenes' in *The Home* magazine that the Association's objects included procuring 'by every lawful means the reduction of excessive prices of necessary commodities'. The Housewives Association took immediate practical steps to protect women from the high cost of food by setting up suburban food markets and establishing cooperative buying schemes for goods such as tea and sugar.[16]

A second main concern was to press for female representation on state and Commonwealth government enquiries into the basic wage and the high cost of living. As Mrs Jordan pointed out to the New South Wales Board of Trade hearing into the cost of living in 1920, the Housewives Association believed strongly that the basic wage should be determined on the basis of the evidence of women witnesses with daily experience in spending the family income and managing the household budget. Other women objected to men determining what was reasonable expenditure on female clothing, especially more personal items of female attire.[17] Members of the Housewives Association and other feminists were relatively successful in their endeavours to get the female consumer's voice heard in cost of living enquiries. Four women were appointed to advise the Board of Trade on working women's clothing needs and expenditures in 1919, and representatives from the Housewives Association and other women's groups gave evidence in 1919 and at the basic wage hearings in 1920. May Mathieson of the Housewives Association was appointed to monitor the prices of dresses and other goods for the Necessary Commodities Control Commission of 1919–20.[18]

'Madam's' intervention into consumer politics had its limits. The *Lone Hand* criticised the Housewives Association's failure to point out that high prices were partly attributable to the inflationary marketing policies of the large drapery stores. The Association ought to 'show the difference between the necessary cost of distribution, and the unnecessary luxury of distribution, such as the costly furnishing of show-rooms, the expensive clothing of attendants and so on, the price of luxuries coming out of the price we pay for clothes and furniture'.[19]A coat wich sold wholesale for £7 5s and retail for £10 represented a 'fairly large sum for the retailer's profit'. The Housewives Association and National Council of Women also attracted criticism from labour women for ignoring the clothing needs of married working-class women.[20] Not only was Madam apparently reluctant to directly criticise retailers and advertisers, but in many ways she supported their efforts to maximise consumption. Female representatives stressed the need for the working woman to possess certain good-quality items in her wardrobe—corsets, costumes, blouses, skirts, umbrellas, boot polish—if she was to maintain a minimum standard of decency and respectability. The retail and advertising industries also remained immune to the National Council of Women's criticism of the extension in the late 1920s of credit facilities such as the cash-order system. A much larger body of women—139 000 housewives—supported retailers by signing a petition in support of the coupon system.[21]

While muted, some direct criticism of the big stores began to appear in magazines and women's organisation's publications in the late 1920s. The Women's League of New South Wales and the Labor Women's Conference both complained of 'unhealthy' basements in city retail houses, and the Country Women's Association of New South Wales unsuccessfully sent copies of certain unspecified resolutions passed at its 1929 conference to the Retail Traders' Association. The *Home* magazine's 'Clearing House' page, devoted to 'the philosophy of home-making', suggested a possible debate on the topic of 'big shops versus little shops—monopoly or competition?'[22] David Jones' Elizabeth Street store attracted particularly vocal criticism, largely on aesthetic grounds, in 1927. Customers found the interior 'barnlike', 'bald' and 'drab', and reported it had the 'barrenness of a storehouse'. Women made unfavourable comparisons between the store's interior and the standards of domestic comfort and design to which they were accustomed. The floor, according to the *Commonwealth Home*, '. . . with its appearance of ingrained dirt and potholes, makes no appeal to the woman used to regarding her own highly-polished floors as the acme of refinement and cleanliness. Lack of resilience and foot comfort does not contribute to popularity.'[23] The stairs, women said, were like factory fire escapes, and the positioning of the lifts required them to walk a long way from the entrance.[24] This critical reaction to the new store suggests that, by the 1920s, shoppers had a clear sense of what they expected in a modern department store, and that their preference for luxury and comfort often failed to coincide with the modern ideas of store design employed by store managements.

This female criticism extended to the fashions and styles of modern dress advertised and sold by the big stores. The confident formulations of a feminist politics of dress which characterised the late nineteenth-century and early twentieth-century women's movement appear to have been submerged beneath other concerns in the 1910s and 1920s. New female clothing styles began to challenge traditional perceptions of conservative and demure womanhood after Paul Poirot's narrow skirts and 'natural' look began to dominate store fashions and catalogues after 1913. Clothing manufacturers began to abandon the noticeably corseted, moulded and constrained female silhouette for one that appeared looser, simpler and more sensuous. The social impact of the new fashions was heightened by a popular dance craze—most notoriously the tango—which encouraged (or provided the excuse for) less restrictive and more revealing dresses. The 'flapper', with her liking for short skirts, dancing, and sexually unconventional behaviour attracted particular disapproval from older women and men concerned that her immoral behaviour threatened traditional definitions of femininity and family life.[25]

Post-World War I Australian society, according to Allen, was characterised by sexual conflict in which the home represented 'conceded, even conquered territory' for men returning from war service. Sexology, Freud, movies and the marketing industry had, by the 1920s, facilitated the social acceptance of the idea that women were sexual creatures. Some women nevertheless effected significant renegotiations of that heterosexuality and of norms and expectations in sexual relations.[26] Women intervened in this newly-sexualised consumerism by commenting on the effects of alcohol and dancing on sexual behaviour, and by specifying appropriate clothing and demeanour for women. Women's opposition to forms of dress and behaviour considered immoral or degrading to womanhood thus constituted a critique of heterosexual consumer culture.

Women reformers' assessments of fashion and dress not only became less favourable after 1910, but were more directly focused on their sexual implications. The Woman's Christian Temperance Union was one of the first organisations to protest in 1913 at the immorality and immodesty—by which they meant (relatively) low necks, short sleeves, and tight and short skirts—prevalent in young women's dress. Members of the National Council of Women quickly followed suit in condemning the 'low tone of society [and] the inordinate love for pleasure and dress so frequently approaching indecency'. The Sydney branch of the YWCA, an organisation not afraid to actively encourage young women to critically engage with controversial issues affecting the status of women, organised a discussion in 1922 on the topic: 'Should a Girl Dance?' In the course of the discussion, fashion and female morality became inextricably intertwined. One member asserted that 'if a girl's style [of dress] is loose, she cannot expect to be treated with every respect'.[27]

One woman's outspoken remarks on modern fashions caused the National Council of Women some embarrassment in 1914. Rose Scott retained among her private collection of papers a clipping of a newspaper article in which Mrs Henry Dobson claimed that modern styles of dress were extreme, immodest, ungainly and indecent, and the women who wore them were foolish and a 'disgrace to humanity'. This outburst prompted one woman, perhaps a member of a rival organisation, to write to the *Sydney Morning Herald* suggesting that members of the National Council of Women would better devote their energies to seeking the cause of modern fashions, rather than indulging in sweeping and largely inaccurate condemnations of their sisters.[28]

A range of views on fashions also existed within the Mothers' Union. Many members were horrified at the unseemly, unladylike, frivolous and 'suggestive' fashions of 1920. Others adopted a more ameliorative tone. One associate member (perhaps a single woman), suggested that fashion was a complex issue. Christian women had a duty to elevate God above self-gratification and therefore could not condone immodest fashions such as short skirts and flesh-coloured stockings. On the other hand, even Christian women did not want to be Puritans: 'we want to have all the beauty and comeliness that we can in our clothes, as in everything else that makes life beautiful'. Echoing her feminist predecessors who argued for a female aesthetics and politics of dress, this Mothers' Union woman believed that dress should be a matter of principle.[29]

Dress became a matter of principle for other women's groups during and immediately after World War I, when shortages and high prices made thrift a desirable policy. Because of her responsibilities as a consumer, the housewife was in the vanguard of the thrift campaign. The Women's Commonwealth Patriotic Association published a series of pamphlets on the subject, including one on 'Thrift in Dress', in which Ruth Beale gave hints to women on ways in which they could avoid waste, shop efficiently and buy economically. Stylish colours, patterns and designs were uneconomical because they quickly went out of fashion. The Association's criticism of extravagant fashions, its advice to women that tailor-made garments were more economical in the long run than ready-made clothes, and its promotion of thrift, economy, and conservativism in dress ran directly counter to retailers' attempts to increase levels of consumer spending.[30]

Beale stated at the outset of her lecture, however, that 'Good appearance is of enormous importance to a woman' and that, despite economic stringencies, her clothes had to be neat, appropriate and becoming. Beale's important qualification suggests that even those women who were opposed to extravagance and immodesty continued to see 'becoming' clothing as essential to female identity. The YWCA strongly opposed the suggestion that standardised clothing schemes be introduced as a thrift measure, because members held the view that women had a duty to express their individuality and 'look as neat and nice as possible'.[31] This basic requirement applied particularly to women in politics. *Table Talk*'s inclusion in 1925 of an article on 'How to Dress for a Political Meeting' did not, as Barbara Cameron suggests, trivialise feminist politics, but signalled women's recognition that clothes were political.[32] Women appeared to have accepted their sex's love of clothes as not only natural but, by the 1920s, psychologically healthy. Using the Freudian notion of repression, Eleanor Allen of the YWCA argued that any woman who suppressed her desire for beautiful clothes was likely to display an unnatural anger against adornment and pretty dresses.[33] Fashionable drapery was no longer seen as a 'feminine luxury' analagous to men's consumption of tobacco or alcohol, as Beatrix Tracy had suggested in 1908, but a psychological, political and social necessity.

A few women attempted to integrate this new consumerist self-consciousness into feminist theory by arguing that women made an economically vital contribution to the social process of consumption. Constance Davey, awarded a Master of Arts in mathematics and economics in 1918 and later a PhD in psychology, formulated in 1919 a theory of consumption in her article on 'The Problem of Spending' in the YWCA's magazine *Association Woman*. Davey argued for an 'economy of right choice and an economy of right use', economies which women failed to exercise when they spent their incomes on luxuries or harmful goods. They could learn to satisfy their wants by the 'harmonious consuming' of goods which cost relatively little. Adopting the language of scientific rationality which men had for so long used to the detriment of women, Davey concluded that women must strive for 'the greatest surplus utility over . . . cost, and this is found by constantly considering their marginal values'.[34]

Other educated women supported the argument for female intervention in the economy on the basis of women's special responsibility for the pursuit of thrift. Janet Mitchell, BA, Thrift Service Director to the Government Savings Bank of New South Wales in 1928, and member of the YWCA, argued in *Rydge's Business Journal* that as women were the nation's major purchasers, 'the greatest field for the thrift education of the future lies in the economic education of women'. This education could be achieved through training courses in household and personal finance and, within the family, through mutually-determined family budgets and the education of children in financial awareness.[35] From the point of view of the Savings Bank, a wife and mother was destined to be a well-trained domestic manager and the educator of good little consumers, rather than an autonomous consumer herself.

Feminists Florence Fourdrinier and Mary Moss devised more radical theoretical connections between women, shopping and politics. Moss proposed that the politics of women's rights should be well grounded in an analysis of consumption. She described how industrialisation had ousted women from their productive function, with the result that men had become the producers and women the consumers. The art of right buying, however, was just as important as the art of right producing, and women must use their consumption powers wisely to improve the quality of goods on sale. Moss argued that commercial interests had exploited feminine qualities derived from women's responsibility for feeding, clothing and sheltering human beings. She argued that these feminine attributes could be reclaimed to govern the sphere of production as well as consumption, in a balance of head and heart.[36]

Florence Fourdrinier's career as a commentator on consumerism included a period in 1919 as editor of David Jones' house organ *Between Ourselves*, and then as editor of the official organ of the Housewives Association, *Ours: a Paper for Australian Homes*. She pointed out in 1921 that the word 'economy' derived from the Greek term for the regulation and management of the household. Women, Fourdrinier asserted, were better shoppers than men because they were familiar with the principles of household management. She urged them to vote as carefully and intelligently as they shopped.[37] The Australian Women's National League took a similar position in August 1931, when it supported the platform of Joe Lyons, leader of the newly-formed United Australia Party. Lyons deplored the fact that consumers, most of whom were women, were not represented by any of the existing political parties and argued that some conception of 'consumer interest' should be impressed upon legislators.[38] The United Australia Party's electoral success four months later may have been in part the result of attracting the support of women consumers.

The voices of consumer advocates were, however, rarely heeded. Grumbles about floor surfaces aside, Sydney women's responses to department stores appeared to be overwhelmingly positive. Women active in campaigns on women's issues collectively patronised the big stores. The National Council of Women of New South Wales, for example, organised lunches in Farmer's restaurant in 1923-24, and groups such as the Country Women's Association and the YWCA eagerly welcomed store management's offers of money, patronage, office space and meeting facilities.[39] Many helped finance their publications with advertisements for the big stores, often with incongruous results. The *Woman*, for example, carried a large advertisement in February 1891 for Grace Brothers' sale alongside an article supporting the Early Closing Bill. Advertisements for Anthony Hordern & Sons appeared on the back cover of the Women's Commonwealth Patriotic Association's 1915–17 series of pamphlets on thrift, and most of the stores were included in the official catalogue of the 1917 National Economy Exhibition.

Neither did advertising attract a sustained feminist critique in the period to 1930. This is not to say that women were unobservant. Consumers who gave evidence at cost of living enquiries, for example, complained that advertising by soft-goods firms was inflationary and often misleading. More typically, the publications of women's organisations incorporated appreciative comments on modern advertising's educative function and 'service to humanity'.[40]

It is perhaps not surprising that consumer culture was seen in a generally positive light by Australian women of the 1910s and 1920s. Unlike their European and American sisters, they lacked the precedent of a substantial critical discourse on consumption and luxury dating from the nineteenth century.[41] Perhaps consumerism and its effects were less visible in Australia's relatively small domestic market. A more likely explanation lies in women's acceptance of the naturalness of separate spheres. Evelyn Caspersz, secretary to the managing editor of the Sydney *Evening News* in 1928, suggested that men edited women's magazines for the same reasons that men dominated the female fashion industry: 'men can see what a woman cannot see about herself in particular, about all women in general. They are women's opposites.'[42] Just as few women disputed the right of male designers such as Paul Poirot to dominate the world of fashion, few challenged the male dominance of marketing and commerce. The majority of women adhered to the comforting notion of sexual complementarity and were probably as keen as men to retain sexual boundaries and cultures which were not directly hazardous.

Most women viewed early twentieth-century developments in retailing as positive, pleasurable and progressive. The expansion of the big stores was a source of civic and national pride in a period in which many Australian women and men wanted evidence that their country could compete in the world of international commerce. The Housewives Association argued in 1922 that 'continuous improvements in methods of production and distribution are the only means by which a country may hope to gain supremacy'. The department store was seen by some as particularly compelling testimony to women's progress. The 'Shop Window' columnist of the *Commonwealth Home* attributed improvements in modern shop architecture to the emancipation of women and their making of shopping into a fine art.[43] The big stores no doubt materially improved shopping conditions and the quality of urban life for many women.

Some women, then, derived a source of personal power and pleasure from the large stores. Others were openly critical of retailers, the fashion industry, irresponsible extravagance in consumption, inappropriate fashions, or theories of national politics and wealth that ignored women's role as consumer. In both cases, women's relationship to mass marketing was active and creative. The politics of shopping gave women a place from which to speak in a culture that demeaned women's consumption work, and increased female visibility and credibility in the struggle for equal rights to citizenship and bodily integrity. These voices may have been scattered, uncoordinated and only rarely dissident in the period before 1930, but they anticipated and constituted an historical continuity with a more formal and coherent feminist critique of mass marketing that developed in the 1970s.

The proliferation of consumer goods offered to the shopper by the 1920s made it impossible for her to refuse to participate in 'the great consumer drama'. Her only option was to exercise choice and to determine particular relationships between objects and individuals.[44] Some contemporaries were well aware of this consumer revolution and its possible effects on women's responses. As

Rydge's Business Journal explained in 1928: 'Where there were once 500 things for a woman to buy there are now 5,000. There are said to be 13,000 items in the average chemist's and fancy goods shop, and 18,000 items in a grocery and hardware store. As a result there is a clash of desires . . . In a mechanical inventive age like ours, the multiplicity of merchandise, together with the myriad show windows and advertising pages, constitutes a high pressure system of selling which no age has ever before known.'[45]

The scale of the marketing revolution irreversibly under way by the 1920s made it likely that women would engage with consumerism predominantly on an individual level. The construction of personal meanings and identities was in itself a significant act of resistance in a department-store culture increasingly devoted to standardised and sexualised representations of modern man and woman.

8 Sexualised consumerism

The 1920s have been characterised in Australian history as a decade of conformity. More and more Australian women and men moved into the cities as male wage-earners bought land and houses in response to the concerted marketing strategies of the real-estate industry. While male breadwinners purchased the family home and possibly a car, women's consumer activities were determined by the needs of the suburban family. As the manufacturing and marketing industries expanded in the post-World War I period, the goods a woman bought, or decided to buy with her husband, were increasingly standardised. Domestic appliances, kitchenware, furniture, processed food and clothing of similar design relentlessly rolled off production lines into the cupboards, shelves and wardrobes of thousands of homes. Radios, movies, magazines and newspapers shaped pervasive and persuasive images of femininity and the Australian consumer dream. A 'dead level Australian culture' reached its apogee.[1]

Within relations between women and men in the 1920s, however, significant rifts were visible. Men abused and beat their wives and daughters behind closed doors in the suburbs, and open public spaces became increasingly hazardous territory for young women. Prostitution and abortion continued to provide police, the judiciary, juries and respectable society with disturbing evidence of women's sexuality, and their determination to control their own fertility. Evidence of old and new forms of female autonomy caused considerable anxiety. Women were increasingly postponing marriage, bearing fewer children and exercising their right to leave their husbands. Women continued to be active in a number of political campaigns, and World War I provided a strong stimulus for single women's workforce participation, especially within the commercial and professional sectors. Women were forging for themselves a central role in modern consumer society.[2]

Department stores and their assistants in the advertising industry helped reconcile sexual conflict with the trend towards cultural homogeneity. In so doing, they gave sexual relations a distinctively modern shape. The activities of department-store managements safely contained and temporarily defused many of the sexual tensions of the post-war decade. In common with the movie, music, leisure and entertainment industries, retailing sexualised society. Department stores in particular distributed in commodity form standardised and commodified images of masculinity and femininity. This chapter examines the ways in which department-store advertising—mail-order catalogues, newspapers and magazines, mannequin parades, store dummies and the promotion of beauty products—sexualised consumerism and standardised gender between 1918 and 1930.

The modern sexual identities promoted by department stores reflected, and undoubtedly influenced, changing ideals of heterosexual attractiveness represented in movies, plays, magazines and popular fiction. The figure of the virtuous housewife was replaced by the youthful, glamorous and slender flapper dedicated to the pursuit of hedonistic consumption. Her physique testified to the self-policing of her body through physical-fitness programmes, beauty regimes, cosmetics and diets. The average woman could emulate the sexually desirable movie star she saw in the pages of her favourite magazine simply by consuming the appropriate products. At the same time, relations between the sexes were increasingly characterised by the cultivation of styles and appearances that operated at a purely sexual level. A conscious sexuality was incorporated into the rituals of male attack and female protection governing courtship and dating. Alert to these shifts in sexual cultures, retail men incorporated a more explicit and inescapable heterosexuality into their sales techniques in the 1920s.[3]

David Jones' magazine for staff, *Between Ourselves*, captured some of these tensions in post-war constructions of womanhood and heterosexuality. In January 1919, probably not uncoincidentally under Florence Fourdrinier's editorship, the magazine supported recent improvements in women's economic and political status, and argued that female department heads, buyers and cashiers had proved to be as competent as men in financial management. Support for the business girl, however, typically drew on the argument that her economic independence would enhance rather than jeopardise her domestic and romantic happiness: she brought to marriage the qualities of common sense and adaptability and could now afford to marry for love. *Between Ourselves* actively promoted modern courtship ideals through regular gossip and personal columns devoted to rumours of departmental flirtations and betrothals, and romantic stories such as that of Muriel, the Gift Girl, who won the greatest gift of all—a husband. A shop assistant's request for a jazz club to be held in the Girls Luncheon Room to which 'every adult girl could be allowed to bring at least one "friend" from outside' under the watchful eyes of senior staff suggests that the store management was anxious to guide its staff through the new rules of heterosocial and sexual conduct. When Bessie from the lace counter threw away her chance of a true romance in 'A Toy Tragedy' by asking the junior from D Department for a kiss on their first date, the pessimistic message for the modern woman trying to balance traditional feminine purity with the more open sexuality of the dating system was clear.[4]

The new sexual knowledges popularised after World War I were largely created and disseminated through a rapidly-expanding and more technologically-sophisticated advertising industry. Advertising agencies such as Patons offered clients a range of services, including market information and advertising space, by the 1920s. Although radio broadcasting became an important mass-communication medium in this decade, newspapers and other printed sources extended their influence by adopting a modern format characterised by bold headlines and more spacious layouts.[5] Department stores were big newspaper advertisers. The amount of column inches in the *Sydney Morning Herald* and *Daily Telegraph* devoted to drapery goods in 1921 was larger than the space given to most other commodities.[6]

Commercial art was by the early 1920s a well-established industry based on formal training in specialised graphic-design techniques.[7] Commercial portraits of women in catalogues such as Grace Brothers' *Model Trader* and David Jones' mail-order catalogue distributed post-war images of a modern, sexualised femininity. The extreme body cant characteristic of the female images of the 1890s was gradually replaced around 1914 by a more upright and less corsetted posture: feet were placed a little further apart and hands were placed assertively on hips. The figures appeared more confident and dynamic, and faces were plumper and healthier, if increasingly similar and youthful. Millinery fashion artists were so used to drawing 'young and pretty' faces by 1918 that it was uneconomical for retailers to include in their advertising hats for 'matrons and other types'.[8] The post-war woman looked out of the catalogue page in a more playful and challenging manner than her predecessor would have dared ten years earlier.

The modernistic style popularised by commercial artists in this period reinforced the abstract nature of commercial femininity. Modernism, the subject of some debate in Australian advertising literature by the late 1920s, promised to attract attention and arouse emotion by expressing the feelings and impressions associated with the commodity. Commercial artists' use of caricature, fragmentation, diagonal lines, off-centre layout, and exaggerated simplicity were designed to attract the consumer's attention and invite her or his active participation in reconstructing the commodity represented.[9]

By the mid-1920s, Australian store catalogues incorporated into their representations of women aspects of modernistic design such as the disproportionately-elongated female silhouette with tapered feet and hands. This modernistic influence on commercial artistic representations of women standardised the female form in striking ways. The change from line drawings to a bolder, cartoon-style of half-tone illustration, together with the use of colour after the war in catalogues such as those of David Jones, tended to erase individual differences and give greater emphasis to women's eyes and lips. Cloche-style hats obliterated women's hair and covered much of their head, so that frequently only the lips or a single curl was visible. Colour and stylistic emphasis thus tended to provocatively fetishise the lips and stress the necessity for cosmetics to complete the feminine look. Women's faces took on a doll-like character, while their bodies assumed a more angular and geometric appearance.

By 1930, uniformly youthful women were presented with *identical* faces and extremely stylised bodies that self-consciously bore little resemblance to reality. Retailers and the artists who served them created images of women on the same principles of mass production as the clothes they were advertising. The ready-to-wear millinery represented in store catalogues from the mid-

Women's costumes, David Jones mail-order catalogue, 1924. These female figures show the influence of modernism on commercial art and the tendency in the 1920s toward standardised and stylistic representations of women. They appear to be less stable and more frivolous than their male counterparts—they are creatures of fashion and leisure. (DAVID JONES (AUSTRALIA) PTY LTD)

1920s, for example, was markedly more uniform in style than the hand-trimmed items depicted in turn of the century catalogues. The women displayed on the fashion page were as much commodities as the clothes and hats they wore.

Store catalogues also encoded masculinity and messages of sexual difference in their pictures of men and men's clothing. Although the lean and stiff male aristocrat was replaced between the 1890s and 1930s by a more solid, almost rectangular silhouette and a chunky masculinity, the male type portrayed in the *Model Trader*, Peapes & Co.'s catalogue and David Jones' mail-order catalogue changed much less drastically than the female. It was not unusual, the *Draper* lamented in 1922, to find designs for male figures in the latest catalogues that were ten years old.[10] Male portraits retained their pseudo-naturalism and a greater range of age-types throughout the 1920s. Catalogue men, with their walking canes, guns and feet placed solidly apart, and thicker body shape, were more stable than women. Men's square and functional hands were placed jauntily in trouser pockets; their legs casually crossed at the ankle or bent at the knee; one foot often slightly raised above the other (placed on a tree stump, for example). All of these images suggested that men could confidently display their bodies in ways forbidden to women.

Men were typically portrayed in action, in contrast to women who appeared to be almost exclusively creatures of leisure. In the *Model Trader* men were placed in city streetscapes, offices, stables, paddocks, stockyards, on golf courses, in cars, riding horses, bathing, hiking, surfing, shaving, digging, fencing or oiling machinery. Even when men and women were sketched engaging in the same activity—smoking—men were pictured lighting up and puffing vigorously, while women's cigarettes dangled languidly from their fingers. Men, firmly located by their occupational status, by the 1910s were shown in catalogues as businessmen, rural workers, delivery men, mechanics and labourers. Catalogues such as Grace Brothers' *Model Trader* of 1921, which showed men swinging axes, shovelling coal, rolling barrels, working on the railroad, mending fences and shoeing horses, advertised a virile and active masculinity.

This polarisation of gender display was noticeably greater in 1930 than it had been twenty years earlier. Retailers may have paid more attention to female figures because their clientele was largely female. Gender asymmetry also suggests that representations of women were more susceptible to aesthetic modification and modernisation than those of men. Jill Carrick points out that it was believed that artists' fusion of the symbol 'woman' with that

Men's clothing, David Jones mail-order catalogue, 1919. Store catalogues were widely distributed throughout country areas and provided images of desirable male and female bodies. Even though they are wearing underclothing, the manliness of the figures in these illustrations is unquestioned. Their bodies take up considerable space and their legs are confidently splayed. They are firmly balanced and capable of action.
(DAVID JONES (AUSTRALIA) PTY LTD)

of 'art' exerted a powerful fascination for the viewer/consumer.[11] The graphic boundaries of femininity were seen to be more amenable to aesthetic invasion.

Fashion photography, evident in drapery trade literature by the 1920s, contributed to the standardisation of the female form. Photographs of models wearing millinery or costumes appeared only rarely in the *Draper* after the turn of the century, retail advertising experts preferring line drawings well into the 1920s because they believed drawings more effectively conveyed aesthetic emphasis. Photographs were considered, by contrast, to be 'stubbornly impartial'.[12] This objectivity of the photograph was, however, an illusion. In claiming to directly represent reality, photographs constructed gender forms more authoritatively than drawings. The New Photography of the 1920s attempted to emphasise the 'essential nature' of objects by drawing attention to their forms and meanings, so that the photograph became the 'most natural way' of selling commodities.[13] Women, traditionally allied with nature, became ideal subjects of fashion photography. Photographs of female models began to appear in the *Draper* from 1915 and, by the late 1920s, occupied whole pages.

Photographs included in the Australian National Gallery's 1986 exhibition of studio photographs taken between 1925 and 1955, 'The Glamour Show', suggest that commercial photographers represented a 'staged and constructed reality' in which the viewer was invited to consume the advertised product, whether that product was inert or human.[14] Portrait-style photographs of female models' heads, particularly in advertisements for millinery, emphatically presented female facial features. Models and film stars displayed physical perfection: surfaces were black, white, matt and smooth; lighting effects accentuated contrasts, light and shadow; and blemishes and irregularities were inconceivable. The self conscious arrangements and glamorisation of both male and female bodies suggests that from its inception commercial photography was organised around the presentation of the feminine.

This shift to a photographic and hence more deliberate representation of femininity was echoed in significant changes to display dummies. In the pre-war period before ready-made clothing dominated drapery goods, dress materials were typically and literally 'draped' on display stands or dressmakers' dummies consisting of a relatively shapeless female torso. Wax models, known to the trade as early as 1902, appear not to have become popular until the period around World War I, when improved production techniques made them more durable and 'lifelike'. Even then, some window-dressers continued to use headless dummies because, as the Champion Window-Dresser of 1924 argued, this method

> . . . leaves something to the imagination, so that the customer can easily visualise her own figure in the frock . . . the simple suggestion of a drape [leaves] the rest to the customer's imagination. She gets a real pleasure in fancying how she will look in this or that material etc. Don't deprive her of that pleasure. She can't imagine herself as the theatrical young lady with the pearly complexion and ruby lips of the wax model.[15]

The female customer, he suggested, had more freedom to construct her own individual fantasy image of her ideal self when the display left 'something to her imagination'.

By the 1920s, the customer had no choice but to attempt to match her bodily appearance with that of the full model in the window. As the headless dummy was gradually replaced after 1914 by wax dummies with heads, prevailing ideas about gender were encapsulated in wax. A female correspondent for the *Draper* described the models in the Paris studio of a large manufacturer of wax figures sold to Australian retailers. Every detail of the female body was observed closely in order to make the figures as lifelike as possible: the way a woman walked, caught objects, handled a powder puff, put on her gloves, carried an umbrella, did her hair, or put pins in a pincushion. The modern elegant woman reproduced in the model, the correspondent drily observed, had to be 'slim, languid, and appear if not ill, at least somewhat tired and as frail as a reed'. Wax figures were given varying complexions and represented mothers, young ladies and babies. Men were carefully reproduced also but, like their catalogue counterparts, were defined by their occupation rather than their life-cycle stage. Male figures included the dandy, the huntsman and the man at his desk.[16]

The wax model was modified in the 1920s to become more alluring. Display figures demonstrated modern hairstyles in 'realistic' fashion, and millinery-display stands in the form of painted heads with natural-looking hair dramatically crystallised contemporary perceptions of female beauty. When realism seemed

Millinery display model, 1926. Advertised in the Draper of Australasia *(June 1926, p. 272) as artistically painted, unbreakable, and with detachable curls, this display bust provided women shoppers with an unambiguous model of female beauty. Her dramatic eyes and mouth could be emulated with the use of cosmetics, her hairstyle could be replicated by the store hairdresser, and her fashionable hat could be purchased in the millinery department.* (STATE LIBRARY OF NEW SOUTH WALES)

to have gone as far as it could go in the late 1920s, surrealist display models constructed in brilliant metallic colours with gold and silver hair became popular. The Women's Page of the *Sydney Morning Herald* reported in 1928 that although Sydney shops had not yet copied London's 'robot figures', they did contain figures of golden papier-mache with 'startlingly sleek shingles and vividly red lips'. Barely nine months later, the fashion had reached Australia, and local wax models had been 'modernised'. Figures were no longer rosy-cheeked and simpering, but slim, boyish and tanned. Their hair was either white or dyed to match the frock displayed. Others 'only faintly resemble the human form, being all angles and fly-away curves, and headless, after the fashion of the futuristic school of artists'.[17]

The headless female body had returned, but in a different form and with distinctly modern meanings. When pre-war display men used headless dummies, the woman customer contributed some of the ideological labour involved in selling the goods by literally putting herself in the picture. She had to construct her 'self' in the clothes. Dummies with perfect modern hairstyles, pearly complexions and perfectly painted ruby lips, on the other hand, provided the customer with a fabricated and unavoidable image of glamorous womanhood. They may have provided models of individual indulgence and modern, vibrant and sensual womanhood, as Leach suggests, but the full-bodied display dummy also precluded the (relatively) free choice of female self-image.[18] It became increasingly difficult for the customer to adjust her own self-image to the feminine window-image without feeling that she had failed to measure up. By the late 1920s the marketing and retail industries had educated the female consumer to consume by imitation so effectively that it mattered little that dummies failed to fit her imaginary body. She knew only that by buying the clothes on display she was buying a sexualised female modernity. Dummies elaborated the sexed messages of a post-war consumer culture in a particularly compelling physical form.

Live mannequins bearing a disturbing similarity to their wax sisters posing in shop windows were also used to entice customers. Attempts by some stores to use their assistants and factory workers as female models in 1916 were not successful. The models were apparently ungainly, wore too much face colour, and had pimply backs. The mannequin parade was soon developed into a highly popular sales technique by some of Sydney's leading fashion houses. The *Sydney Morning Herald* attributed the high cost of clothes in 1919 to 'the mannequin who paraded so gracefully up and down the Wilton pile carpet before Venetian framed mirrors'. The *Draper* praised Farmer's in 1918 for its dramatic presentations featuring a lady's boudoir and the office of a costume and millinery showroom. By the late 1920s these live presentations drew on popular forms of entertainment and visual spectacles to include dances, songs, films, orchestral accompaniment and even operatic arias. Underwear featured prominently. Hordern Brothers emphasised the fashion appeal of corsets in a live display of foundation garments produced in conjunction with Berlei called 'Modelling the Mode', while Mark Foys' mannequin parade of intimate garments, 'The Magic of Silk and the Secret of Warmth', managed to combine practicality with sensuality.[19]

The language and images used in advertisements for women's fashion goods sold by department stores presented mundane garments such as those aimed at the 'business girl' market as glamorous and desirable commodities. A voile frock, for example, was 'prettily trimmed, faggot stitching and hand embroidery. Collar is sailor shape and bodice full. Waist has velvet belt and skirt is pleated.' Cotton crepe kimonos temptingly featured chrysanthemum or cherry blossom designs in Vieux Rose, Sky, Saxe, Lavender and Helio. This seductive language of fashion extended to the explicit descriptions of female underclothing which appeared daily on the front pages of most major newspapers in the post-World War I period. The Bandeau Brassiere for the Smart Business Girl who wore a blouse and skirt was made in heavy net lace, and the Gossard lace-in-front corset, which provided the necessary support to counteract the harm caused to business girls by hours of standing and sitting, featured 'extreme low bust, free hip . . . in palest Pink, figured Broche'.[20]

Women's bodies were sexualised in other ways through the consumer culture promoted by department stores. A uniform female external appearance and bodily form was codified between 1918 and the mid-1920s in a series of state and commonwealth government enquiries into the basic wage and cost of living for adult woman workers.[21] Retailers' evidence of women's buying preferences and costs figured prominently in court hearings, and many witnesses confirmed that they bought their clothes from the big-city stores. In their attempts to specify the appropriate contents of the working-woman's wardrobe, arbitration court officials, male counsel and female expert witnesses drew on easily-accessible presentations of clothing advertised by the big drapery stores. These material objects, images and advertising narratives put into cultural circulation a set of clearly sexed and implicitly sexual messages which inextricably linked a woman's choice of clothing to her sexual identity.

Labour activist Imelda Cashman described the way in which at the hearings an elderly judge and four male barristers would gravely 'examine an article upside down, or pinch it timidly between two fingers and pass it on, or smile when a bit of lace was seen', and suggested that the courtroom at times resembled a bargain sale at a fashionable drapery house.[22] The men of the court appeared to derive a voyeuristic sexual pleasure from the opportunity to examine and touch feminine articles of underwear, and to interrogate witnesses on their corset-wearing habits or preference for lacy camisoles. A housekeeper was pressed for details:

> Talking about corsets, what's wrong with those at 5s 11d a pair?
> They are all right. They can be washed and dried if they get dirty.
> What would a girl do while they were being washed and dried?
> Mr. Cantor: Stay at home or in bed. (Laughter)
> Witness: They can be washed and dried in about two hours.[23]

Women's purchasing activities and the alien language of female fashion became the source of a cross-class male camaraderie in the courtroom. Men involved in the arbitration system, in conjuction with those in the advertising, retailing and newspaper industries, effectively sexualised the working-woman's wardrobe by appropriating, publishing, and hence putting into discourse details relating to intimate female rituals of consumption.[24]

Details of the quantities and costs of articles 'deemed to be essential for a working-woman's wardrobe' submitted by female witnesses and representatives reveal the culturally significant role of department stores in promoting modern images of femininity. The regimen of clothing supplied in 1919 by a committee of four women representing employers and employees included standard articles such as costumes, skirts, blouses, frocks, hats, hose, shoes, accessories, underwear, haberdashery and toilet articles.[25]

Some items—a sportscoat, sandshoes and bathing costume—

suggest that the working woman was expected to purchase commodities that would enable her to devote some time to rest, recreation and healthy physical activities. Women workers were only too keen to take the opportunity to exercise their physical freedom. The 'Ground Floor Girls' at David Jones, for example, attempted to get the company to extend its boys' camping holidays to female staff, and many women enjoyed the store's physical-culture classes. Women's periodicals such as *Woman's World* also promoted the provision of physical training for women workers in articles such as 'Keeping Fit for Business, the City Girl's Problem'.[26]

The ideal modern feminine body which emerged from debates within the English physical culture movement in the decade after the War, as Jill Julius Matthews shows, was distinctively marked by its slenderness, physical freedom and beauty. The modern feminine body was not only healthy, beautiful, and heterosexually-oriented, but manifestly the outcome of appropriate consumer activities. The purchase of bathing costumes, sporting and holiday wear, much in evidence in newspaper and magazine advertisements and promoted in articles such as 'Clothes for the Sportswoman', promised the woman worker a healthy modern persona.[27]

The inclusion in the regimen of items such as a hairbrush, comb, toilet soap, talcum powder, vaseline, face cream and face powder suggests that it was considered essential for a working woman to purchase commodities that would make her look beautiful as well as healthy. Women other than prostitutes, actresses or ladies of high fashion did not routinely wear cosmetics before the War, and the toiletry and perfumery section of the fancy-goods department of the big stores sold only a limited range of items such as face powders, creams, rouge and lip salves.[28] From around 1910, however, retail managements promoted the ideal of the 'cream-complexioned girl, whose face represents the result of hours of steaming, and massage, and skin-food, and all the rest of the tricks of the beauty parlour . . . [in preference to] the leather-skinned and brick-dust-hued child of Nature'.[29]

No longer reviled as the accoutrements of women of dubious morals, cosmetics began to achieve a profitable respectability in the 1920s. The incorporation of cosmetics and beauty products into the consumer repertoire of the post-war middle-class and respectable working-class woman was due in large part to the promotional efforts of department-store managers. Although cosmetics had been worn by fashionable American women without stigma from the late nineteenth century, department stores made them widely available and more socially acceptable to relatively provincial markets. Lipstick, powder compacts, powdered and cream rouge, liquid face powder, vanishing cream, eyebrow pencils and astringents were, by the late 1920s, part of the department store's standard cosmetic counter and the 'draper's perquisite and excellent business'.[30]

American department stores asked Helena Rubinstein in 1918 if they could sell her products. In Australia, Elizabeth Arden pioneered the profitable relationship between department stores and cosmetics by selecting one major retailer in each state capital. Her products were sold exclusively in Sydney through David Jones. The store's Elizabeth Arden department, first appropriately introduced into the Elizabeth Street store, achieved a rate of gross profit of 42.3 per cent in 1930, 13.9 per cent above the average for all departments.[31] An Elizabeth Arden advertisement of 1927 consisted of a photographer's sphinx-like portrait of a model's face displaying inscrutability, symmetrical and clearly-defined features, and mask-like perfection. The accompanying text emphasised the cosmetics' ability to transform unremarkable and blemished women into flawless individuals while, paradoxically, imposing on them a standardised femininity.

The sale of cosmetics in the 1920s was part of a wider cultural project focusing on female beauty. Female stars promoted by an international film industry set standards of female beauty and sexual appeal which were repeatedly displayed to female consumers in picture houses and magazines throughout the country. Because women were implicitly encouraged to see if they 'measured up' to these standards, beauty became competitive. David Jones initiated a competition in 1921 to find the store's Most Charming Girl in possession of a 'classically correct countenance'; the *Evening News* sponsored a beauty contest in 1922 to find Australia's Most Beautiful Girl; and the first Miss Australia contest was held in 1926.[32]

Sydney's department stores provided services for the woman who could afford to pay for the pleasure of having the new beauty products and techniques personally applied to her body. Once only available to wealthy women who patronised exclusive salons, the beauty industry catered to a mass female market by the 1920s. David Jones incorporated a beauty parlour and hairdressing salon into its Elizabeth Street store in an attempt, according to Charles Lloyd Jones, to democratise beauty and help women of 'moderate means' to improve their appearance. Marcus Clark employed a ladies' hairdresser, and Buckinghams opened a ladies' hairdressing salon and beauty parlour in 1929. The sewing requisites that had traditionally been displayed on the draper's haberdashery counter were replaced in the department store by articles of female adornment such as belts, shingle combs, hair wavers, clasps and hair slides. Stores also made money out of men's desire to be personally presentable. David Jones' Elizabeth Street store included a barber's shop and a man's manicure parlour.[33]

Despite the concerted efforts of manufacturers, advertisers and department-store managers to intervene in the cultural construction of beauty and femininity, these sexual messages were not necessarily inscribed unmodified onto women's bodies. Women used clothing and beauty products to adapt or remake their female identity. Women's open use of cosmetics, and their abandonment of restrictive clothing and corsets suggests they took an active role in appropriating what they wanted from the repertoire of commodities and meanings associated with sexualised consumerism. Kathy Piess argues, for example, that women 'linked cosmetics use to an emergent notion of their own modernity' defined by their capacity to consume.[34]

The significance women attached to beauty did not necessarily coincide with the ideas of retail and advertising men. Women workers' decision to include powder and face cream on their lists of necessary expenditures in spite of public accusations of female vanity and promiscuity suggests that cosmetics not only disciplined the body and served an important function within the sexual economy, but were essential to their individual self-definition as woman and worker. As columnist 'Peggy' remarked to her colleagues in the Western Australian public service in 1914, 'one scarcely likes to emerge from the office all grease and perspiration, especially after five when the ladies of leisure frequent the town looking as fresh as possible'.[35] Newspaper accounts of basic wage hearings which drew attention to 'The Inevitable Powder Puff' may have contributed to public disapproval of women's habit of powdering in public, but they also reinforced the increasingly acceptable notion that beauty products were necessary requisites of modern femininity.[36]

The New South Wales Board of Trade cost of living enquiries provide a unique glimpse into the ways in which working-class women may have used consumption to fashion their own identities. Women complicated and contested the marketing industry's prescriptions of the working-woman's wardrobe and body by suggesting that sexual identity competed with other needs in their consumption activities. Economic and practical considerations were important to women with limited time and income for shopping, mending and washing clothes. They were frequently too tired at the end of a day's work to make their own clothes and preferred to buy ready-made clothing.

The working woman of the 1920s needed to buy appropriate clothing at the cheapest possible cost. Edith Rimmer, clothing factory worker, told the 1918 enquiry that she usually bought her clothes at Bondi Junction, a suburban shopping centre, which proved less expensive than shopping in the city stores. Elizabeth Daw, tailoress, looked at shop windows and carefully compared prices of clothes in newspapers before buying. Although price was important, these consumers found that sale goods were not always the bargains they seemed. 'Rough chip hats at 1s 9d', considered one witness, would indeed be rough. Durability, comfort and wearing quality were essential criteria. Alice Ward, kitchen worker and waitress, and Susan Willcox of the Federated Clothing Trade Union, preferred a costume for work wear because it was always 'neat and serviceable', could be worn in summer and winter, saved wear on other clothing and required minimal laundering.[37]

Female witnesses argued, however, that material factors such as durability and cost were not sufficient criteria in selecting appropriate items for their wardrobes. A smart and fashionable appearance was also necessary if a working girl was to secure a position. Elizabeth Daw told the court that she wanted to wear something which would not make her look 'about ten years behind the times'. Susan Willcox agreed that: 'it is really essential for a girl to look medium, to look neat. An employer is always looking for the better class of girl who comes along; it adds to the appearance of his place.'[38] Willcox indicated her understanding that the economic livelihoods of most women, whether in paid employment or not, depended on their sexual attractiveness. Willcox's testimony also suggests that the desire to look and feel feminine was not necessarily unwillingly imposed on women by a masculine culture. When challenged on working-women's partiality for decorative rather than plain underwear, Willcox asserted that 'she might as well be dead, if she could not get a little trimming on her camisole, say'. Moreover, only a woman who had deliberately elected to repress her sexual identity would forgo trimmed camisoles:

> Well, the only people's under-garments I have ever seen without any trimming on are the girls who are going into a convent. They are not allowed to have the trimmings on. She has to wear strong black or dark clothes without the slightest trimming on them, because she has to renounce the world.[39]

Willcox and other female shoppers clearly had no intention of renouncing the pleasures of a sexualised culture. They considered it their right as women and as consumers to have the freedom to purchase attractively feminine drapery commodities that enhanced their sexual identity.

Professional and middle-class women witnesses at the cost of living enquiries did not always approve of the sexualised clothing that working-class members of their sex elected to buy. Annie Golding, for example, was worried that 'Girls like a little broader and a little better lace [on an underskirt], and they will have it even if they have to go short of their food, I am sorry to say; they will have their appearance nice'.[40] Labor activist Imelda Cashman refused to make an allowance in her estimations for 'special dresses for theatres'.[41] Arguing that girls were victims of their nervous systems and suffered when they 'felt shabbily dressed', a female physician stated that it was essential that girls should be 'decently but not elaborately dressed'.[42] The common feminist argument of the 1920s that a living wage for women enabling economic independence from men was the necessary prerequisite for women's deliverance from 'sexual bondage' underlay the evidence of many of these expert witnesses.[43]

Their stress on female decency is particularly significant in the context of the sexualised consumer culture that was fully articulated in this period. Many women resented the opportunity the hearings allowed men to gain voyeuristic pleasures from the revelation of intimate details of women's personal clothing and toilet habits. Women unionists, labour activists and members of women's organisations such as the National Council of Women and the Housewives Association of New South Wales were critical of men's intervention and attempts to regulate the female business of fashion, dress and shopping. Women, feminists argued, were more qualified than men to enquire into the cost of living because they shopped, budgeted and managed the household economy.[44] Men were, moreover, simply incapable of understanding the female culture of feminine clothing and personal needs.

Feminists also implied that it was improper for women to disclose such intimate details to men in public. The presence of men in the courtroom, women suggested, inhibited female witnesses from giving the necessary information. A petition was circulated among women in New South Wales shortly after the conclusion of the first enquiry which stated that:

> . . . had the enquiry been conducted before women members instead of men members of the Board of Trade, evidence would have been forthcoming from female witnesses as to their items of expenditure on articles of wearing apparel and otherwise which could not, in the opinion of most women, be given *with propriety* by female witnesses before a tribunal composed solely of men.[45] (my emphasis)

Labor leader Kate Dwyer, normally confident of arbitration's benefits for women workers, disapproved of 'four or five men deciding whether a bit of lace on a working girl's camisole was a reasonable expenditure when considering her basic wage'.[46] Other labour women were critical of the exclusive focus on single women and argued that the court should also take into account the less glamorous clothing needs of married women workers.[47]

If feminists had a qualified success in their endeavours to feminise enquiries into the cost of living and basic wage, their victory was won on the battlefield of female representation and the recognition of the housewife's contribution to the economy rather than sexual propriety. As Rose Scott discovered in her unsuccessful battle in 1913 with the New South Wales Ladies Amateur Swimming Association over the admittance of male spectators to women's swimming carnivals, it was difficult for feminists to counter the growing tide of a masculinist sexual libertarianism without being dismissed as old-fashioned or wowserish. Like Scott, the women who criticised the masculinism of the Board of Trade took an early stand against what Allen calls the 'increasing legitimation of the male desire to stare and the demand that this desire be visually gratified'.[48]

It is perhaps significant that this male license to openly stare at—and to touch and talk about—women's bodies and the fetishised commodities associated with them coincided with sexual anxieties and tensions arising out of women's new public freedoms, and her visibility as a waged worker and consumer in the post-war period. The representation of the woman worker as a sexually-attractive object of male desire, clothed in lacy camisoles and corsets and displaying the body beautiful, demeaned and degraded women sexually. This sexualisation, in which department-store managers were fully complicit and instrumental, also effectively defused any male anxieties about what appeared to be women's growing sexual and economic independence.

That women gave alternative meanings to their wardrobes, and in some cases actively opposed this sexualisation by insisting on decency and propriety suggests that retail men and their helpers in the marketing industry encountered some resistance in their attempts to shape modern consumer culture in their own image. Rarely, but significantly, women directly criticised retailers' and advertisers' sexual exploitation of their bodies. Miss Montefiore of the Civic League committee suggested as early as 1908 that the League pay attention to 'the exhibition of women's underclothing in Drapers' windows and also of such advertisements'. A columnist complained in the *Shop Assistants Magazine* in June 1926 that intimate underwear was 'displayed on wax figures as a matter of no moment' and again in October that chocolates were sold with women's ankles, knees or other seductive parts of her anatomy. It was impossible, Callisto wrote in 'Woman to Woman and Others', for anything to be advertised in posters, newspapers or magazines without a woman or part of her being somewhere in the scene. The 'prevailing impression of too many of these is a leer and a guffaw of sensuality'.[49]

By the 1920s sex was used to sell, and sexual identity had to be bought. Consumer activity, especially the purchase of clothing, accessories, beauty products and services, was indispensible to the creation and maintenance of heterosexuality and the personae of handsome man and beautiful woman. While sexed commodities had constructed sexed identities in 1880, by 1920 the meanings associated with this purchased masculinity and femininity were much clearer and less amenable to individual negotiation than they had been in the late nineteenth century. The sexual information routinely encoded in the design, display and sale of manufactured and standardised commodities created unambiguously-sexed messages which could then be communicated to customers. The private desires and temptations characteristic of the old-style drapery house were exploited and transformed by twentieth-century department-store managers and advertisers into a publicly sexualised consumerism.

Part IV: 1930–90

9 Romance to pornography

The department store had by 1930 institutionalised and popularised a sexualised Australian consumer culture. In the decades that followed, the department store's pioneering role in the development of modern selling techniques was taken over by a national marketing industry and mass-media networks. This chapter suggests some of the major changes in the history of sexualised consumerism from 1930 to 1990. These developments can be broadly grouped into three periods: an emphasis on romance in the 1930s and 1940s; a more explicit and intense sexualisation from 1950 to 1980; and the interdependence of the marketing and pornography industries from the 1980s.

1930–50

The department store began to slip from its pre-eminent position within a sexualised culture of consumption between the depression and the post-war years. Rival selling organisations better suited to the rationalised business culture of the 1930s and 1940s aroused 'the deep-seated dissatisfaction and disease now seen as the crucial element in loosening the customers' purse strings'.[1] Signalling the end of the big stores' hegemony in Sydney, representatives of chain variety stores such as Coles (established in 1914) and Woolworths (1924) joined the Retail Traders' Association of New South Wales in the late 1920s. Chain stores which dispensed with expensive customer services and operated on the basis of a high turnover with a low profit margin represented serious competition. Chain-store managements introduced highly standardised and functional principles of display and customer-assistant interaction that laid bare the processes of selling.[2] The powerful mystique, persuasive gender displays and sexual-spatial organisation typical of the department store were replaced by a more streamlined approach to selling.

Despite major changes in the structures of distribution after 1930, the physical spaces and material goods displayed in the department store continued to tempt the consumer and circulate notions of womanliness and manliness. The traditional distinctions between men's and women's spaces were not only maintained but in some cases strengthened. David Jones' George Street store was renovated, extended and re-opened in 1935 as a 'modern men's store'. The male spaces of the 1930s and 1940s suggested a technical and streamlined masculinity that linked men firmly to the machine age. The Sydney Bon Marché's men's and boyswear department in 1948, for example, featured fixtures and fittings in yellow walnut and a parquetry floor of deep-red jarrah inlaid with herringbone design. The footwear section had chrome-plated tubular steel furniture. Under similar design influences, David Jones' Market Street store opened in 1938 was furnished in marble, silver-ash woodwork, and aluminium fittings. Fletcher Jones' 1938 'Modern Manner Overcoat Style Exhibition' presented male models against a 'futuristic, glittering metallic background'.[3] The alliance between modernity and technology became a masculine alibi for marketing fashion to men.

At the same time, romance, beauty and glamour were increasingly incited in sales efforts directed at women. Store managements provided their sales assistants in 1934 with courses in the correct use of cold creams, powders and shampoos, and Manka Rubinstein visited Australia in 1937 to lecture women on beauty culture and promote her sister Helena's costly products. The popular appeal of romantic movie stars was used in store promotions such as the Bon Marché's quest in December 1938 to find a Deanna Durbin look-alike. The promotion increased its sales by twenty per cent. Advertisers were told that stressing the romantic appeal of goods such as cameras, musical instruments, jewellery and perfume heightened their desirability. Window displays that incorporated human-interest stories revolving around mother-love, self-sacrifice, courtship and marriage were said to be particularly effective. Retailer K.C. Corbett provided a lyrical description of Farmers' 1938 autumn windows, whose small statues, warm lighting, rose-coloured silk background and beautiful model in a richly-coloured gown 'told a classic love story' that was dramatic and exciting. Corbett suggested that businessmen keep a scrapbook of effective brand-name advertisements, such as those for Lux and Lifebuoy soaps, which promised success in romance to their purchasers.[4]

Brand-name product advertisements, rather than those for the big stores, were the new models of progressive marketing. The slow decline of the department store with its predominantly local or state-wide market coincided with the rise of the Australian advertising profession and of nationally-marketed brands after the 1930s.[5] Goods were promoted by brand advertising paid for by manufacturers and devised with the assistance of a host of product designers, copywriters, commercial artists, advertising agents, market analysts, newspaper and magazine proprietors, radio networks, and packaging and display experts. It was increasingly these men who asserted in publications such as *Rydge's Business Journal* that women were attracted by style and beauty, susceptible to flattery and emotional appeals, and impervious to reason.[6]

Professional marketing men such as Berlei's John T. Humphrey actively appropriated the construction of sexual meanings. Berlei provided stores with coordinated sets of window displays, advertising copy and radio scripts in the belief that few retailers were '*expert* advertising men'. The company's 1940 window displays featured a row of identical dummies of naked female upper torsos and larger-than-life photographs of glamorous female models wearing brassieres. The displays illustrate the increasingly influential and explicit role played by manufacturers in promoting an ideal female body and breast shape. The Hollywood theme reinforced women's expected function as the object of the male gaze. In the background were two beautiful women photographed to look as if they were on a movie screen, while in the foreground a man looked appreciatively through a movie camera at partially-undressed models.[7]

Marilyn Lake argues that World War II provided a strong stimulus to the sexualisation of women already evident in the advertisements of the 1930s. Appeals to feminine charm and grace typical in 1910s and 1920s advertisements were replaced by the late 1930s by the direct offer of 'sex appeal'. Reflecting the interwar impact of Hollywood models of sexual relations, women who were once depicted in advertisements surveying themselves in a mirror were now more likely to be explicitly scrutinised by men and exhorted to be youthful and heterosexually attractive. Wartime conditions allowed the prewar sexualisation of women created by consumer culture to flourish.

1950–80

The consumer culture which had emerged in Australia by the 1920s and reached a plateau during the economic disruptions of depression and war, extended its influence in the years of relative prosperity. Significant changes in consumption and distribution patterns further eroded the department store's influence on the culture of consumption. Consumers increasingly preferred to spend their discretionary income on durable goods such as homes, large household items, electrical appliances, motor vehicles and on rent, gas, electricity and fuel. Expenditure on food, clothing, footwear and other items typically sold by department stores correspondingly decreased.[9]

The popularity of supermarkets and self-service stores, first introduced in the 1920s, in which women assumed many of the tasks previously performed by the retailer or his assistants, and the decline in home delivery services made shopping an even more time-consuming task.[10] Large suburban shopping centres became important from the late 1950s as places in which women congregated to shop and, often unsuccessfully, seek relief from domestic isolation, dissatisfaction and boredom.[11] Shopping centres rendered anachronistic emporium-style modes of selling, and further displaced the department store as a site of contemporary sexual meanings. The big stores did, of course, continue to attract a loyal and appreciative clientele. But their grandeur and authority had unmistakably begun to crumble.

The Australian marketing industry, facilitated by post-war immigration, high employment and advances in mass production, was well into its stride by the 1950s. According to Stella Lees and June Senyard, a new world of marketing evident in industries such as market research, selling, public relations and advertising tried to change the buying habits of generations. A new breed of tertiary-educated male marketing experts, managers and businessmen attempted to expand markets by promoting new products or by repackaging traditionally male products such as cigarettes to appeal to women.[12] Psychologists helped advertising companies such as the George Patterson advertising agency to find out more about women's likes and dislikes, views and attitudes. The 1972 Patterson Report, revealingly subtitled *Wooing the Australian Woman*, promised to provide manufacturers and marketing experts with all the information they needed to understand the Australian woman, representing 80–100 per cent of their business, as 'a complete human being'.[13]

These marketing men attempted to sell their products in a culture increasingly receptive to the open expression of sexuality. The 'sexual revolution' of the 1970s brought sexual matters which had long been hidden from polite society into open discourse.[14] A dating system incorporating the remnants of older courtship practices was gradually made redundant by increasing social acceptance of women's right to initiate and enjoy heterosexual activity. Ideas embodied in the women's liberation movement's advocacy of female sexual autonomy, the hippy counter-culture's promotion of the idea of 'free love', and a proliferating sexological literature were materially supported from the 1960s by the availability of the oral contraceptive pill and greater access to legal abortion. No longer confined to marriage, sex was increasingly uncoupled from reproduction and attached to personal goals of pleasure and freedom.

The advantages for women of this revolution in sexual mores were dubious. Sheila Jeffreys argues that post-World War II sexual libertarianism made it harder for women to resist or explore alternatives to heterosexuality as an institution of male power.[15] Jill Julius Matthews notes for Australia that much of the 'permissive' social legislation enacted between 1950 and 1980 guaranteed the servicing of men's sexual needs and pleasures. The ideology of permissive consumerism that shaped post-World War II constructions of femininity encouraged the men of the marketing industry to represent women as seductive as well as nurturant.[16]

Although commodities assumed a more explicitly erotic significance, they invoked a sexual desire that could never be fulfilled. The experience of pleasure and fulfilment promised by these sexualised commodities was, moreover, different for women and men. For men, sexual identity was constructed around notions of potency; for women, it centred on a receptiveness based on female narcissism.[17] A survey of *Popular Mechanics* readers conducted in

1967, for example, described its male consumers as young, hobby-minded and sports-minded family men with above-average incomes, homes and cars. In answer to the question 'What Makes Men Buy?', a leading market researcher concluded that men were attracted to certain makes of car by the promise of sexual power. 'The throaty roar of the young man's sports car could be his vicarious expression of the male's instinctive mating cry.' The reasons given for women's purchases, on the other hand—self-indulgence, altruism, romantic aspirations, and the desire to be attractive—implied dependence rather than power.[18]

These characterisations of female personality differed from earlier versions in their explicit acknowledgement of female sexuality. 'Sex', for example, was directly nominated as one of the answers to the marketing industry's persistent question: 'What Makes Women Buy?' According to marketing expert Rena Bartos, advertisements of the 1960s and 1970s referred to an assertive female sexuality perceived to be characteristic of contemporary heterosexual relationships in which women took the initiative.

However, men were still threatened by the idea of female sexuality rampant. Sexual references in advertising were generally coyly implicit and reliant on suggestion and innuendo. Market researchers suggested that women were not motivated by 'pseudo-erotic scenes in commercials' but by romance and the subtle (still feminine) desire to buy products which would enhance their sexual attractiveness. Sexual allusions were of the double entendre kind. In one American advertisement for wine, a photograph of a young woman was captioned 'Had any lately?'; while in Paris an advertisement for underwear showed a naked young man, with the copy placed 'where the eye would be drawn by curiosity'. Despite the protests of academics, government officials and clergymen, *Advertising in Australia* reported in 1967 that sex was ubiquitous in advertising.[19]

The spectacular growth of the cosmetics industry from the 1950s demonstrated the success of marketing sexual attractiveness to women. One survey found 77 per cent of all British women between the ages of sixteen and 64 used face powder and 76 per cent used lipstick. A large proportion of these sales were to teenage girls. The teenage girl was repeatedly told in popular magazines of the period that cosmetics and other beauty products would allow her to achieve the portable charm and glamour that defined modern femininity. Men, too, were persuaded that toiletries and 'good grooming' were indispensable to business and sexual success. One advertisement captioned 'Seal of Approval', showing the imprint of female lips on a bottle of shaving lotion, stressed the importance of appropriate consumption to heterosexual success. In a period notable for its hysterical homophobia, advertising excluded and denied lesbian and male homosexual identities. Manufacturers were careful 'not to give the impression of effeminacy [but] emphasise the "rugged masculinity"' of the men represented in advertising.[20]

The mass media played a key role in promulgating ideas about sex and sexuality from the 1950s. Daily newspapers and national magazines such as the *Australian Women's Weekly* continued to be important sources of sexual knowledges, but were supplemented from the 1920s by radio and from the 1950s by television, movies, point-of-sale displays, package design and other visual forms of advertising. Radio had been closely linked to the retail industry since Farmer & Company established its own radio broadcasting station, 2FC, in 1923. A major advertising medium from the 1930s, its role, at least in evening advertising, was being eroded by the late 1950s. The introduction of television into Australia in 1956 coincided, as Virginia Nightingale points out, with shopping-centre developments and price-cutting wars in the grocery trade. While prices were advertised in the press, the broadcast media was established as the site for brand advertising. The television programme became a display case for commodities.[21]

Because advertisers needed to know with increasing precision the numbers and kinds of potential customers these media reached, market research became an important source of knowledge about the female consumer—specifically, the housewife—in Australia in the post-World War II years. Market reseachers' portrait of the housewife in many ways countered the trend towards greater heterosexual explicitness in advertising and marketing. She was portrayed as domesticated, obtuse, duplicitous, predominantly concerned with family and personal affairs, and often incapable of knowing her own mind or her reasons for buying. A persistent tension existed in market-research literature between men's desire to manage female consumer behaviour and women's apparent refusal to cooperate or respond as advertisers wished. Housewives' clear dislike of an advertisement for sheets featuring an attractive blonde model, for example, suggests some female opposition to advertisers' blatant use of sex in selling.[22]

A coordinated and politically effective modern consumer movement drawing (albeit largely without acknowledgement) on the nineteenth-century tradition of women's consumers' leagues was finally established in the 1960s. Australia's *Choice* magazine, for example, was first published in 1960. From the late 1960s, feminists exposed the isolation of the housewife and her relegation to the mindless and repetitive duties associated with being 'Mrs Consumer'. Feminist critiques of images of women in advertising, such as Patricia Edgar and Hilary McPhee's 1974 *Media She*, signalled a concerted and organised female opposition to the marketing industry's exploitation of female sexuality that by the 1980s had some impact on notions of acceptable advertising standards.[23]

1980 to the 1990s

Despite these critiques of the marketing industry's sexualisation of women and commodities, it was nevertheless difficult by the 1980s to find an advertisement which did not refer to women's sexual identity. Women were finally being allowed into more powerful positions in marketing and selling but, according to Game and Pringle's 1983 study of gender at work, men in the retail industry continued to ensure that the 'real' managerial positions remained theirs.[24] Manufacturers and distributors continued to sex-type commodities and assume that female consumers had very different preoccupations to men. The gift-wrap paper and greetings cards designed for men, for example, cannot be confused with those aimed at women. In 1991, Australian university students were offered sexed sample bags of selected consumer goods. In addition to some items such as toothpaste and sweets common to both bags, the female bags contained deodorant, sanitary napkins, Slim-a-Soup, Special K cereal, leaflets advertising Lean Cuisine, and a home pregnancy test kit. The women's sample bag encapsulated the 1990s feminine ideal of a woman who was slender, fit, healthy, sweet-smelling and sexually available. The male bag gave commodity form to a muscular and robust masculinity: it contained regular Cup-a-Soup, Nutri-Grain Iron Man cereal, and shaving cream. Student unions criticised the bags as 'highly sexist' and refused to distribute them.[25]

The symbolic character and sexual meanings of consumer goods have changed since the 1880s, but continue to be central to the sexual organisation of the contemporary world. The 'Dress for Success' fashion adopted by many women professionals, for example, is explained by anthropologist Grant McCracken as women's attempt to imitate and appropriate the clothing of a higher social group—men—to claim equal status. He interprets new men's fashions, such as the 1983 'heroic' look, as men's need to recover authority and re-establish sexual boundaries which women's move into male jobs and clothing styles threatened to blur. McCracken concludes that the conservative function of consumer goods and 'the thoroughness with which this society has inscribed the cultural categories and principles of "maleness" and "femaleness" in the object code and material world' has in large part been responsible for the persistence of sexism.[26]

Descriptions of the female consumer similarly suggest that while the marketing industry's perceptions of women have changed considerably since the 1970s, the market continues to be perceived as sexed, and sexual distinctions in consumer behaviour continue to be maintained. References to the female consumer as irrational and easily tempted, taken for granted by an earlier generation of retailers, were by the 1980s less common.[27] The marketing industry at last realised that it was not in its interests to continue to deny women's intelligence and discernment, nor to take lightly women's new economic independence. Marketing texts and journals began in the late 1970s to pay attention to 'the changing demographics of women' which indicated the complexity and unpredictability of the contemporary female market. Not only were women increasingly combining paid and unpaid work, but their consumer behaviour depended on whether they were single women, working wives, heads of household, 'empty nesters', stay-at-home housewives or plan-to-work housewives, career women or just-a-job working women. Marketing experts and consumer researchers started to take notice of women's responses to sexism in advertising, stereotypical representations of the housewife in marketing research, and changing images of men in print advertisements.[28] Some of these new attitudes filtered down to retailers. Car dealers, for example, asserted in 1991 that the female car buyer was generally more practical and more critical of after-sales service than men. The *Courier Mail* reported the results of a Queensland survey which found that 37 per cent of female customers believed they had encountered 'sharpie' car salesmen, and 66 per cent said that they had been treated with disdain. As women reportedly influenced over 75 per cent of new vehicle sales, dealers were well advised to take notice of their criticism.[29]

Other commentators believed a 'new improved sexism' had entered advertising. Describing the physical perfection and sexually ambivalent status of an attractive, naked man featured in a 1988 advertisement for sheets, Peter Ruehl of the *Australian Financial Review* decided that this 'male bimbo' represented a major change in advertising thought:

> When you're pushing sheets, a little androgyny goes a long way. Or blue jeans, swimsuits and talcum powder. This guy and his cousins are turning up all over the place. Oddly enough, while the peak of the so-called permissive era has passed, the medium that determines what we eat, how we look, and what we wash our toilets with—advertising—has inserted (sorry, this is catching) this kind of libidinous renegade into the public psyche.[30]

Whatever the anticipated market, 'the basic message is sex by whichever method you choose to enjoy it'. Some consumer researchers suggested that men were increasingly depicted in advertisements in decorative roles while others called for a closer investigation of 'consumer lovemaps'. These new directions in consumer research suggest that the industry was indeed beginning to recognise the profitability of exploring the connections between (hetero)sexuality and consumption.[31]

This open celebration of sex as 'provocative, sensuous, titillating . . . but never ever sentimental', in the words of an advertising brochure quoted by Ruehl, had its darker side. Some advertisements, entered the realms of the pornographic. Naomi Wolf shows that as women moved into positions of power in the 1970s and 1980s, products were sold using the conventions of high-class pornography. These glossy, dramatic and artistic images of women, explicitly portrayed them as the objects of male sexuality and the victims of sexual violence. Wolf argues that sexual hostility is endemic and essential to consumer culture: 'The last thing the consumer index wants men and women to do is to figure out how to love one another: the $1.5 trillion retail-sales industry depends on sexual estrangement between men and women, and is fuelled by sexual dissatisfaction'.[32] Wolf thus suggests that those in the marketing and consumption industries, like those in the pornography business, profit not just from sexuality and sexual difference but more dangerously from deeply misogynistic representations of women. It is perhaps the intensity of this misogyny that most clearly differentiates contemporary forms of marketing from early twentieth-century manifestations of sexualised selling.

Shifting definitions of the sexual were evident in the transformation of the almost exclusively female territory of the department store into the less clearly sexed but more explicitly sexualised discourses and public spaces characteristic of public patriarchy.[33] Those department stores that had survived into the 1970s, particularly older stores left stranded by central business-district concentration and new regional shopping-centre developments, were often dilapidated shells of their formerly bustling selves. Their fates varied. Stores like Grace Brothers (Broadway, Sydney) and McWhirters (Fortitude Valley, Brisbane) which had, in the early twentieth century, constituted the heart of suburban shopping centres bravely limped on. Meanwhile, industry restructuring and intensive remodelling designed to capture (or recapture) the upper end of the market saved inner-city stores such as Melbourne's Myer store and David Jones' Sydney 'Most Beautiful Store in the World'.[34] Some, like Mark Foy's, retained their facades but many, including the palatial Anthony Hordern & Sons building, failed to withstand the power of urban developers and fell to the demolition crews in the late 1980s.

A visit to a suburban shopping mall or urban pedestrian shopping precinct, often incorporating a department store, became the modern way to shop.[35] Property developers sought new markets by constructing inner-city retail centres such as Melbourne Central (incorporating the Daimaru department store), Sydney's Sky Garden mall and Brisbane's Myer Centre which offered the consumer and her children entertainment as well as spectacle.[36] Large corporations moved into 'leisure retailing'; that is, the sale of non-standard craft items and gifts, fast-food facilities and various activities, entertainments and exhibitions designed to attract consumers—couples and families, as well as women—at weekends and at other recreational times. The old McWhirters department store was transformed in 1989 into a much lighter and more colourful McWhirters Marketplace featuring craft barrows, small retail outlets, a produce market, a large dining area and several coffee shops, and an artspace in which local artists produced and sold their creations.[37]

In the shift from department store to festive marketplace, the sexual meanings of shopping were transformed. A visit to a leisure retail complex was presented as superior to the usual trip to the supermarket for the weekly groceries. Supermarket shopping (still largely women's work and therefore associated with femininity and domestic drudgery), shopping centres and complexes, brand names and corporations, and the television advertising on which they were dependent, took much of the sex out of household shopping.[38] Leisure shopping, on the other hand, was presented as a creative, aesthetically pleasing and relaxing activity in which the consumer could demonstrate his or her skills in selecting unusual, exotic or personalised items. As one female shopper interviewed for a 1991 television documentary entitled 'Born to Shop' explained:

> One of the things about shopping is that . . . it's a way of expressing yourself, because in our society, where there is so much to choose from, what you choose is kind of like an artistic decision. So that's one of the things that shopping is, it's being creative.[39]

Because leisure shopping incorporated this element of creativity, it was an activity in which men as well as women could engage. The traditional distinction between men's and women's departments were erased and the commodities on display were not as clearly sexed. The store was no longer, in Susan Porter Benson's phrase, 'an Adamless Eden' denoting both work and pleasure, but a heterosexual space almost exclusively devoted to leisure.

In providing men with leisure goods and services, festive markets and shopping malls gave a new and more socially acceptable form to an older tradition of male consumption. In one Canadian shopping centre, strategically placed store mannequins turned out to be, on closer inspection, real women standing in awkward poses for extremely long periods of time in a bizarre spectacle of female beauty.[40] In a postmodern world, the real woman became disturbingly indistinguishable from her lifeless representation. The retail industry and the sex industry, moreover, occupied similar territory. Brisbane's Fortitude Valley, particularly the area known as the 'sin triangle', has long been known as the 'red light' district of Brisbane, and may in the future be home not only to McWhirters Marketplace but to a proposed 'adult entertainment zone'. As one local alderman observed, the Brisbane City Council found it difficult to tell the difference between a fruit shop and a sex shop. The proposal created opposition from local women who felt threatened by the presence of men in search of commercialised sex. Men's incursion into what was once clearly female retail territory may also be cause for female concern.

Some marketing experts realised that women frequently reacted negatively to a blatant sexual sell articulated from a male vantage point. Although sex is still a potent selling tool for some products, 'marketers are convinced that a growing segment of the buying public, many of them women, are fed up with the hard sell of sex. They long for something more. The result is the marketing of romance'.[41]

A focus on romance, emotion and relationships was reported to be more effective than sex in advertising to 1980s women with enhanced social status, economic power and 'purchasing clout'. This neo-romanticism in some ways returns to the domestic and family-oriented images of the 1940s, and might be interpreted as a conservative attempt to persuade women to give up their gains in the workplace and return to the home.

More optimistically, the supplementation of advertisements using 'hard' sex by a more feminised concept of romance and alternative models of desire suggests that advertising does not have to be confined to a monolithic model of heterosexuality grounded in male sexual fantasies and experiences to meet marketing men's criteria of success. The 'feminism of pleasure' that emerged in the 1980s in response to pessimistic analyses of women as victims proposed that female sexualities (heterosexual and lesbian) be conceived of as products of culture and therefore as complex, contradictory and diverse. Women are represented in accounts such as Rosemary Pringle's *Secretaries Talk* as autonomous sexual subjects who use their sexuality in the pursuit of personal desires and power. Libertarian feminists thus clearly differ from radical or cultural feminist scholars opposed to heterosexist and phallocentric models of female sexuality and the persistence of sexual hierarchies and inequalities.[42]

There may nevertheless be value in critically evaluating the empowering and pleasurable possibilities offered to today's female consumers in non-exploitative forms of advertising. Forms of contemporary women's culture based on romance such as Mills and Boon novels and soap operas provide significant spaces for women to construct alternative readings and creatively appropriate their sexual messages.[43] Romantic marketing themes might also provide women with opportunities to place themselves in advertising narratives as sexual subjects, rather than as the inevitable objects of male sexual pleasure.

Conclusions

Sex and sexual difference have been central to successful retailing since at least the late nineteenth century. The intensity and precise manifestations of the relationship between sex and selling have, however, changed markedly over the last century. From the late nineteenth century to the early twentieth, retailers conducted their businesses as if they were private, bourgeois and domestic retreats from the world of commerce. The cultivation of a mass market defined by sex, and based on adding the custom of working- and middle-class women to that of the wealthy changed the discrete sexual culture of the nineteenth-century emporium. As their enterprises expanded and the need to manage consumer behaviour became more pressing, retail owners and a rising generation of managers rationalised and paid more scientific attention to differences of sex in buying habits and aptitudes.

Notions of masculinity, but more especially a femininity defined by sexual attractiveness, were by the 1920s standardised and widely circulated by department stores. The particular significance of the late 1910s and 1920s as a critical period in the sexualisation of selling may be attributable to a range of intersecting cultural influences: the popularisation of Freudian and other psychological explanations for human behaviour; the influence of sexology and sex experts; the gradual dominance of working-class models of heterosexual and heterosocial interaction; and the commercialisation of sex evident in arenas such as the prostitution industry. The growing economic and sexual independence of women themselves may have provoked a masculinist response in the form of sexual trivialisation. There may also be some link between the enforced but deep fraternal bonding experienced by men during and immediately after World War I, and the crisis in heterosexuality evident in marketing men's industrious attempts to reduce women to creatures of sex.

By 1930 sexualised forms of selling were well established in a variety of marketing institutions, knowledges and media. Retail proprietors and managers, wholesalers and manufacturers, newspaper and magazine editors, advertising agencies, salesmanship writers and display and marketing experts took for granted the need to tailor their promotional activities to the fact of a sexed, predominantly female, consumer population. As the pre-eminent institution of distribution in this period, the department store initiated and decisively influenced the development of distinctively modern and sexed selling techniques. The need of big-store owners and managers to rationalise, streamline and make more profitable their operations as enterprises expanded after the turn of the century spawned a predominantly male army of experts parasitic upon their success. It was these men who, in their efforts to scientifically dissect and explain customer behaviour, effectively defined consumer culture's ideals of modern manhood and womanhood.

Since at least the middle of the nineteenth century, when the drapery-shop proprietor personally served and courteously attended to his lady customers, retailers had sought women's custom using dialogue and demeanour similar to those deemed appropriate to men in the courting of prospective marriage partners. Considerable changes took place in the manner of that wooing as retailers adopted mass-marketing methods in the first two decades of the twentieth century. New methods of winning the attention and loyalty of the customer mirrored and may have effected changes taking place in courtship codes visible in the streets and other public spaces beyond the store.

Late nineteenth-century courtship and selling rituals were acted out as familial transactions conducted in domestic bourgeois spaces (conventionally the parlour) in which men, but especially women, were subject to considerable surveillance and chaperonage. Heterosexual interaction was marked, ideally if not in practice, by female sexual restraint and premarital chastity. Although women had nominal freedom of choice of marriage partner, family expectations, social conventions and economic necessity severely circumscribed that freedom. Negotiations over the marriage contract—a contract actually grounded, as Pateman shows, in the sexual subordination and slavery of women[1]—depended on sexed criteria such as moral standing, decency and business prospects (for men) and virtue, purity and submissiveness (for women). Men were assumed to be the active, even aggressive partner. The seduced and abandoned woman common in much popular literature and criminal court proceedings of the period was represented as morally flawed and defiled, but also pitiable as the unwitting and helpless victim of unrestrained male ardour. Female shoppers were similarly depicted in trade literature as passive victims of the merchant prince.

These codes of premarital heterosexual interaction had shifted markedly by 1930. Working-class patterns of courtship began to subsume older middle-class codes at the same time as the traditionally exclusive drapery-store clientele was expanded by large numbers of shoppers of both middle- and working-class status comprising a mass market for staple consumer goods. Both courting and selling now typically took place in open, more impersonal, and less domestic spaces which clearly displayed the goods for close inspection and comparison, and gave the impression of greater freedom of choice and movement. Family obligations and economic considerations were replaced or overlaid by more personal and individualised goals of self-fulfilment.

Both marriage and consumption promised to provide women with an individual sexual identity. No longer expected to be passionless—at least within marriage—women's courting activities were represented as sexual experiences. Dating, in which a series of sexual partners was expected, gradually replaced an older tradition of monogamous courtship. The act of purchase, similarly, was depicted as a promiscuous form of female sexual abandon and sensual gratification. In this modern female sexuality, women found it more difficult to retreat behind the persona of 'victim' in sexual transactions. The modern woman, whether a rape defendant or a housewife yielding to the department-store's temptations, was frequently seen to be guilty of consent.

By providing such appealing and accessible models of the modern man and modern woman, and by suggesting their appropriate social and spatial relationship, the department store effectively reformulated heterosexuality in the first two decades of the twentieth century. Its male managerial personnel intervened in relations between women and men largely unconsciously, and in concert with other popular media such as newspapers, magazines, fiction, plays, songs, posters and movies. The department store, like other cultural forms, articulated and securely placed in cultural currency notions of desire and sexual desirability. The department store's distinctive contribution, however, was to display those ideas in material form and offer them for sale as permanent reminders of sexual status. Retailers and trade experts publicised a multitude of sexual differences in dress, body shape, physical appearance, temperament and lifestyle that made clear the social distinction between male and female. The rigid demarcation between male and female, characteristic not only of the department store but of most known human societies, acted as a taboo against the sameness of men and women, a taboo necessary to the institutional maintenance of heterosexuality and male dominance.

Such constructed sex differences were not politically neutral. Representations of femininity in the period to 1930 inevitably positioned women as subordinate to an assumed male standard of normal human conduct. Women were depicted in sales literature as passive, easily tempted, infinitely seducible and creatures of emotion and passion; men, on the other hand, were rational, logical and active. The industry's adoption of psychological and other scientific languages from the 1910s reinforced these constructions of women as 'other' and securely placed men as the subject, and women as the object of knowledge.[2] The department-store's standards of sexual attractiveness also had vastly different implications for men and women. Women had to consume more goods and services to achieve modern ideals of beauty and glamour and hence attractiveness to men. More importantly, their purchased desirability made them the objects of male derision, voyeurism and even violence.

At the same time, however, these specifically modern constructions of womanhood created discursive spaces in which female resistances, negotiations or refusals might be enacted. Women created or creatively appropriated a range of ideal female consumer types: the scientific shopper, household manager, educated housewife, consumer expert, bargain-hunter, fashionable working woman, ethical or political dresser. Women could choose any of these models to enhance their personal self-esteem and pleasure, or to give women as a sex a more authoritative voice in political matters. Although retailers and advertisers appeared to be firmly in control of consumer culture, the very existence of an extensive and prolonged advice literature attempting to define and manage female behaviour is testimony to the persistent tensions between male retail manager and female shopper. As the *Patterson Report* acknowledged, women's changing tastes and preferences 'constantly re-shape the marketplace with an ever-changing pattern of demand which makes the marketing of goods a much more hazardous and unpredictable enterprise than many observers would have us believe'.[3]

Female shoplifting and women's inexplicable tendency to steal goods which appeared to be 'of no use to the individual' was perhaps an even greater headache for retailers in 1991 than it was at the turn of the century.[4] Whether in the shape of a shoplifter, a political shopper or simply a 'difficult' customer, the men of the distribution and promotional industries encountered considerable female resistance in their push for profits.

Although they were very much in the minority, some women in the 1910s and 1920s actively opposed the sexualisation of selling and the marketing industry's objectification of women. They probably failed to realise the magnitude of their task. The increasing emphasis placed by retailers, advertisers and sales professionals on differences of sex and sexuality decisively marked the transition from a late nineteenth-century culture of separate sexual spheres to a modern heterosexual consumer culture. By the 1920s it was evident in a number of discourses that public reticence about sex had declined and (predominantly married) female sexual expression was socially accepted. This 'new presence of the erotic in the public realm' was linked to the emergence of a consumer society. The acceptance of pleasure, self-gratification and personal satisfaction were easily translated to the province of sex.[5] Just as transferable in the opposite direction were sexual knowledges to selling. While historians have pointed to the increasing commercialisation of sex in the early twentieth century, this book suggests that the sexualisation of commerce was equally significant.

Subsequent shifts in the marketing of sex as romance in the 1940s, to the promise of erotic fulfilment in the 1960s, to pornographic advertisements and the retreat to 'relationships' in the 1990s suggest that the ties binding the discourses of sex and selling have strengthened, or at least become more visible, during the course of the twentieth century. Patterns of interaction between the sexes, influenced by the sexual revolution's libertarian ideals and permissive codes of premarital conduct, have since the 1920s made female sexual behaviour both more accepted and more difficult to negotiate outside conventional heterosexuality. Since the late 1970s, however, the steady march of sexualised consumerism has lost some of its sense of direction. Postmodernity's parade of a multiplicity of marketing and sexual discourses makes the retail industry's contribution to sexed subjectivities and restrictive models of femininity less predictable.

How can this glimpse inside yesterday's department stores help today's consumers negotiate their world? This historical study suggests, first, that the rules of sex-appropriate and sexual behaviour are created not only by images and representations, but in corporate offices, boardrooms, meeting rooms and executive suites. It is behind these doors and in the individual histories, corporate decisions and internal literature generated by the (still mostly) male managers and directors of the advertising, marketing and retailing industries that heterosexuality is not only constructed and reproduced but constantly modified and elaborated.

The more open those inside conversations about the nature of men and women are to outside scrutiny, the more the consumer will be able to effectively argue with and intervene in the processes of her construction. There is a case to be made, for example, for requiring marketing, retailing and advertising companies to publish and make widely available internal policies and decisions affecting the representation of men, women and sexuality in advertising material. State and federal governments must also ensure sufficient resources for the maintenance and extension of consumer action and protection groups such as consumer affairs bureaus, and attempt to incorporate into their briefs consistent attention to issues of sex.

The valuable work undertaken by feminists in organisations such as Media Switch in monitoring and objecting to sexually exploitative advertisements might usefully by supplemented by, for example, guaranteeing female and, more importantly, feminist representation on advertising standards bodies. Such organisations currently rely on legal definitions of obscenity to define what is unacceptable. As Catharine Mackinnon argues, obscenity law protects the system of male power (hidden behind concepts such as 'morality' and 'sensibilities') more effectively than it protects women from exploitation. The real issue 'is how male sexuality is presented, so that anything can be done to a woman, but obscenity is sex that makes male sexuality look bad'.[6] Sexually exploitative advertisements tend to be banned only when they transgress phallocentric notions of 'public decency' which do not always coincide with feminist readings. Criteria based on obscenity law need to be replaced therefore with policies explicitly grounded in the feminist critique of male sexualities.

This study exposes the lie behind mass markets, consumer cultures and commercial institutions assumed to be free of sex. It has long been a masculine project to eradicate the potentially-destabilising elements of sex and femininity from concepts and knowledges men prefer to present as authoritative, objective and value-free. But sex cannot be erased so easily from social life and culture. Commerce—and economics and politics—is sexed, and mass markets and consumer cultures are unavoidably structured around sexual difference. Social policies and political programmes designed to regulate marketing, selling and consumption need therefore consistently and conscientiously to disaggregate consumer populations into their component male and female constituencies. Government and private industry also need to take into account that consumer decisions and patterns of consumer spending are the outcome of negotiations and communications between or (more rarely) among the sexes.

Sex is probably as unlikely to be excluded from marketing as it is to be expunged from other sexual cultures. Rosemary Pringle suggests in her study of secretaries that instead of attempting to remove sex from the office, feminists might try to creatively appropriate and harness that sexuality to critical or oppositional projects.[7] Feminist literature and theories might usefully be incorporated into the curricula of marketing courses and training programmes. Feminist analyses of the body, of sexual representations in a variety of media and cultures, of men and the construction of masculinity, of women and popular culture, as well as theories of sexuality, the sex industry, lesbianism and critiques of fashion and beauty would all equip marketing students with the critical techniques and knowledges necessary to shift definitions of the sexual in directions more in harmony with the diversity of female needs and desires.

This study of the history of consumer culture has shown that women have always taken the opportunity to intervene, negotiate and resist. Women workers who regularly spend their lunch breaks trying on clothes with no intention of buying them have their predecessors in the flappers who frustrated shop assistants by endlessly trying on hats, and even earlier in the 'cranky shoppers' of the 1890s. The strategies of department-store owners and managers have consistently been countered by the tactics of women as shoplifters, browsers, difficult customers and 'urban guerrillas in the consumer city'.[8] If the history of the interplay between retailers' strategies and women's trickery and tactics is one of an ongoing struggle over the sexual meanings of consumption, then the tradition of the militant consumer and the difficult customer is worth rescuing. The failure of the marketing industry's century-long battle to seduce and tempt the female consumer into utter submission is largely attributable to such individual acts of female insubordination.

Endnotes

Abbreviations

AONSW: Archives Office of New South Wales, Sydney
DJA: David Jones Archives, Sydney
Draper: Draper of Australasia
GBA: Grace Brothers Archives, Sydney
ML: Mitchell Library, Sydney
MRANSW: Master Retailers' Association of New South Wales
JMRANSW: Journal of the Master Retailers' Association of New South Wales
NSWPP: New South Wales Parliamentary Papers
RTANSW: Retail Traders' Association of New South Wales
JRTANSW: Journal of the Retail Traders' Association of New South Wales
SAM: Shop Assistants Magazine
SMH: Sydney Morning Herald

Introduction

1 Jan McGuinness, 'Shoppers, take heart', *The Bulletin*, 18 June 1991, p. 97
2 H. Pasdermadjian, *The department store: its origins, evolution and economics*, Newman Books, London, 1954, p. 12; James Jeffreys, *Retail trading in Britain 1850–1950: a study of trends in retailing with special reference to the development of co-operative, multiple shop and department store methods of trading*, Cambridge University Press, Cambridge, 1954; Lawrence

Neal, *Retailing and the public*, Allen & Unwin, London, 1932, p. 15; Frances Pollon, *Shopkeepers and shoppers: a social history of retailing in New South Wales from 1788*, RTANSW, Sydney, 1989, p. 51

3 Marilyn Lake, 'Socialism and manhood: the case of William Lane', *Labour History*, no. 50, May 1986, pp. 54–62 and 'The politics of respectability: identifying the masculinist context', *Historical Studies*, vol. 22, no. 86, Apr. 1986, pp. 116–31; Judith Allen, 'Evidence and silence: feminism and the limits of history', in *Feminist challenges: social and political theory*, eds Carole Pateman and Elizabeth Gross, Allen & Unwin, Sydney, 1986 and ' "Mundane men": historians, masculinity and masculinism', *Historical Studies*, vol. 22, no. 89, Oct. 1987, pp. 617–28; Anne-Maree Collins, 'Woman or beast: bestiality in Queensland 1870–1949', *Hecate*, vol. 17, no. 1, 1991, pp. 36–42

4 See, for example, John Ferry, *The history of the department store*, Macmillan, New York, 1960; Keith Dunstan, *The store on the hill*, Macmillan, Melbourne, 1979; Lesley Hordern, *Children of one family: the story of Anthony and Ann Hordern and their descendants in Australia 1825–1925*, Retford Press, Sydney, 1985; Ambrose Pratt, *Sidney Myer: a biography*, Quartet, Melbourne, 1978; Nicholas Brash, Anne Burke and Colette Hoeben, *The model store 1885–1985*, Kevin Weldon & Associates, McMahons Point, 1985; Frances Pollon and Philip Geeves, *A romance with retailing: an early history before 1900 and progress to 1913*, RTANSW, Sydney, 1983

5 Carole Pateman, *The sexual contract*, Polity Press, Oxford, 1988, p. 113

6 Michael Miller, *The Bon Marché: bourgeois culture and the department store 1869–1920*, Princeton University Press, Princeton, 1981; Daniel Boorstin, *The Americans: the democratic experience*, Random House, New York, 1973; Neil Harris, 'Museums, merchandising and popular taste: the struggle for influence', in *Material culture and the study of American life*, ed. Ian M.G. Quinby, W.W. Norton, New York, 1978; Howard Wolfers, 'The big stores between the wars', in *Twentieth century Sydney: studies in urban and social history*, ed. Jill Roe, Hale & Iremonger, Sydney, 1980

7 Neil Harris, 'The drama of consumer desire', in *Yankee enterprise: the rise of the American system of manufactures*, eds

Otto Mayr and Robert C. Post, Smithsonian Institution Press, Washington DC, 1981; Rosalind Williams, *Dream worlds: mass consumption in late nineteenth-century France*, University of California Press, Berkeley, 1982; Daniel Horowitz, *The morality of spending: attitudes towards the consumer society in America 1875–1940*, Johns Hopkins University Press, Baltimore, 1985; Elizabeth Ewen and Stuart Ewen, *Channels of desire: mass images and the shaping of American consciousness*, McGraw Hill, New York, 1982; Simon J. Bronner (ed.), *Consuming visions: accumulation and display of goods in America 1880–1920*, W.W. Norton, New York, 1989; Wolfgang F. Haug, *Critique of commodity aesthetics: appearance, sexuality and advertising in capitalist society*, translated by Robert Bock, Polity Press, Cambridge, 1986; Susan Strasser, *Satisfaction guaranteed: the making of the American mass market*, Pantheon, New York, 1989

8 On women and consumer capitalism see Batya Weinbaum and Amy Bridges, 'The other side of the paycheck: monopoly capital and the structure of consumption', in *Capitalist patriarchy and the case for socialist feminism*, ed. Zilla R. Eisenstein, Monthly Review Press, New York, 1979; Nona Y. Glazer, 'Servants to capital: unpaid domestic labour and paid work', *Review of Radical Political Economics*, vol. 16, no. 1, 1984, pp. 61–87; On shop assistants see Jennifer MacCulloch, ' "This store is our world": female shop assistants in Sydney to 1930', in *Twentieth century Sydney: studies in urban and social history*, ed. Jill Roe, Hale & Iremonger, Sydney, 1980; Theresa McBride, 'A woman's world: department stores and the evolution of women's employment 1870–1920', *French Historical Studies*, vol. 10, no. 2, Fall 1978, pp. 664–83; Lee Holcombe, *Victorian ladies at work: middle-class working women in England and Wales 1850–1914*, David & Charles, Newton Abbott, 1973; Carole Elizabeth Adams, *Women clerks in Wilhelmine Germany: issues of class and gender*, Cambridge University Press, Cambridge and Melbourne, 1988

9 Rosemary Pringle, 'Women and consumer capitalism', in *Women, social welfare and the state*, eds Cora Baldock and Bettina Cass, Allen & Unwin, Sydney, 1983

10 Susan Porter Benson, *Counter cultures: saleswomen, managers*

and customers in American department stores 1890–1940, University of Illinois Press, Urbana, 1986

11 Joan W. Scott, 'Gender: a useful category of historical analysis', *American Historical Review*, vol. 91, no. 5, Dec. 1986, pp. 1053–75

12 David Chaney, 'The department store as a cultural form', *Theory, Culture and Society*, vol. 1, no. 3, 1983, pp. 25–7

13 Sheila Jeffreys, *Anti-climax: a feminist perspective on the sexual revolution*, Women's Press, London, 1990, p. 3

14 See, for example, Moira Gatens, 'A critique of the sex/gender distinction' in *Beyond Marxism? Interventions after Marx*, eds Judith Allen and Paul Patton, Intervention Publications, Sydney, 1983; Elizabeth Grosz, 'Notes toward a corporeal feminism', *Australian Feminist Studies*, special issue 'Feminism and the body', no. 5, Summer 1987, pp. 1–16

15 Rosemary Pringle, *Secretaries talk: sexuality, power and work*, Allen & Unwin, Sydney, 1988

16 Rachel Bowlby, *Just looking: consumer culture in Dreiser, Gissing and Zola*, Methuen, New York and London, 1985, p. 20

17 John R. Gillis, *For better, for worse: British marriages, 1600 to the present*, Oxford University Press, New York, 1985, p. 270; Janet McCalman, *Struggletown: public and private life in Richmond 1900–65*, Melbourne University Press, Carlton, 1984, pp. 131, 145

18 Francoise Ducrocq, 'From poor law to jungle law: sexual relations and marital strategies (London, 1850–1870)', in *Women in culture and politics: a century of change*, eds Judith Friedlander, Blanche Weissen Cook, Alice Kessler-Harris and Carroll Smith-Rosenberg, Indiana University Press, Bloomington, 1986, pp. 39–41

19 Beth L. Bailey, *From front porch to back seat: courtship in twentieth century America*, Johns Hopkins Press, Baltimore, 1988, pp. 3–19, quote on p. 3. In the absence of historical studies of Australian courtship practices, I am assuming that the major trends, if not perhaps the precise timing, of American courtship were also evident in Australia. Scattered evidence of relations between single women and men, and more fully-documented studies of the histories of sexual relations and sexuality in both cultures, suggest striking similarities.

20 John D'Emilio and Estelle Freedman, *Intimate matters: a history of sexuality in America*, Harper & Row, New York, 1988,

ch.8; McCalman, *Struggletown*, pp. 146–7; Russell W. Belk and Gregory S. Coon, 'Can't buy me love: dating, money and gifts', in *Advances in consumer research*, eds Rebecca H. Holman and Michael R. Solomon, vol. 18, Association for Consumer Research, Provo, UT, 1991, p. 522; Ellen K. Rothman, *Hands and hearts: a history of courtship in America*, Basic Books, New York, 1984, pp. 205, 225; Kathy Peiss, '"Charity girls and city pleasures: historical notes on working-class sexuality, 1880–1920', in *Desire: the politics of sexuality*, eds Ann Snitow, Christine Stansell and Sharon Thompson, Virago, London, 1984

21 D'Emilio and Freedman, *Intimate matters*, ch. 10; Sheila Jeffreys, *The spinster and her enemies: feminism and sexuality 1880–1930*, Pandora, London, 1985. For similar developments in Australia see Ann Curthoys, 'Eugenics, feminism and birth control: the case of Marion Piddington', *Hecate*, vol. 15, no. 1, 1989, pp. 73–89; Alison Mackinnon and Carol Bacchi, 'Sex, resistance and power: sex reform in South Australia c. 1905', *Australian Historical Studies*, vol. 23, no. 90, Apr. 1988, pp. 60–71; Kerreen Reiger, *The disenchantment of the home: modernizing the Australian family 1880–1940*, Oxford University Press, Melbourne, 1985, chs. 8–9; Rosemary Auchmuty, 'The truth about sex', in *Australian popular culture*, eds Peter Spearritt and David Walker, Allen & Unwin, Sydney, 1979.

22 Judith Allen, ' "Our deeply degraded sex" and "the animal in man": Rose Scott, feminism and sexuality 1890–1925', *Australian Feminist Studies*, nos. 7/8, Summer 1988, pp. 65–91; Lucy Bland, 'Marriage laid bare: middle class women and marital sex', in *Labour and love: women's experience of home and family, 1850–1940*, ed. Jane Lewis, Basil Blackwell, Oxford, 1986; Rothman, *Hands and hearts*, pp. 232–67

23 Jeffreys, *The spinster and her enemies*; Beverley Kingston, *My wife, my daughter and poor Mary Ann: women and work in Australia*, Thomas Nelson, West Melbourne, 1975, pp. 130–36

24 Margaret Jackson, ' "Facts of life" or the eroticization of women's oppression? Sexology and the social construction of heterosexuality', in *The cultural construction of sexuality*, ed. Pat Caplan, Tavistock Publications, London, 1987, pp. 56–57, 60–61; Marie Carmichael Stopes, *Married love: a new contribution to the solution of sex difficulties*, Putnam, London, 1942 [1918], pp. 59–62, 66, 94

25 *The romance of the house of Foy*, published in connection with the Golden Jubilee of Mark Foy's Ltd, Sydney, 1935
26 Rothman, *Hands and hearts*, pp. 232–37, 244; Bailey, *From front porch to back seat*, p. 24
27 Lesley Hordern, *Children of one family*; George Forbes, *History of Sydney from the foundation of the city in 1788 up to the present time 1926*, William Brooks, Sydney, 1926; *JRTANSW, May 1923, June 1932*
28 Other Sydney big stores which began as drapery shops in this period included Edward Arnold (1858), E. Way (1864), Peapes & Shaw (1865), and W.T. Waters (1890). Some shops that began by selling hardware and ironmongery (Lassetters, 1863; Nock & Kirby, 1873), menswear (Murdochs, 1893) and grocery (Civil Service Co-operative Stores, 1871) were also among the big stores by the late nineteenth century. For more details see Gail Reekie, 'Sydney's big stores 1880–1930: gender and mass marketing', PhD thesis, University of Sydney, 1987, pp. 17–41.
29 Historians have tended to anachronistically apply the term 'department store' to any store selling clothing, drapery, accessories, household goods and other non-perishables from the second half of the nineteenth century. It was not commonly in use in the Australian retail trade, however, until the 1920s. Late nineteenth century and early twentieth century drapery shops that expanded their premises and increased the variety of their stock were known as drapery houses or drapery establishments, emporiums or universal providers. From the turn of the century they were also known simply as the 'big stores'. I use 'big stores' as a generic term for those inner city shops, usually drapery shops, that expanded into what were commonly known by the 1920s as department stores and which constituted the membership of the Council of the Master Retailers' Association (later the Retail Traders' Association) of New South Wales

1 Private desires

1 *Australian Town and Country Journal*, 24 Apr. 1886, p. 84; quoted in Lesley Hordern, *Children of one family: the story of Anthony and Ann Hordern and their descendants in Aus-*

tralia 1825–1925, Retford Press, Sydney, 1985, p. 237; see also pp. 98, 200

2 *Australian Dictionary of Biography*, vol. 10

3 Frances Pollon, *Shopkeepers and shoppers: a social history of retailing in New South Wales from 1788*, RTANSW, Sydney, 1989, pp. 128–29

4 Advertisement for David Jones in *The new atlas of Australia*, ed. Robart McLean, John Sands, Sydney, 1886?, n.p.; Pollon, *Shopkeepers and shoppers*, p. 152

5 See, for example, advertising card 1880 in DJA; comment on circulars in *Australian Storekeepers' Journal*, July 1895, p. 92; examples of posters for David Jones, Mark Foy's and Lassetters in *Art and Architecture*, vol. 2, 1905; reference to advertising manager in Farmer & Co. minute book, 15 Apr. 1897, GBA

6 *Woman's Voice*, 6 Apr. 1895, p. 211

7 *The romance of the house of Foy*, published in connection with the Golden Jubilee of Mark Foy's Ltd, Sydney, 1935, p. 39

8 Thomas J. Redmond, *The history of Anthony Hordern & Sons Ltd*, Anthony Hordern & Sons Printers, Sydney, 1938, p. 109; David Jones Ltd board minutes, 8 Apr. 1907, DJA BRG 1/32/1; advertisement for Lowes Ltd in *Sunday Sun*, 17 Sept. 1905

9 *Australian Storekeepers' Journal*, Mar. 1895, p. 9

10 *Draper*, Apr. 1903, p. 152; Hordern, *Children of one family*, p. 203; William Leach, 'Strategists of display and the production of desire', in *Consuming visions: accumulation and display of goods in America 1880–1920*, ed. Simon J. Bronner, W.W. Norton, New York, 1989, p. 106

11 See the reminiscences of women such as Eugenie McNeil, *A bunyip close behind me: recollections of the nineties*, retold by her daughter Eugenie Crawford, Hawthorn Press, Melbourne, 1972

12 Elaine Abelson, *When ladies go a-thieving: middle class shoplifters in the Victorian department store*, Oxford University Press, New York, 1989, ch. 1

13 *The letters of Rachel Henning*, ed. David Adams, Penguin, Ringwood, [1951–52] 1988, p. 270

14 McNeil, *A bunyip close behind me*, p. 69

15 'Rolling and blocking' were technical terms referring to the handling and display of large bolts of material. J.W. Hayes,

The draper and haberdasher: a guide to the general drapery trade, Houlston & Sons, London, 1878, ch. 4.

16 See various correspondence and agreements between the partners of David Jones and female employees 1887–92 in DJA BRG 1/8, BRG 1/13 and BRG 1/24. For details of the work of Sydney shop assistants see Jennifer MacCulloch, ' "This store is our world": female shop assistants in Sydney to 1930' in *Twentieth century Sydney: studies in urban and social history*, ed. Jill Roe, Hale & Iremonger, Sydney, 1980; Gail Reekie, ' "Humanising industry": paternalism, welfarism and labour control in Sydney's big stores 1890–1930', *Labour History*, no. 53, Nov. 1987, pp. 1–19

17 See, for example, article on the millinery showroom, *Lone Hand*, Nov. 1907, p. 85

18 *Australian Storekeepers' Journal*, Apr. 1899, p. 93; *Draper*, Aug. 1901, p. 6; J. W. Hayes, *The draper and haberdasher*, pp. 11, 16

19 Beatrix Tracy, 'The shop girl', *Lone Hand*, 1 Sep. 1908, pp. 523–30, reproduced in Beverley Kingston, *The world moves slowly: a documentary history of Australian women*, Cassell Australia, Stanmore, 1977, p. 116; *Woman's Budget*, 27 Feb. 1906, p. 18; Peter Bailey, 'Parasexuality and glamour: the Victorian barmaid as cultural prototype', *Gender and History*, vol. 2, no. 2, Summer 1990, pp. 148–72

20 T.A. Coghlan, 'Information respecting the Census and Industrial Returns Act 1891', *Votes and proceedings of the Legislative Assembly of New South Wales* 1891–92, vol. 7; Deborah S. Gardner, 'A paradise of fashion: A.T. Stewart's department store 1862–1875', in *A needle, a bobbin, a strike: women needleworkers in America*, eds Joan M. Jensen and Sue Davidson, Temple University Press, Philadelphia, 1985

21 Obituary of Josephine O'Keefe in *Daily Telegraph*, 16 Apr. 1931, newspaper cuttings, DJA; David Jones Board minutes 26 Mar. 1907, DJA BRG 1/32/1

22 Karen Halttunen, 'From parlor to living room: domestic space, interior decoration and the culture of personality' in *Consuming Visions*, ed. Simon J. Bronner, W. W. Norton, New York, 1989

23 *Australian Storekeepers' Journal*, Apr. 1899, p. 93

24 The description of the extravagance of ladies' gowns displayed

in a city costumiere's showrooms is contained in an article on sweated female labour in the dressmaking industry in *Australian Worker*, 7 Jan. 1905

25 Mariana Valverde, 'The love of finery: fashion and the fallen woman in nineteenth century social discourse', *Victorian Studies*, vol. 32, no. 2, Winter 1989, pp. 169–88; Judith A. Allen, *Sex and secrets: crimes involving Australian women since 1880*, Oxford University Press, Melbourne, 1990, pp. 118–27

26 *Draper and Warehouseman*, May 1894, p. 3 and Nov. 1894, p. 8; *Australian Storekeepers' Journal*, Jan. 1900, p. 3 and Feb. 1900, p. 51

27 *Australian Town and Country Journal*, 24 Apr. 1886, p. 84; *Australian Field*, Sep. 1894, p. 267; *Australian Town and Country Journal*, 14 Nov. 1906, reprinted in Anthony Hordern & Sons, *While I live I'll grow: being an account of the foundation and growth of Australia's mammoth business*, Sydney, n.d.

28 *Australia*, 6 June 1907, p. 15

29 *Australian Storekeepers' Journal*, Jan. 1899, p. 3; *Draper* Aug. 1901, p. 15; Hayes, *The draper and haberdasher*, pp. 20–21

30 *Draper and Warehouseman*, Sep. 1894, p. 3; New South Wales Department of Labour and Industry, *Reports on the working of the Factories and Shops Act* 1900, pp. 5, 9; Early Closing Association of New South Wales, *A few facts concerning the hours worked by shop assistants in Sydney and suburbs*, 1898; T.A. Coghlan, 'Census and Industrial Returns Act 1891', p. 1079

31 *Australian Worker*, 1 Mar. 1906. See also 'Shopgirl's plea to the wives of workingmen', *Australian Worker*, 6 June 1907

32 *Draper*, Jan. 1902, p. 5, and editorial Feb. 1902

33 *Draper and Warehouseman*, Aug. 1893, pp. 5–6; *Draper*, Aug. 1901, p. 5; Sept. 1902, p. 329; Feb. 1904, p. 35

34 John D'Emilio and Estelle B. Freedman, *Intimate matters: a history of sexuality in America*, Harper & Row, New York, 1988, p. 179; Ellen K. Rothman, *Hands and hearts: a history of courtship in America*, Basic Books, New York, 1984, pp. 198–200

35 Annie S. Swan, *Courtship and marriage and the gentle art of home-making*, Hutchinson, London, 1894, pp. 14–15

36 Letter to Edward Lloyd Jones from William Newman, 5 Sep. 1892, DJA BRG 1/24

37 *Draper and Warehouseman*, May 1894, p. 3; *Draper*, Apr. 1904, p. 125, Sep. 1905, p. 316

38 *My Lady's Journal*, Mar. 1906, p. 29

39 By fashion, I mean the arbitrary but socially and economically valued differences of style created by designers and manufacturers, and distributed by retailers on a seasonal basis. For a discussion of fashion as a system of difference, see Jean Baudrillard, *For a critique of the political economy of the sign*, Telos Press, St. Louis, 1981, pp. 78–79.

40 Transcript of evidence presented at the shop assistants case heard before the New South Wales Arbitration Court 1907 (hereafter Shop assistants case 1907), AONSW, 2/95–98, vol. 43, p. 799

41 Beatrix Tracy, 'The shop girl', p. 117

42 Valerie Steele, *Fashion and eroticism*, Oxford University Press, New York, 1985

43 *Happy Homes*, Oct. and Dec. 1891, n.p.

44 *The Woman*, Feb. 1892, p. 3; Mar. 1892, p. 6; Rose Scott, speech on Dress and Character, n.d., Scott family papers, ML MSS 38/29, pp. 339–51

45 Excerpts from the *Dawn*, Jul. 1891 and Sept. 1893 in Olive Lawson, *The first voice of Australian feminism: excerpts from Louisa Lawson's The Dawn 1888–1895*, Simon & Schuster, Brookvale, NSW, 1990, pp. 237–40; *Dawn* Apr. 1904, p. 6

46 *Woman's Voice*, 9 Feb. 1895, p. 174; 6 Apr. 1895, p. 211

47 *Australian Storekeepers' Journal*, Apr. 1895, p. 9; June 1896, p. 167; *Draper and Warehouseman*, Oct. 1894, p. 5

48 William Leach, 'Transformations in a culture of consumption: women and department stores, 1890–1925', *Journal of American History*, vol. 71, no. 2, Sep. 1984, p. 320

49 *Woman's Voice*, 23 Mar. 1895, p. 197

50 Scott, speech on Dress and Character; *Woman's Voice*, 18 May 1895, p. 244; report of a lecture presented to the National Council of Women, probably 29 Oct. 1908 [thanks to Jennifer MacCulloch for helping me date this reference], unmarked newspaper clipping, Scott family papers, ML MSS 38/50; *The Wardrobe*, Oct. 1905, p. 6

51 Reports by inspector Annie Duncan in New South Wales Department of Labour and Industry, *Report on the working of the Factories and Shops Act* 1896, p. 1394; 1897, pp. 1374, 1395; 1899, p. 15; 1900, p. 5; letter from Senior Showroom Employees, Grace Brothers, to Rose Scott, 1897, in Rose Scott

correspondence, ML MSS, pp. 243–4; *SMH*, 13 Oct. 1898, clipping in collection of documents relating to the Early Closing Association of New South Wales, ML; Paper on Early Closing read by Rose Scott at a meeting of the National Council of Women, reported in *Evening News*, 19 Nov. 1898, in Scott family papers, ML MSS 38/50. For a general account of the early closing movement see Denise Roberts, 'The movement for the early closing of shops in New South Wales 1890–1899', BA Hons thesis, University of New South Wales, 1981.

52 *Woman's Voice*, 9 Feb. 1895, pp. 170–71

53 Rose Scott, speech on Early Closing, Scott family papers, ML MSS 38/28, pp. 267–69

54 *Report on the working of the Factory and Shops Act* 1900, p. 5; *Australian Worker*, 6 June 1907, p. 15; Scott, Speech on Early Closing, pp. 267–9

55 Beatrix Tracy, 'The shop girl', p. 118

2 *Sex, class and the mass market*

1 For example, W. Hamish Fraser, *The coming of the mass market, 1850–1914*, Macmillan, London, 1981; Barbara Little, 'Retail trade and distribution in Sydney 1880–1914', PhD thesis, University of Sydney, 1979

2 Methodological problems in assessing the relationship between the development of mass marketing and changes in disposable income include extreme variations in individual and household income patterns, life cycle changes in expenditure, wide ranges in price and quality, and the difficulty of distinguishing 'necessary' from 'luxury' commodities.

3 Jean Baudrillard, 'The ideological genesis of needs', *For a critique of the political economy of the sign*, Telos Press, St. Louis, 1981

4 John Mackinolty, 'The Married Women's Property Acts', in *In pursuit of justice: Australian women and the law 1788–1979*, eds Judy Mackinolty and Heather Radi, Hale & Iremonger, Sydney, 1979, pp. 73–74

5 P.G. Macarthy, 'Wages in Australia 1891 to 1914', *Australian Economic History Review*, vol. 10, no. 1, Mar. 1970, pp. 70–71

6 Little, 'Retail trade and distribution in Sydney', pp. 21, 33, 231, 234

7 'Interim report of the Royal Commission of Inquiry into the Alleged Shortage of Labour in the State of New South Wales 1911', in *NSWPP* 1911–12, vol. 2, 3rd session; Commonwealth Bureau of Census and Statistics, *Labour and Industrial Branch Reports* 1912, p. 84. The cost of living was set in the 1920s by the 1920 Royal Commission into the Basic Wage. Figures calculated from Commonwealth *Labour Reports* 1921–30
8 T.A. Coghlan, *The wealth and progress of New South Wales*, Government Printer, Sydney, 1902, p. 775; *Labour Reports* 1912, 1914, 1928
9 *Magnet*, 15 Mar. 1910, p. 2
10 Elsie Jones, 'Fertility decline in Australia and New Zealand 1861–1936', *Population Index*, vol. 37, 1971, pp. 308, 314; Peter McDonald, Lado Ruzicka and Patricia Pyne, 'Marriage, fertility and mortality', in *Australians: historical statistics*, ed. Wray Vamplew, Fairfax Syme & Weldon, Sydney, 1987, p. 42; Colin Forster, 'Aspects of Australian fertility, 1861–1901', *Australian Economic History Review*, vol. 14, no. 2, 1974, pp. 105–23
11 Neville Hicks, *This sin and scandal: Australia's population debate 1891–1911*, Australian National University Press, Canberra, 1978, p. 23; Royal Commission on the Basic Wage, 1920, *Australia: Parliamentary Papers* 1920–21, vol. 4, p. 53; A.B. Piddington, *The next step: a family basic income*, Macmillan, Melbourne, 1921, p. 15
12 McDonald, Ruzicka and Pyne, 'Marriage, fertility and mortality', p. 42
13 *SAM*, Aug., Nov., Dec. 1926; *Woman's World*, Apr. 1922, p. 6
14 For details of women's work in this period see Jill Julius Matthews, *Good and mad women: the historical construction of femininity in twentieth century Australia*, Allen & Unwin, Sydney, 1984; Beverley Kingston, *My wife, my daughter and poor Mary Ann: women and work in Australia*, Nelson, Melbourne, 1975; Desley Deacon, *Managing gender: the state, the new middle class and women workers 1830–1930*, Oxford University Press, Melbourne, 1989. For similar trends in Britain see Lee Holcombe, *Victorian women at work: middle-class women in England and Wales 1850–1914*, David & Charles, Newton Abbott, 1973.
15 *SMH*, 26–28 Nov. 1918; *Draper*, Dec. 1918, p. 426

16 *Draper*, Dec. 1923, p. 742; *Brisbane Courier*, 28–31 Jul. 1931

17 *Draper*, Oct. 1924, p. 558, June 1929, p. 262

18 Gail Reekie, 'The shop assistants case of 1907 and labour relations in Sydney's retail industry', in *Foundations of arbitration: the origins and effects of state compulsory arbitration 1890–1914*, eds Stuart Macintyre and Richard Mitchell, Oxford University Press, Melbourne, 1989; Edna Ryan, *Two-thirds of a man: women and arbitration in New South Wales 1902–1908*, Hale & Iremonger, Sydney, 1984

19 *Woman's World*, 1 Nov. 1922, p. 18

20 Charles Lloyd Jones and Desmond Robinson, 'Customers are human', typescript, c. 1958, DJA; *Australian Storekeepers' Journal*, June 1896, p. 161; *Draper*, May 1903, p. 191. The reference to the different operating principles of the cash and credit traders occurs in the evidence of George Wright of Farmers, Department of Labour and Industry's Necessary Commodities Commission, transcript of proceedings, 19 Feb. 1920, AONSW 2/5728, p. 43. The *Draper*, June 1924, p. 365, gave advice on dressing windows to attract both credit and cash customers. For details of time-payment schemes see Little, 'Retail trade and distribution in Sydney', p. 274, and (for Melbourne) Graeme Davison, *The rise and fall of marvellous Melbourne*, Melbourne University Press, Melbourne, 1978, p. 196.

21 Under the cash-order system, a finance company issued the borrower with an order to a nominated store (usually a drapery house) to supply her with goods to a certain value. The retailer paid the finance company fifteen per cent of the value of the order in return for the custom, while the borrower paid five per cent as a premium and five per cent as a first instalment. Interstate Commission of Australia, Prices Investigation no. 11 Report, Clothing, 1919, in *Commonwealth Parliamentary Papers* 1917–19, vol. 5, pp. 429, 435; *SAM*, June 1926, p. 34; Little, 'Retail trade and distribution in Sydney', p. 130.

22 Matthews, *Good and mad women*, pp. 65–73. See also Michael Gilding, 'Economic relations in the bourgeois family, Sydney, 1870–1940', *Australia 1888 Bulletin*, no. 9, Apr. 1982.

23 Kerreen Reiger, *The disenchantment of the home: modernizing the Australian family 1880–1940*, Oxford University Press, Melbourne, 1985, ch. 3; Deacon, *Managing gender*, ch. 8; Desley Deacon, 'Taylorism in the home: the medical profes-

sion, the infant welfare movement and the deskilling of women', *Australian and New Zealand Journal of Sociology*, vol. 21, no. 2, 1985, pp. 161–73

24 New South Wales Department of Labour and Industry, *Reports on the Working of the Factories and Shops Act* 1900, p. 9

25 *SAM*, Nov. 1926. For a discussion of the interests of women's organisations in consumer-related issues see Meredith Foley, 'The women's movement in New South Wales and Victoria, 1918–1938', PhD thesis, University of Sydney, 1985, chs. 4, 5.

26 Ellen McEwen, 'The Newcastle coalmining district of New South Wales, 1860–1900', PhD thesis, University of Sydney, 1980, p. 346

27 New South Wales, Department of Labour and Industry, *Report on the working of the Factories and Shops Act* 1907, p. 32

28 New South Wales Board of Trade, cost of living enquiry, males and females general, 1920, transcript of evidence, AONSW 2/5775, p. 66. See also evidence of Caroline Martin (p. 156) and Mrs Jordan for the Housewives Association (p. 487). *Draper*, Jan. 1908, p. 27; *Commonwealth Home*, Aug. 1928, p. 35

29 Calculated from figures in Glen Withers, Anthony M. Endres and Len Perry, 'Labour', in *Australians: historical statistics*, ed. Wray Vamplew, p. 147

30 Article in *SMH*, quoted in *JRTANSW*, Mar. 1929, p. 51

31 Evidence of Frank Smith at shop assistants case 1907, vol. 43, p. 858; *Men's Wear*, Jan. 1924, clipping in Peapes & Co. papers ML MSS 2161, box Y812; *SAM*, Dec. 1926, p. 20; *Draper*, 1928, p. 495; Herbert Casson, *The art of customer-finding*, Cornstalk Pub. Co, Sydney, 1928, ch. 5; Herbert Casson, *Better salesmanship and twelve tips on finance*, Corstalk Pub. Co, Sydney, 1928, p. 47

32 Report of the Sydney City and Suburban Sewage Health Board, in *Votes and proceedings of the New South Wales Legislative Assembly* 1875–76, vol. 5, pp. 595, 599, 626; references to suburban shopping in *Reports on the Factories and Shops Acts* from 1897; New South Wales Legislative Assembly, *Royal Commission re Saturday Half-Holiday* 1909, Appendix D. See also Kerreen Reiger, "Clean and comfortable and respectable": working-class aspirations and the Australian 1920 Royal Com-

mission on the Basic Wage', *History Workshop Journal* no. 27, Spring 1989, pp. 97–102.

33 R. Twopeny, *Town life in Australia*, London, 1883, p. 56; evidence presented at New South Wales Board of Trade enquiries into the cost of living for adult female workers 1918, transcript of proceedings, AONSW 2/5768, pp. 21, 58, 65; *Compendium of Living Wage Declarations and Reports*, 1921, pp. 52–53; details of the cost of a tailored costume come from Necessary Commodities Control Commission, 10 June 1920, AONSW 2/5729, pp. 3–4

34 Cost of living enquiry, general, 1920, p. 157; Cost of living enquiry, women, 1918, p. 148

35 Cost of living enquiry, women, 1919, p. 754

36 Janet McCalman, *Struggletown: public and private life in Richmond 1900–1965*, Melbourne University Press, Carlton, 1984, p. 143

37 See, for example, advertisements for 'working man's' stores in the *Australian Worker* after 1906; Shop assistants case 1907, vol. 43, p. 865; cost of living enquiries, women, 1918; women, 1919; and general, 1920

38 Evidence of Leslie Conway of Sydney Snows, Cost of living enquiry, women, 1919, p. 623

39 Cost of living enquiry, women, 1919, p. 753

40 References to Anthony Hordern & Sons in evidence given at shop assistants case 1907, vol. 44, p. 1050; and to the ladies' trade in shop assistants case 1907, vol. 43, p. 719; vol. 42, p. 105. Retailers' attempts to secure female customers of all classes are referred to in *JRTANSW*, Jan. 1929, p. 15; *Draper*, Feb. 1926, p. 44; Sept. 1930, p. 479.

41 'The future policy of the company', Report of the Executive to the Directors of David Jones, 12 July 1916, David Jones Board minutes, DJA BRG 1/32

42 Cost of living enquiry, women, 1918, p. 98

43 Eugenie McNeil, *A bunyip close behind me: recollections of the nineties*, retold by her daugher Eugenie Crawford, Hawthorn Press, Melbourne, 1972, p. 69; Lesley Hordern, *Children of one family: the story of Anthony and Ann Hordern and their descendants in Australia 1825–1925*, Retford Press, Sydney, 1985; Davison, *The rise and fall of marvellous Melbourne*, p. 201

44 H. Pasdermadjian, *The department store: its origins, evolution and economics*, Newman Books, London, 1954, p. 126
45 *Draper*, May 1922, pp. 212–13

3 Scientific selling

1 Newspaper clipping, n.d., in Women's Political Educational League Item 2, Scott family papers, ML MSS 38/43; details of William Hughes' career in *Australian Dictionary of Biography* vol. 9, p. 394; shop assistants case 1907, vol. 45, p. 1843; *Australian Worker*, 23 May 1907, p. 1; New South Wales Department of Labour and Industry, *Reports on the working of the Factories and Shops Act* 1912, p. 34; *SMH*, 11 Sep. 1905, p. 7
2 *Draper and Warehouseman*, Nov. 1892, editorial
3 Interim Report of the Royal Commission of Inquiry into the Alleged Shortage of Labour in the State of New South Wales 1911, *NSWPP* 1911–12, vol. II, 3rd session, pp. 29, 127, 148
4 Summarised in the *Draper*, June 1918, pp. 208–09
5 Minutes of the MRANSW 13 Jul. 1903, RTANSW Archives; Sydney Chamber of Commerce, *Annual Report* 1920; *JMRANSW, June 1921; JRTANSW*, June 1925
6 *Proceedings and resolutions of the first Australian convention of advertising men,* Brisbane, 1918, National Library of Australia MS 1014, p. 55
7 *Draper*, Feb. 1922, p. 56
8 *Draper*, Oct. 1925, p. 459, Oct. 1930, p. 565; *JRTANSW*, Aug. 1929, p. 12
9 *JRTANSW, Jan. 1930, p. 61*
10 Kerreen Reiger, *The disenchantment of the home: modernizing the Australian family 1880–1940*, Oxford University Press, Melbourne, 1985; Desley Deacon, 'Taylorism in the home: the medical profession, the infant welfare movement and the deskilling of women', *Australian and New Zealand Journal of Sociology*, vol. 21, no. 2, July 1985, pp. 161–73; Helen Bourke, 'Industrial unrest as social pathology: the Australian writings of Elton Mayo', *Historical Studies*, vol. 20, no. 79, Oct. 1982, pp. 217–33
11 Editorial on the shop assistants arbitration court case, *Draper*, Aug. 1907, p. 363
12 *Draper*, Nov. 1917, p. 534; Housewives Association of New South Wales organ *Ours*, Aug. 1922, p. 19

13 *Sydney Technical College Handbook*, 1935
14 *Draper*, June 1922, p. 274
15 John Spierings, 'Magic and science: aspects of Australian business, management, advertising and retailing, 1918–40', PhD thesis, University of Melbourne, 1989, pp. 501–02
16 A.R. Harwood, 'Report to the directors of David Jones Ltd', 1913, pp. 1–2, DJA; 'Future policy of the company', in David Jones Board Minutes, 1916; Board Minutes 12 March 1924, DJA BRG 1/32/1
17 Nicholas Brash, Anne Burke and Colette Hoeben, *The model store 1885–1985*, Kevin Weldon & Associates, McMahons Point, NSW, 1985, p. 182; *Rydge's Business Journal*, Jan. 1929, pp. 23–25, 69
18 *Fifth Convention of the Advertising Association of Australia and New Zealand*, 1925, p. 31, NLA MS 1014
19 Obituary of Eleanor Donaldson, *SMH*, 15 Aug. 1986
20 John Spierings, 'Realising dreams: elements of advertising in Australia between the wars', unpub. paper, 1986, p. 1; *Brisbane Courier*, 3 Sep. 1918, clipping in Advertising Association of Australia and New Zealand records, NLA MS 1014. See also Ann Stephen, 'Agents of consumerism: the organisation of the Australian advertising industry 1918–1938', in *Media Interventions*, eds Judith Allen et al, Intervention Publications, Leichhardt, NSW, 1981.
21 *JRTANSW*, Jul. 1929, p. 39
22 *Second Convention of Advertising Men, 1920*, Advertising Association of Australia and New Zealand, NLA MS 1014; *Draper*, Sep. 1920, p. 296; Helen Bourke, 'Industrial unrest as social pathology'.
23 See, for example, a series of articles on 'The human instincts in business', Feb. 1921–Jan. 1922 and references to industrial psychology in *Draper*, May 1920, p. 99, Sep. 1920, p. 296; *Australasian Journal of Psychology and Philosophy*, vol. 3, no. 3, Sep. 1925, pp. 211–18; *JRTANSW*, Nov. 1929, p. 19
24 *Draper*, Aug. 1902, p. 319
25 *Reason Why*, Aug. 1908, p. 21; E. Gewurz, *Wisdom and success in advertising*, T. C. Lothian, Melbourne, 1910, p. 11
26 *Draper*, Jan. 1921, pp. 2–3
27 *JRTANSW*, Jan. 1930, pp. 53–61
28 Desley Deacon, 'Political arithmetic: the nineteenth century

Australian census and the construction of the dependent woman', *Signs*, vol. 11, no. 1, 1985, pp. 27–47; Jill Julius Matthews, *Good and mad women: the historical construction of femininity in twentieth century Australia*, Allen & Unwin, Sydney, 1984, pp. 72–73; Gabriella Turnatori, 'Between public and private: the birth of the professional housewife and the female consumer', in *Women and the state: the shifting boundaries of public and private*, ed. Anne Showstack Sassoon, Hutchinson, London, 1987

29 Beatrix Tracy, 'The shop girl', in *The world moves slowly*, ed. Beverley Kingston, p. 118; *Draper*, May 1915, p. 129; summary of Bright and Hitchcock's (Geelong) training scheme in *Draper*, Nov. 1917, p. 353. See also salesmanship curricula in *Sydney Technical College Handbook*, 1935.

30 *Draper*, Nov. 1917, p. 353

31 Sheila Jeffreys, *The spinster and her enemies: feminism and sexuality 1880–1930*, Pandora, London, 1985, ch.9

32 Lustre Hosiery Ltd, *The craft of retail selling: dedicated to the great army of men and women who fill a most important niche in the realm of merchandising*, Sydney, n.d. (?1920s), pp. 14–17; William Beable, *Behind the counter: a practical guide for shop assistants*, Angus & Robertson, Sydney, 1930, ch. 10; *Rydge's retail merchandising course*, Sydney, 1937, pp. 123–24; *Draper*, Sep. 1921, pp. 380–81

33 *Rydge's Business Journal*, Mar. 1931, p. 166

34 *Reason Why*, Feb. 1909, p. 16; *Draper*, May 1921, p. 194; *Men's Wear*, Jan. 1924, p. 19, in Peapes Ltd records, Box Y812, ML MSS 2161; Herbert Casson, *The art of customer-finding*, Cornstalk Pub. Co., Sydney, 1928, p. 84

35 Kinduno, '"Coy and hard to please": appealing to the woman buyer', *Advertiser's Monthly*, Jan. 1930, pp. 28–29

36 *Rydge's retail merchandising course*, p. 16; Lustre Hosiery, *The craft of retail selling*, p. 22; *Rydge's Business Journal*, Mar. 1931, pp. 166–68; *SMH*, 13 Jan. 1919, p. 1

37 Roland Marchand, *Advertising the American dream: making way for modernity*, University of California Press, Berkeley, 1985, pp. 162, 168, 191. Marchand found that working-class men were not portrayed as consumers in American advertisements. The Australian evidence contradicts this. See, for example, Grace Brothers' *The model trader*, 1921.

38 G.T.W. Patrick, 'The psychology of women', *Popular Science Monthly*, vol. 47, 1895, reproduced in *The psychology of women: selected readings*, ed. Juanita Williams, Norton, New York, 1979
39 *Draper and Warehouseman*, May 1984, p. 3; *Draper*, May 1918, p. 188
40 Article from the *Dry Goods Economist* reprinted in *JRTANSW*, Dec. 1929, p. 61; *Draper*, Apr. 1907, pp. 155–56; May 1918, p. 188; Lustre Hosiery, *The craft of retail selling*, p. 24
41 *Draper*, Mar. 1918, p. 97; *JRTANSW*, Aug. 1929, p. 27
42 *Draper*, May 1921, p. 217
43 Lustre Hosiery, *The craft of retail selling*, p. 23
44 *Draper*, Oct. 1918, p. 345
45 Advertisement for David Jones, *SMH*, 13 Jan. 1919, p. 3; article by Phil Warner, *Advertiser's Monthly*, Nov. 1929, p. 5; *Rydge's Business Journal*, Jan. 1928, p. 54
46 Suggestions for 'reason why' copy for men in the *Draper*, Mar. 1927, p. 115; Apr. 1925, p. 180; the 'boot to suit you' quote comes from the *Draper*, May 1921, p. 170; references to men's assumed receptivity to current affairs themes in *Draper*, Aug. 1920, p. 271; Jul. 1921, p. 284; Mar. 1927, p. 115; 'lofty sentiments' quote from *Draper*, Jul. 1916, p. 246
47 Casson, *The art of customer-finding*, pp. 82, 85
48 Kinduno, 'Appealing to the woman buyer', p. 29
49 Lustre Hosiery, *The craft of retail selling*, p. 15; *Draper*, June 1922, p. 277
50 *Draper*, Jan. 1921, p. 5
51 *JRTANSW*, Dec. 1929, p. 65
52 Judith A. Allen, *Sex and secrets: crimes involving Australian women since 1880*, Oxford University Press, Melbourne, 1990, pp. 87–88
53 Martin Pumphrey, 'The flapper, the housewife and the making of modernity', *Cultural Studies*, vol. 1, no. 2, 1987, pp. 179–94
54 Allen, *Sex and secrets*, ch. 5. Echoes of this tension may be detected in formal psychological texts on sex differences, many of which were written in direct response to disturbing changes in the sexual order and the 'masculinisation' of women.
55 *Draper*, May 1921, p. 217; *Rydge's retail merchandising course*, p. 112

56 Gail Reekie, 'Market research and the post-war housewife', *Australian Feminist Studies*, no. 14, Summer 1991, pp. 15–27. Australian retailers and advertisers first became interested in market research towards the end of the 1920s, but in this period depended primarily on statistical and mathematical knowledges of the market. Psychology did not become a major market research methodology until the 1950s and 1960s.

4 Sexed commodities

1 Adrian Forty, *Objects of desire: design and society 1750–1980*, Thames & Hudson, London, 1986, p. 66
2 Ann Game and Rosemary Pringle, *Gender at work*, Allen & Unwin, Sydney, 1983, pp. 60–62
3 *Draper*, Dec. 1908, p. 415
4 *Australian Storekeepers' Journal*, Apr. 1895, p. 9; June 1896, p. 167; *Draper*, Oct. 1923, p. 627; Aug. 1927, p. 359
5 *Between Ourselves*, Feb. 1919, back cover
6 For a useful summary see Ann Curthoys, 'The sexual division of labour: theoretical arguments', in *Australian women: new feminist perspectives*, eds Norma Grieve and Ailsa Burns, Oxford University Press, Melbourne, 1986
7 See, for example, Harrods (London) when it moved into drapery and ladies' fashions at the end of the nineteenth century (Sean Callery, *Harrods Knightsbridge: the story of society's favourite store*, Ebury Press, London, 1991, p. 94)
8 Farmer & Co. Engagement book 1873–1889, GBA; Peapes & Co. Applications for engagement, Peapes & Co. papers, Box Y812, ML MSS 2161; shop assistants case 1907, vol. 43, p. 1517; *Draper*, Aug. 1906, p. 263
9 Shop assistants case 1907, vol. 42, p. 123
10 Shop assistants case 1907, vol. 42, p. 95
11 Susan Porter Benson, *Counter cultures: saleswomen, managers and customers in American department stores 1890–1940*, University of Illinois Press, Urbana, 1986, p. 23
12 Shop assistants case 1907, vol. 44, pp. 1040–42, 1089–90
13 *New South Wales Industrial Arbitration Reports* 1907, p. 145
14 Game and Pringle, *Gender at work*, p. 60.
15 Shop assistants case 1907, vol. 43, p. 947; vol. 45, p. 1675; vol. 43, p. 887

16 Shop assistants case 1907, vol. 43, p. 947; vol. 44, p. 1358
17 Shop assistants case 1907, vol. 43, pp. 701, 824, 887, 947; vol. 44, pp. 1058, 1198, 1358; vol. 45, p. 1675
18 The *Magnet*, Dec. 1909, p. 3
19 David Jones Board Minutes 20 June 1916; David Jones 'The future policy of the company', report of the executive submitted to the Board of Directors 18 Jul. 1916, in Board Minutes, DJA; personnel file of Mrs Searle 1923–24, DJA
20 *Australian Storekeepers' Journal*, Apr. 1898, p. 107; Lesley Hordern, *Children of one family: the story of Anthony and Ann Hordern and their descendants in Australia 1825–1925*, Retford Press, Sydney, 1985, p. 253; *Australian*, 6 June 1907, pp. 14–15; Thomas J. Redmond, *The history of Anthony Hordern & Sons Ltd*, 1938, p. 91
21 *JRTANSW, June 1925, p. 376*
22 *JRTANSW*, Feb. 1928, p. 47; 'Interim Report of the Royal Commission of Inquiry into the Alleged Shortage of Labour in the State of New South Wales', *NSWPP*, 1911, vol. 1, part 2, p. 80
23 'The future policy of the company', 1916, pp. 3–4
24 See, for example, David Jones, *A visit to David Jones: reviewing the George Street store, the country order department and the Marlborough Street factory*, 1923, DJA BRG 1/134
25 *JRTANSW*, Oct. 1927, p. 53
26 *Lone Hand*, Nov. 1911, p. 12
27 Helene E. Roberts, 'The exquisite slave: the role of clothes in the making of the Victorian woman', *Signs*, vol. 2, no. 3, 1977, pp. 558–65; David Kunzle, 'Dress reform as anti-feminism', *Signs*, vol. 2, no. 3, 1977, pp. 577–79
28 Valerie Steele, *Fashion and eroticism*, Oxford University Press, New York, 1985, p. 208
29 Moira Gatens, 'A critique of the sex/gender distinction', in *Beyond Marx? Interventions after Marx*, eds Judith Allen and Paul Patton, Intervention Publications, Sydney, 1983, p. 150
30 See, for example, corset advertisement in *Australian Storekeepers' Journal*, Sep. 1896, p. 276
31 *Draper*, Apr. 1921, p. 159
32 *Draper*, Apr. 1921, pp. 157, 159
33 *Draper*, Dec. 1924, p. 698; May 1925, p. 244; *JRTANSW*, Dec. 1929, pp. 41–43; *Home*, Mar. 1924, p. 1
34 *Draper*, Jul. 1919, p. 278; Dec. 1923, pp. 742, 763; Aug. 1930,

p. 413; for Brisbane, see advertisements for McWhirters in *Courier Mail*, 28 Jul. 1931

35 *JRTANSW*, Dec. 1927, p. 31; Sep. 1926, p. 17; June 1929, p. 55; *Courier Mail*, 29 Jul. 1931

36 *Draper*, Sep. 1926, p. 432

37 Personnel files of Mrs Elizabeth Dumas (1910) and Mrs E. Hammond (1912), DJA; *Draper*, Jul. 1919 p. 229; Aug. 1919, pp. 198–99; (reference to cancer) Apr. 1921, p. 157 ; *SMH*, 30 Sep. 1918; *SAM*, Jul. 1926, pp. 10, 23

38 *Draper*, Sep. 1918, p. 312. On fracturing and reassembly see Jean Baudrillard, 'Fetishism and ideology: the semiological reduction', in his *For a critique of the political economy of the sign*, Telos Press, St. Louis, 1981.

39 *Draper*, May 1923, p. 294

40 *Courier Mail*, 29 Jul. 1931

41 Sue Best, 'Berlei corsets and the (un)making of the modern body', *Continuum*, vol. 5, no. 1, 1991, p. 191

42 *Draper*, Jan. 1918, pp. 19–20

43 Eugenie McNeil, *Ladies didn't: recollections of an Edwardian girlhood*, retold by her daughter Eugenie Crawford, Penguin, Ringwood, 1984, pp. 81–82; *Lone Hand*, Nov. 1911, p. 12 (see also article on millinery in the same journal, Nov. 1907); *Woman's News*, Jan. 1905, p. 7

44 *Draper*, Aug. 1921, p. 352

45 *Lone Hand*, Nov. 1911, p. 12

46 Letter to David Jones & Co. from Edward Wilcox, 22 Jul. 1892, DJA BRG 1/13

47 Herbert Casson, *The art of customer-finding*, Cornstalk Pub. Co., Sydney, 1928, p. 142

48 *JRTANSW*, Dec. 1929, p. 61; William H. Beable, *Behind the counter: a practical guide for shop assistants*, Angus & Roberson, Sydney, 1930, pp. 57–58

49 On the shift to the selling of ideas, see Wolfgang Haug, *Critique of commodity aesthetics: appearance, sexuality and advertising in capitalist society*, Polity Press, Cambridge, 1986. Warner's article is in *Advertiser's Monthly*, Nov. 1929, p. 5; *Rydge's Business Journal*, Dec. 1928, p. 812; Casson, *The art of customer-finding*, p. 141; Alex Whyte, 'The psychology of selling', *Rydge's Business Journal*, Feb. 1928.

50 Necessary Commodities Control Commission, transcript of evi-

dence, 17 May 1920, AONSW 2/5729, p. 33; *Draper*, Aug. 1929, p. 410; David Jones Trading Results 1921 and 1930, DJA BRG 1/140

51 *Draper*, July 1917, p. 215

52 Shop assistants case 1907, vol. 43, p. 499; New South Wales Board of Trade, cost of living enquiry, males and females, general, 1920, AONSW 2/5775, pp. 233–36; details of maximum added percentage allowed on landed cost of clothing in *JRTANSW*, Feb. 1927, p. 33; *Report of the Royal Commission on the Basic Wage* 1920, p. 30. (Boys' clothing was estimated to cost more per year than girls' clothing.)

53 Shop assistants case 1907, vol. 44, pp. 975, 1340–41, 1220–21; Necessary Commodities Control Commission 1919, p. 7 and throughout; Interstate Commission of Australia, Prices Investigation no. 11 Report, Clothing, *Commonwealth Parliamentary Papers* 1917–19, vol. 5, p. 434

54 Evidence of George Wright, Necessary Commodities Control Commission, 19 Feb. 1919, pp. 37, 41; Report of the Fair Profits Commission 23 Apr. 1920, in Sargood Gardiner papers, Box 1, University of Melbourne Archives

55 Shop assistants case 1907, vol. 43, p. 583

56 Shop assistants case 1907, vol. 42, p. 457; vol. 45, p. 1453; 'Royal Commission on the Shortage of Labour 1911', p. 80

57 *JRTANSW*, Sep. 1924, p. 81

58 Calculated from David Jones departmental trading results 1921 and 1930, DJA BRG 1/140

5 Windows and interior displays

1 *JRTANSW*, Jan. 1928, p. 41

2 Farmers: *Draper*, Dec. 1902, p. 443. Buckinghams: *Draper*, Apr. 1903, p. 136. Anthony Hordern & Sons: *Australian*, 6 June 1907, p. 15. Marcus Clark: *My Lady's Journal*, Mar. 1906, p. 28. David Jones: Charles Lloyd Jones and Desmond Robinson, 'Customers are human', unpub. typescript, c. 1958, DJA; plan of Elizabeth Street store departments 1927, DJA BRG 1/574. Lassetters: *Town and Country Journal*, 13 May 1908. McDowell and Hughes: *Draper*, Mar. 1915, p. 83. Robert Reid: catalogues 1899–1912 in Robert Reid papers, Australian National University Archives of Business and Labour 81/310A.

3 *Draper*, Aug. 1914, p. 370; *Draper*, Apr. 1922, p. 183; *Draper*, Sep. 1914, p. 406. The quotation is from *Draper*, May 1918, p. 188
4 *Draper*, May 1915, p. 164; *Draper*, Aug. 1906, p. 263; *Draper*, Dec. 1929, p. 648
5 *Draper*, Sep. 1905, p. 316
6 *Draper*, Oct. 1925, p. 167
7 Advertisement for Farmers, *The Home*, Mar. 1924, p. 50; Anthony Hordern & Sons Ltd, *Annual Report*, 1930, Fisher Library.
8 Vivien Stewart, 'The way they were: a Sydney department store in the 1920s', *Heritage Australia*, vol. 9, no. 4, Summer 1990, pp. 20–23
9 *Draper*, Oct. 1904, p. 347
10 Susan Porter Benson, *Counter cultures: saleswomen, managers and customers in American department stores 1890–1940* University of Illinois Press, Urbana, 1986, pp. 38–47
11 *Products of Bray and Holliday Ltd*, Adshead Rose Publicity, Sydney, n.d. ?1924–29
12 *Commonwealth Home*, Oct. 1927, p. 29; *SMH*, 2 Jan. 1929, p. 4; *JRTANSW*, July 1929, p. 27; Ian Fell, 'Shops: the architectural treatment of modern shop design', B.Arch. thesis, University of Sydney, 1928, Fisher Library, pp. 6–8, 11
13 Karen Halttunen, 'From parlor to living room: domestic space, interior decoration, and the culture of personality', in *Consuming visions: accumulation and display of goods in America 1880–1920*, ed. Simon J. Bronner, W.W. Norton, New York, 1989, pp. 170–72
14 For example, newspaper report of David Jones' Elizabeth Street store, *Sun*, 27 Nov. 1927, DJA
15 William Leach, 'Transformations in a culture of consumption: women and department stores, 1890–1925', *Journal of American History*, vol. 71, no. 2, Sep. 1984, pp. 323–25
16 *SMH*, 24 Nov. 1919, p. 4
17 Rosalind Williams, *Dreamworlds: mass consumption in late-nineteenth century France*, University of California Press, Berkeley, 1982, pp.67–92
18 *Draper*, Apr. 1903, p. 136; *My Lady's Journal*, Mar. 1906, p. 28; *Draper*, Oct. 1918, p. 333; *Labor Daily*, 28 Nov. 1928, p. 5
19 Halttunen, 'From parlor to living room', p. 189

20 *SAM*, Sep. 1926, p. 25; *Labor Daily*, 28 Nov. 1928, p. 5; *Sun*, 29 Nov. 1927
21 Leach, 'Transformations in a culture of consumption', p. 331
22 *Draper*, Aug. 1902, p. 279; newspaper clipping 1905 in Peapes & Co. papers, ML MSS 2161 Box Y812; *Sydney Mail*, 13 Sep. 1905, p. 678; *Sydney Mail*, 19 Dec. 1923 in Peapes & Co. papers; *Draper*, Nov. 1928, p. 551; *Labor Daily*, 28 Nov. 1928, p. 5
23 David Jones board minutes 27 Aug. 1919, DJA BRG 1/32/1; *Draper*, Feb. 1914, p. 47; *Sydney Technical College Handbook*, 1916
24 A woman window-dresser, probably an exception, was employed by a Sydney jewellery and optical goods shop in 1938 (*Rydge's Business Journal*, Mar. 1938, p. 172).
25 *Sun Pictorial*, 22 May 1930, clipping in DJA
26 William Leach, 'Strategists of display and the production of desire', in *Consuming Visions*, ed. Simon J. Bronner, p. 132
27 *Draper*, Aug. 1902, p. 323; Oct. 1918, p. 335; *Draper*, Jan. 1914, p. 31
28 *Draper*, Aug. 1930, p. 462; Nov. 1928, p. 549
29 For example, *Draper*, Jan. 1914, p. 31; Aug. 1924, p. 493
30 Rydge's Business Journal, *Rydge's retail merchandising course*, Sydney, 1927, p. 267; advertisement for Mark Foy's, *SMH*, 30 Sep. 1918
31 *Draper*, Oct. 1904, p. 374; *Draper*, Sep. 1920, p. 308
32 Alan Foley and W.J. Hewett, *Textbook of window dressing and display*, A Lawrence & Co, Sydney, 1922–23, pp. 90, 96, 98; *JRTANSW*, Dec. 1929, p. 65
33 The drawing room tableau is described in *Commonwealth Home*, Sep. 1928, p. 39.
34 Rachel Bowlby, *Just looking: consumer culture in Drieser, Gissing and Zola*, Methuen, London, 1985, pp. 29–34
35 Leach, 'Transformations in a culture of consumption', pp. 328–29
36 *Commonwealth Home*, Sep. 1928, p. 35; *Helen's Weekly*, Jan. 1928, p. 39
37 M. Barnard Eldershaw, *Tomorrow and tomorrow and tomorrow*, Virago, London, [1947] 1983, pp. 46–47
38 *Draper*, Mar. 1923, p. 141
39 *SAM*, June 1926, p. 23
40 *Commonwealth Home*, Sep. 1928, p. 39

41 *Draper*, May 1917, p. 131
42 Sheila Jeffreys, 'Indecent exposure', in *Women against violence against women*, eds Dusty Rhodes and Sandra McNeill, Onlywomen Press, London, 1985, p. 83; Sandra McNeill, 'Flashing: its effect on women', in *Women, violence and social control*, eds Jalna Hanmer and Mary Maynard, Macmillan, London, 1987, p. 108

6 *Managing women's desires*

1 *The romance of the house of Foy, published in connection with the Golden Jubilee of Mark Foy's Ltd, 1885–1935*, Sydney, 1935, pp. 39–40; Charles Lloyd Jones, 'The history of David Jones Limited', reprinted from the *Journal of the Royal Australian Historical Society*, vol. 41, 5, 1955, pp. 6–7, DJA; Charles Lloyd Jones and Desmond Robinson, 'Customers are human', unpub. typescript, c. 1958, DJA
2 On women's desire for personal adornment see *Draper*, Dec. 1920, p. 400; Oct. 1922, pp. 481–82; on women and fashion, see *Home*, June 1920, pp. 29–30; *JRTANSW*, Nov. 1921, p. 532; *Draper*, Aug. 1919, p. 287. Some attention began to be paid to fashions in men's clothes in the 1920s (see *SMH* editorial, 'Clothes and the man', 17 Aug. 1929, p. 14), but did not substantially alter the strong relationship between femininity and fashion.
3 *Draper*, Jan. 1921, p. 5; *SMH*, 13 Sep. 1929, p. 11; extract from the autobiography of Edward Bok, editor of the *Ladies' Home Journal* 1890–1919, reproduced in the *Draper*, Oct. 1922, pp. 481–82
4 Lustre Hosiery Ltd, *The craft of retail selling*, n.d., ?1920s, Sydney, pp. 17, 22, 23; *JRTANSW*, Oct. 1922, p. 81; Jan. 1930, pp. 53–61
5 *Commonwealth Home*, Feb. 1928, pp. 29–30; *Draper*, Oct. 1918, p. 334; May 1924, p. 278; Mar. 1922, p. 126
6 Lloyd Jones and Robinson, 'Customers are human', pp. 84–85, DJA; *Sun*, 27 Nov. 1927, clipping, DJA; *Draper*, Nov. 1928, p. 543; *Rydge's Business Journal*, 1 Aug. 1928, pp. 519–21. On the role of department stores in shaping cultural tastes and aspirations see John E. O'Connor and Charles F. Cummings, 'Bamberger's department store, *Charm* magazine, and the cul-

ture of consumption in New Jersey 1924–1932', *New Jersey History*, no. 102, 1984, pp. 1–33

7 The reference to the Nock and Kirby promotion is in *Herself*, Mar. 1929; details of Christmas promotions in *Draper*, Jan. 1930, p. 15; Mar. 1930, p. 125

8 *National Economy Exhibition. Organised by the Women's Commonwealth Patriotic Association. Official Catalogue*, Sydney, 1917; YWCA, *Annual Report*, 1919–20, p. 2; 1920–21, p. 2; CWA, *Report*, 1928, p. 25; 1931, p. 16.

9 Susan Porter Benson, *Counter cultures: saleswomen, managers and customers in American department stores 1890–1940*, University of Illinois Press, Urbana, pp. 258–65

10 *SAM*, Feb. 1927. p. 17; quotation from *SAM*, Aug. 1927, p. 4; *Draper*, Nov. 1923, p. 660; Nov. 1928, p. 543; *JRTANSW*, Oct. 1928, p. 49

11 *Between Ourselves*, Dec. 1919, p. 24

12 *Between Ourselves*, June 1920, p. 15

13 *Dajonian*, Oct. 1932, DJA

14 *Sunday Sun*, 11 Feb. 1934, clipping, DJA

15 *Between Ourselves*, Feb. 1920, pp. 16–17; 'History and policy of David Jones Limited', speech by Mr Stark to the Improvement Class, Mar. 1925, BRG 1/496, DJA

16 *Draper*, May 1920, p. 104; *SAM*, May 1926, pp. 7, 34

17 *JRTANSW*, Oct. 1923, p. 90; Berlei Limited, *Fifty-two practical aids to better salesmanship* (collection of salesmen's [*sic*] manuals), 1926

18 *Draper*, June 1918, p. 213; reference to the playlets in *Draper*, May 1918, p. 155

19 Wolfgang F. Haug, *Critique of commodity aesthetics: appearance, sexuality and advertising in capitalist society*, translated by Robert Bock, Polity Press, Cambridge, [1971] 1986, pp 38–39

20 Correspondence and newspaper clippings in the Department of the Attorney-General and of Justice, Special Correspondence Bundles—Papers re Shoplifting, First Offenders (Women) Act, and Women's Legal Status Bill 1905–39, AONSW 3/3165 [hereafter Attorney-General's shoplifting file].

21 Attorney-General's shoplifting file. The quote is from the chairman of the Metropolitan Branch of Stipendiary Magistrates, memo, 22 Mar. 1922.

22 Judith Allen, 'Women, crimes and policing in New South Wales

1880–1939', PhD thesis, Macquarie University, 1984, pp. 119–21

23 Extract from *Hansard*, 23 Sep. 1919, Attorney-General's shoplifting file; Judith Allen, 'Breaking into the public sphere: the struggle for women's citizenship in NSW 1890–1920', in *In pursuit of justice: Australian women and the law 1788–1979*, eds Judy Mackinolty and Heather Radi, Hale & Iremonger, Sydney, 1979

24 Memo from the chairman, Metropolitan Branch of Stipendiary Magistrates, 9 Aug. 1922; minutes of deputation, 11 June 1926, Attorney-General's shoplifting file

25 Allen, 'Women, crimes and policing', p. 125

26 *SMH*, 3 Dec. 1929, DJA

27 *Truth*, 15 Dec. 1929, clipping, Attorney-General's shoplifting file; *SMH*, 3 Dec. and 10 Dec. 1929; *Guardian*, 27 Sep. 1929, clippings, DJA

28 *SMH*, 14 May 1929, clipping, DJA

29 Elaine Abelson, *When ladies go a-thieving: middle-class shoplifters in the American department store*, Oxford University Press, New York, 1989

30 Allen, 'Women, crimes and policing', p. 116

31 *SMH*, 27 Sep. 1929, clipping, DJA

32 *Truth*, 15 Dec. 1929, clipping, Attorney-General's shoplifting file

33 *JRTANSW*, Aug. 1928, p. 4; *Rydge's Business Journal*, June 1960, p. 585; *SMH*, 31 May 1929; memo from Detective Inspector John Pattinson, 28 Aug. 1928, Attorney-General's shoplifting file; statement by Chief Stipendiary Magistrate Gates, *SMH*, 20 Jul. 1929, clipping, DJA

34 SMH, 7 Dec. 1929; *Telegraph*, 12 June 1929, clippings, DJA

35 Abelson, *When ladies go a-thieving*, p. 173

36 I was unable to locate any articles on kleptomania or shoplifting in the main psychological and medical journals published in Australia in the period to 1930

37 *Draper*, Jan. 1915, p. 5; Feb. 1915, p. 33; *Evening News*, 16 Aug. 1926, clipping, Attorney-General's shoplifting file

38 Judith A. Allen, *Sex and secrets: crimes involving Australian women since 1880*, Oxford University Press, Melbourne, 1990, p. 152

39 Attorney-General's shoplifting file; *SMH*, 22 Aug. 1928, p. 15

40 Attorney-General's shoplifting file; *Draper*, Apr. 1928, p. 158
41 Notes from Under Secretary, 12 Dec. 1929 and Crown Solicitor, 17 Oct. 1928; memo 9 Oct. 1928, Emily Austin in Nancy Green case papers, Attorney-General's shoplifting file
42 See, for example, *SMH*, 15 and 23 Jan. 1913, clippings, Attorney-General's shoplifting file; also press reports of court cases involving store employees, for example, *SMH*, 1 May 1929, clipping, DJA
43 Unmarked clipping (?Feb. 1929), DJA
44 *SMH*, 2 and 5 Feb. 1929; *Daily Telegraph*, 12 Feb. 1929; *Sun*, 4 Mar, 1929, clippings, DJA; quote and headline from unmarked clipping (? Feb. 1929), GBA
45 Master Retailers' Association of New South Wales, minutes, 19 Nov. 1908 and 25 Feb. 1909, RTANSW archives; report on deputation to Minister for Justice 1913, Attorney-General's shoplifting file
46 Minutes of deputation 11 June 1926 and 21 Aug. 1928, Attorney-General's shoplifting file; Mary Dain's case reported in *SMH*, 10 Dec. 1929, clipping, DJA
47 *JRTANSW*, Mar. 1929, p. 7
48 *SMH*, 5 Mar. 1929, clipping, DJA
49 *SMH*, 1 May 1929, clipping, DJA
50 Memo, 13 Sep. 1934, Attorney-General's shoplifting file
51 *SMH*, 20 Jul. 1929, clipping, DJA
52 *Sun*, 5 Jan. 1928, clipping, GBA; *SMH*, 25 Apr. 1929, p. 4

7 *Madam intervenes: women and consumer politics*

1 *Draper*, Nov. 1921, p. 480
2 Herbert Casson, *The art of customer-finding*, Cornstalk Pub. Co, Sydney, 1928, pp. 75–77; Rydge's Business Journal, *Rydge's retail merchandising course*, Sydney, 1937, p. 378; *Advertisers' Monthly*, Mar. and Aug. 1930 (unfortunately, no details of the content of the lectures on women's responses to advertising were provided); *Draper*, Jul. 1926, pp. 286–87. The quote is from *Draper*, Sep. 1928, p. 422.
3 William Leach, 'Transformations in a culture of consumption', *Journal of American History*, vol. 71, no. 2, Sep. 1984, p. 342. See also William Leach, *True love and perfect union: the feminist reform of sex and society*, Basic Books, New York, 1980,

ch.9; Valerie Steele, *Fashion and eroticism*, Oxford University Press, New York, 1985; Elizabeth Wilson, *Adorned in dreams: fashion and modernity*, Virago, London, 1985.

4 Carmel Shute, 'Australian women and the Great War: aspects of ideological change, with particular emphasis on Queensland', BA Hons thesis, History Department, University of Queensland, 1973, p. 155. See also Anne Summers, *Damned whores and God's police: the colonization of women in Australia*, Penguin, Harmondsworth, 1975, pp. 379–96.

5 For details of women's political activity in this period see Summers, *Damned whores and God's police*; Barbara Cameron, 'The flappers and the feminists: a study of women's emancipation in the 1920s', in *Worth her salt: women at work in Australia*, eds Margaret Bevege, Margaret James and Carmel Shute, Hale & Iremonger, Sydney, 1982; Kerreen Reiger, *The disenchantment of the home: modernizing the Australian family 1880–1940*, Oxford University Press, Melbourne, 1985; Sabine Willis, 'Homes are divine workshops', and Pat Gowland, 'The Women's Peace Army', in *Women, class and history: feminist perspectives on Australia 1788–1978*, ed. Elizabeth Windschuttle, Fontana, Melbourne, 1980; Meredith Foley, 'The women's movement in New South Wales and Victoria, 1918–1939', PhD thesis, University of Sydney, 1985; Jill Matthews, 'Education for femininity: domestic arts education in South Australia', *Labour History*, no. 45, Nov. 1983, pp. 30–53

6 Quoted in Summers, *Damned whores and God's police*, p. 388

7 Militant Women's Group, *Woman's road to freedom*, Proletarian Press, Sydney, 1927, p. 16

8 National Council of Women of New South Wales, *Biennial Reports*, 1923–24, 1925–26; Australian Labor Party, minutes of Second Interstate Conference of Labor Women, Canberra, May 1930; YWCA Sydney, *Annual Reports*, 1916–17, 1919–20, 1921–22. The YMCA, by contrast, appeared to have had no interest in shop assistants or in industrial welfare work more generally.

9 National Council of Women of New South Wales, *Biennial Reports*, 1919–20, pp. 12–13; 1925–26, p. 17; *JRTANSW*, Sep. 1925, p. 83; *Ours* (organ of the Housewives Association), Aug. 1922, p. 19

10 Alice Kessler-Harris, *Out to work: a history of wage-earning women in the United States*, Oxford University Press, New

York, 1982, pp. 166–171; Sarah Smith Malino, 'Faces across the counter: a social history of female department store employees 1870–1920', PhD dissertation, Columbia University, 1982; Judith Smart, 'Feminists, food and the fair price: the cost of living demonstrations in Melbourne, August–September 1917', *Labour History*, no. 50, May 1986, pp. 113–31; editorial on women's boycotts in *Draper*, Jul. 1920

11 Civic League minute book 18 Aug., 20 Oct. 1909, ML MSS 2024/1; *The Woman* (official organ of the Australian Women's National League), Dec. 1920, p. 307. The aims of the League were stated as: loyalty to Empire, to combat socialism, to educate women in politics and safeguard the interests of home, women and children.

12 Women's Co-operative Society Ltd., *Rules*, Balmain, 1911; *Australian Congress of Consumers' Co-operative Societies*, Sydney, 1920; *Daily Telegraph*, 3 Oct. 1929, *SMH*, 20 and 21 Sep. 1929, clippings, DJA

13 For example, column by Housewife, *Sydney Mail*, 13 Sep. 1913; 'Purely Business' by Shopper, *Australian Worker*, 30 Jan. 1929; Women's Column, *SMH*, 30 Sep. 1930; *Ours*, Jul. 1921; *My Lady's Journal*, Feb. 1906; *Helen's Weekly*, Oct. 1927

14 *Everylady's Journal*, 6 Jan. 1919

15 *JRTANSW*, May 1928, p. 3, Feb. 1929, p. 5; *Worker*, 13 Mar. 1929, p. 15; Australian Labor Party, minutes of Second Interstate Conference of Labor Women at Canberra, May 1930; *Herself*, June 1930, p. 34; Foley, 'The women's movement in New South Wales and Victoria 1918–1939', ch. 4; Women's Commonwealth Patriotic Association, series of pamphlets on thrift, Sydney, n.d. (?1915–17); Women's Column, *SMH*, 30 Sep. 1918

16 *The Home*, Dec. 1920. pp. 90, 92. For a full discussion of the Housewives Association, see Foley, 'The women's movement of New South Wales and Victoria, 1918–1939', ch. 4.

17 New South Wales Board of Trade, cost of living enquiry, males and females general, 1920, transcripts of proceedings, AONSW 2/5775, p. 487; Kate Dwyer at First Interstate Conference of the National Council of Women, unmarked newspaper clipping, Scott family papers, ML MSS 38/50

18 New South Wales Board of Trade, *Compendium of Living Wage Declarations and Reports*, 1921, pp. 53–54; Foley, 'The women's movement in New South Wales and Victoria, 1918–1939', p. 119

19 *Lone Hand*, Feb. 1920, p. 38
20 Mary Gilmore, 'For working women', *Australian Worker*, 27 May 1920, p. 9
21 National Council of Women, *Biennial Report*, 1926–28, p. 22; *SMH*, 29 Mar. 1928, p. 11, 15 Aug., p. 11
22 National Council of Women of New South Wales, *Biennial Report*, 1926–28, p. 49; Australian Labor Party, minutes of Second Interstate Conference of Labor Women, Canberra, 1930; *Home*, Mar. 1926, p. 18
23 *Commonwealth Home*, 2 Apr. 1928, pp. 29–30
24 'Lily's letter to London', *Commonwealth Home*, Jul. 1928
25 Alexandra Joel, *Best dressed: 200 years of fashion in Australia*, Collins, Sydney, 1984, pp. 45–50; Barbara Cameron, 'The feminists and the flappers', pp. 258–62
26 Judith A. Allen, *Sex and secrets: crimes involving Australian women since 1880*, Oxford University Press, Melbourne, 1990, pp. 155–56
27 *White Ribbon Signal* (organ of the WCTU), May 1913, pp. 8–9; Report of Honorary International Secretary Rose Scott, National Council of Women, New South Wales, *Biennial Report*, 1913–14, p. 8; *Association Woman*, Nov. 1922, p. 8
28 *SMH*, 21 Jan. 1914, clipping, Scott family papers ML MSS 38/50, item 2, p. 87
29 *Mothers in Australia*, Dec. 1920, p. 14; quotation from *Mothers Union*, June 1918, pp. 15–16
30 Women's Commonwealth Patriotic Association, *Thrift in Dress*, 1915–17, pp. 3–4, 11
31 *Association Woman*, Sep. and Oct. 1918
32 Quoted in Cameron, 'The flappers and the feminists', p. 267
33 *Association Woman*, June 1921, pp. 5–6
34 *Association Woman*, Dec. 1919, pp. 5–6. For details of Constance Davey's life see *Australian Dictionary of Biography*, vol. 8, pp. 216–17
35 *Rydge's Business Journal*, Nov. 1928, pp. 737–30
36 *Herself*, June 1928, n.p.; Jul. 1928, p. 9
37 *Ours*, Dec. 1921, p. 2
38 *The Woman*, Aug. 1931, p. 154
39 National Council of Women of New South Wales, *Biennial Report*, 1923–24, p. 8; YWCA *Annual Reports*, 1919–20, p. 2 and 1920–21, p. 2; CWA *Report*, 1928, 1931

40 Report of the Royal Commission on the High Cost of Living no. 4 (General), *Victoria: votes and proceedings, Legislative Assembly*, 1923–24, vol. 2, p. 1077; New South Wales Board of Trade, inquiry into the cost of living of adult female workers 1918, transcripts of proceedings, AONSW 2/5768, p. 97; *Association Woman*, Feb. 1921, p. 14; *Herself*, July 1928, p. 3

41 There appears to have been little reaction in the nineteenth and early twentieth centuries from Australian intellectuals to consumerism and its social effects. Compare with the rich French literature (Rosalind Williams, *Dream worlds: mass consumption in late nineteenth century France*, University of California Press, Berkeley, 1982); similar sources for the United States (Daniel Horowitz, *The morality of spending: attitudes towards the consumer society in America 1875–1940*, Johns Hopkins University Press, Baltimore, 1985); and Germany (Warren G. Breckman, 'Disciplining consumption: the debate about luxury in Wilhelmine Germany, 1890–1914', *Journal of Social History*, vol. 24, no. 3, 1990, pp. 485–505).

42 *Newspaper News*, Jul. 1928, p. 17

43 *Ours*, Aug. 1922, p. 12; *Commonwealth Home*, Jul. 1928

44 Neil Harris, 'The drama of consumer desire', in *Yankee enterprise: the rise of the American system of manufactures*, eds Otto Mayr and Robert C. Post, Smithsonian Institution, Washington DC, 1981, p. 212

45 *Rydge's Business Journal*, Aug. 1928, p. 519

8 Sexualised consumerism

1 Heather Radi, '1920–29', in *A New History of Australia*, ed. F.K. Crowley, Heinemann, Richmond, 1974, p. 389

2 Judith A. Allen, *Sex and secrets: crimes involving Australian women since 1880*, Oxford University Press, Melbourne, 1990, pp. 126–27; W.A. Sinclair, 'Women and economic change in Melbourne 1871–1921', *Historical Studies*, vol. 20, no. 79, October 1982, pp. 288–90; Martin Pumphrey, 'The flapper, the housewife and the making of modernity', *Cultural Studies*, vol. 1, no. 2, 1987, p. 186

3 Peter Bailey, 'Parasexuality and glamour: the Victorian barmaid as cultural prototype', *Gender and History*, vol. 2, no. 2, Summer 1990, 148–172; Sandra Lee Bartky, 'Foucault, feminin-

ity, and the modernization of patriarchal power', in *Feminism and Foucault*, eds Irene Diamond and Lee Quinby, Northeastern University Press, Boston, 1988; Paula Fass, *The damned and the beautiful: American youth in the 1920s*, Oxford University Press, New York, 1978, pp. 279–88. For similar developments in Australia see Beverley Kingston, *My wife, my daughter and poor Mary-Ann: women and work in Australia*, Thomas Nelson, West Melbourne, 1975, p. 134; Jill Julius Matthews, 'Building the body beautiful', *Australian Feminist Studies*, no. 5, Summer 1987, p. 19; Barbara Cameron, 'The flapper and the feminists', in *Worth her salt: women at work in Australia*, eds Margaret Bevege, Margaret James and Carmel Shute, Hale & Iremonger, Sydney, 1982.

4 'Is the modern business girl any value to the nation?', *Between Ourselves*, Jan. 1919, pp. 14–15; continued Apr. 1919, p. 8; notes under 'Personal', *Between Ourselves*, May 1919, p. 16; 'Muriel the gift girl', *Between Ourselves*, Dec. 1920, pp. 10–11; letter to the editor, *Between Ourselves*, Sep. 1919, p. 10; 'A toy tragedy', *Between Ourselves*, June 1919, p. 16

5 Ann Stephen, 'Agents of consumerism: the organisation of the Australian advertising industry, 1918–1938', in *Media Interventions*, eds Judith Allen et al, Intervention Publications, Leichhardt, 1981, pp. 79–85

6 Analysis of display advertising in *Advertising in Australia*, Jul. 1921, pp. 15–25

7 J.V. Barker, 'The advertising art of Australia', *Technical Gazette of New South Wales*, vol. 13, part 2, 1923, pp. 73–80

8 *Draper*, June 1918, p. 207

9 'Modern art applied to advertising', *Advertiser's Monthly*, May 1930, p. 25; Edward Perugini, 'Effects of modernistic art', *Advertiser's Monthly*, Dec. 1929, pp. 5–6; N.R.[*sic*] 'Applying the factor of suggestion: effective use of background motifs revealed', *Advertiser's Monthly*, Dec. 1929, pp. 29–30. On the use of modernism in advertising see Roland Marchand, *Advertising the American dream: making way for modernity 1920–1940*, University of California Press, Berkeley, 1985, p. 182.

10 *Draper*, Dec. 1922, p. 591

11 Jill Carrick, 'Turn of the century posters: representing women', *Arena*, no. 79, 1987, pp. 108–18

12 *Draper*, May 1924

13 Ann Stephens, 'Mass produced photography in Australia during the inter-war years', *Art Network*, no. 9, Autumn 1983, p. 40
14 Australian National Gallery, *The glamour show: studio photographs 1925–1955*, 10 May–14 Sep. 1986, catalogue
15 *Draper*, June 1924, p. 365
16 *Draper*, May 1921, p. 172
17 *SMH*, 26 Apr. 1928, p. 5; 2 Jan. 1929, p. 4
18 William Leach, 'Strategists of display and the production of desire', in *Consuming visions: accumulation and display of goods in America 1880–1920*, ed. Simon J. Bronner, W.W. Norton, New York, 1989, p. 113
19 *Draper*, Aug. 1916, p. 271; *SMH*, 24 Nov. 1919, p. 4; *Draper*, Dec. 1918, p. 425; *Draper*, May 1929, p. 258; Aug. 1930, p. 413
20 Advertisement for frock, *SMH*, 27 Nov. 1918; kimono, *SMH*, 16 Dec. 1918; brassiere, *SMH*, 26 Nov. 1918
21 Kerreen Reiger's work on the 1920 basic wage commission, which focuses on working-class married women's notions of family comfort and respectability, provides a useful comparison (' "Clean and comfortable and respectable": working-class aspirations and the Australian 1920 Royal Commission on the Basic Wage', *History Workshop Journal*, no. 27, Spring 1989, pp. 97–102)
22 *Printing Trades Journal*, 17 Dec. 1918, pp. 286–88
23 *SMH*, 16 Nov. 1918
24 Gail Reekie, 'Decently dressed? Sexualised consumerism and the working woman's wardrobe 1918–1923', in *Women, work and the labour movement in Australia and Aotearoa/New Zealand*, eds Raelene Frances and Bruce Scates, special issue, *Labour History*, no. 61, 1991, pp. 42–56
25 New South Wales Board of Trade, *Compendium of Living Wage Declarations and Reports*, 1921, pp. 52–53
26 *Between Ourselves*, Sep. 1919, pp. 5, 15; May 1920, p. 11; the *Dajonian*, Oct. 1932, DJA; *Woman's World*, Mar. 1922, p. 25
27 *Woman's World*, Sep. 1922, p. 20. See Matthews, 'Building the body beautiful', pp. 18–19
28 See, for example, sections devoted to perfumery and toilet goods in the Christmas supplements of the *Draper*, Oct. 1916, Oct. 1922 and Oct. 1924; also Robert Reid (wholesaler) price list of haberdashery and fancy goods, 1911, Robert Reid

papers, Australian National University Archives of Business and Labour 81/310B

29 Mere Man in *The Magnet* (Mark Foy's magazine), Aug. 1910, p. 5

30 *Draper*, Sep. 1928, pp. 459–62; *SAM*, Aug. 1926, p. 10, *Draper*, Sep. 1929, p. 516. On changing ideals of beauty see Lois Banner, *American Beauty*, Alfred A. Knopf, New York, 1983

31 Helena Rubinstein, *My life for beauty*, Bodley Head, Sydney, 1964, pp. 40, 56, 60, 62; *The Home*, Dec. 1925, p. 9; David Jones Trading Results, 1930, DJA BRG 1/140

32 *Between Ourselves*, Feb. 1921, p. 16; *The Home*, Sep. 1922, p. 75; Alexandra Joel, *Best dressed: 200 years of fashion in Australia*, Collins, Sydney, 1984, pp. 69–70

33 David Jones' beauty parlour, *Sun*, 29 Nov. 1927, clipping, DJA; Marcus Clark reference book 1929, Marcus Clark papers, Australian National University Archives of Business and Labour 74/31/1; Buckinghams' beauty parlour, *Draper*, Oct. 1929, p. 534; haberdashery items, *Draper*, Oct. 1926, p. 445; barber shop, plan of Elizabeth Street store, 1927, DJA BRG 1/574

34 Kathy Piess, 'Making faces: the cosmetics industry and the cultural construction of gender, 1890–1930', *Genders*, no. 7, Spring 1990, p. 143. See also Fass, *The damned and the beautiful*, pp. 282–83

35 Cited in Gail Reekie, 'Female office workers in Western Australia 1895–1920: the process of feminisation and patterns of consciousness', in *The work place: Time Remembered, special issue no. 5*, ed. Lenore Layman, Murdoch University, Perth, 1982, p. 16

36 *Melbourne Era*, 18 Aug. 1923

37 Cost of living enquiry, women, 1918, pp. 21, 58, 97, 98, 148; *Printing Trades Journal*, 17 Dec. 1918, p. 287

38 Cost of living enquiry, women, 1918, p. 169

39 Cost of living enquiry, women, 1918, p. 169

40 Cost of living enquiry, women, 1919, p. 692

41 *SMH*, 25 Nov. 1919, p. 6

42 *SMH*, 27 Nov. 1919, p. 7

43 Marilyn Lake, 'Sexuality and feminism: some notes on their Australian history', *Lilith*, no. 7, Winter 1991, p. 32

44 See Meredith Foley, 'The women's movement in New South

Wales and Victoria 1918–1938', PhD thesis, University of Sydney, 1985, ch.4

45 *SMH*, 12 Dec. 1918

46 Speech at First Interstate Conference of the National Council of Women, unmarked newspaper clipping in Scott family papers ML MSS 38/50. For details of Kate Dwyer's life and career see *200 Australian women: a Redress Press anthology*, ed. Heather Radi, Redress Press, Sydney, 1988, pp. 78–79.

47 *Australian Worker*, 27 May 1920, p. 9

48 Judith Allen, '"Our deeply degraded sex" and "the animal in man": Rose Scott, feminism and sexuality 1890–1925', *Australian Feminist Studies*, no. 7/8, Summer 1988, p. 85

49 Civic League minute book, minutes 16 Sep. 1908, ML MSS 2024/1; *SAM*, June 1926; Oct. 1926, p. 24

9 Romance to pornography

1 John Spierings, 'Magic and science: aspects of Australian business, marketing, advertising and retailing, 1918–40', PhD thesis, University of Melbourne, 1989, p. 465

2 *JRTANSW*, Jul. 1933, p. 3; Spierings, 'Magic and science', p. 481

3 *Rydge's Business Journal*, Apr. 1948, p. 335; Ruth Thompson, 'David Jones' centenary celebrations 1838–1938', *Australia 1938 Bulletin*, no. 3, Dec. 1980, p. 12; *Rydge's Business Journal*, Sep. 1934, pp. 856–57

4 *Rydge's Business Journal*, Nov. 1934, pp. 1068–69; Dec. 1938, p. 914; Aug. 1938, pp. 578–79, 624; Jan. 1940, pp. 15, 58–59; Apr. 1938, pp. 251–53

5 Spierings, 'Magic and science', p. 465

6 *Rydge's Business Journal*, Aug. 1934, pp. 750–52

7 *Rydge's Business Journal*, Mar. 1940, pp. 186–87

8 Marilyn Lake, 'Female desires: the meaning of World War II', *Australian Historical Studies*, vol. 24, no. 95, Oct. 1990, p. 283

9 Greg Whitwell, *Making the market: the rise of consumer society*, McPhee Gribble, Melbourne, 1989, pp. 29–31

10 *Rydge's Business Journal*, Mar. 1950, pp. 241–42; Ann Game and Rosemary Pringle, *Gender at work*, Allen & Unwin, Sydney, 1983, pp. 63–70, 119–26; Nona Y. Glazer, 'Servants to capital: unpaid domestic labor and paid work', *Review of Radical Political Economics*, vol. 16, no. 1, 1984, pp. 61–87; Meaghan Morris, 'Things

to do with shopping centres', in *Grafts: feminist cultural criticism*, ed. Susan Sheridan, Verso, London, 1988

11 Ralph Herbert and Michael Emmison, 'Social contacts amongst suburban housewives', *Australian Journal of Social Issues*, vol. 12, no. 4, 1977, pp. 307–15

12 Stella Lees and June Senyard, *The 1950s . . . How Australia became a modern society, and everyone got a house and a car*, Hyland House, Melbourne, 1987, ch. 3

13 George Patterson Pty Ltd, *The Patterson report or 'wooing the Australian woman'*, G. Patterson, Sydney, 1972

14 Judith Allen, for example, refers to the steady process of disclosure evident in the policing of sex crimes after 1940 (*Sex and secrets: crimes involving Australian women since 1880*, Oxford University Press, Melbourne, 1990, ch. 8)

15 Sheila Jeffreys, *Anti-climax: a feminist perspective on the sexual revolution*, Women's Press, London, 1990, esp. ch. 3

16 Jill Julius Matthews, *Good and mad women: the historical construction of femininity in twentieth century Australia*, Allen & Unwin, Sydney, 1984, pp. 89–91, 96–9

17 Ann Game and Rosemary Pringle, 'The making of the Australian family', *Intervention*, vol. 12, 1979, pp. 93–95

18 *Advertising in Australia*, supplement to *Newspaper News*, 17 Feb. 1967, p. 27; 'What makes women buy', *Advertising in Australia*, supplement to *Newspaper News*, 19 Aug. 1966, pp. 14–16, 26; 'What makes men buy', *Advertising in Australia*, supplement to *Newspaper News*, 10 May 1968, p. 8

19 Rena Bartos, *Marketing to women around the world*, Harvard Business School Press, Boston, 1989, p. xiii; 'What makes women buy', p. 16; 'Sex and Madison Avenue', *Advertising in Australia*, supplement to *Newspaper News*, 4 Aug. 1967, pp. 8–13

20 'Cosmetics faces a fragrant future', *Advertising in Australia*, supplement to *Newspaper News*, 11 Nov. 1966, pp. 8–11, 25; Lesley Johnson, 'The teenage girl and the social definition of growing up for young Australian women 1950 to 1965', *History of Education Review*, vol. 18, no. 1, 1989, pp. 1–12

21 Sidney Baume, 'Current trends in advertising', *Rydge's Business Journal*, Oct. 1957, pp. 970–71; Peggy Nightingale, 'Women as audiences', in *Television and women's culture: the politics of the popular*, ed. Mary Ellen Brown, Currency Press, Sydney, 1990, pp. 31–34

22 Gail Reekie, 'Market research and the post-war housewife', *Australian Feminist Studies*, no. 14, Summer 1991, pp. 15–27

23 Robert O. Hermann, 'The consumer movement in historical perspective', in *Consumerism: search for the consumer interest*, eds David A. Aaker and George S. Day, Macmillan, New York, 1974, 2nd ed.; Julie Rigg, 'The loneliness of the long distance housewife: Mrs Consumer', in *In her own right*, ed. Julie Rigg, Nelson, Melbourne, 1969; Patricia Edgar and Hilary McPhee, *Media She*, William Heinemann, Melbourne, 1974

24 Pringle, 'Women and consumer capitalism', p. 98; Game and Pringle, *Gender at work*, p. 72

25 *Australian*, 13 Feb. 1991, p. 17

26 Grant McCracken, *Culture and consumption: new approaches to the symbolic character of consumer goods and activities*, Indiana University Press, Bloomington, 1988, pp. 97–132

27 Some lone voices, possibly female, criticised the tendency of early copywriters to assume that women were 'vain, credulous and illogical' (*SPC*, Organ of the Sydney Publicity Club, Nov. 1930, p. 3)

28 See, for example, *Journal of Marketing*, vol. 41, no. 3, July 1977, special issue on women; Rosemary Scott, *The female consumer*, Associated Business Programmes, London, 1976; articles on women's income and spending habits in *American Demographics*, Apr. 1988, Aug. 1989, Sep. 1989; Bartos, *Marketing to women around the world*; Maralinda Wolheter and H. Bruce Lammers, 'An analysis of male roles in print advertisements over a 20 year span: 1958–1978', *Advances in Consumer Research*, vol. 7, 1980, pp. 760–61

29 *Courier Mail*, 25 Apr. 1991

30 *Australian Financial Review*, 20 Sep. 1988, pp. 1, 8

31 Wolheter and Lammers, 'An analysis of male roles in print advertisements', p. 761; Stephen J. Gould, 'Towards a theory of sexuality and consumption: consumer lovemaps', *Advances in Consumer Research*, vol. 18, 1991, pp. 381–83. See also Russell W. Belk and Gregory S. Coon, 'Can't buy me love: dating, money and gifts', *Advances in Consumer Research*, vol. 18, 1991, pp. 521–27.

32 Naomi Wolf, *The beauty myth*, Chatto and Windus, London, 1990, p. 114

33 On the distinction between private and public patriarchy, see

Sylvia Walby, *Theorizing patriarchy*, Basil Blackwell, Oxford, 1990

34 Gail Reekie, 'The most beautiful store in the world', *Australian Left Review*, Feb/Mar 1988, pp. 37–39

35 See, for example, Frederick W. Langrehr, 'Retail shopping mall semiotics and hedonistic consumption', *Advances in Consumer Research*, vol. 18, 1991, pp. 428–33

36 Barbara Johnstone, 'The selling machines: technologies of vision and the fine art of selling', BA Hons thesis, Griffith University, 1991

37 The following discussion of leisure retailing is based on Gail Reekie, 'Changes in the Adamless eden: the spatial and sexual transformation of a Brisbane department store 1930–1990', in *Lifestyle shopping: the subject of consumption*, ed. Robert Shields, Routledge, London, in press.

38 'Mum's still the boss of the family purse', *Rydge's*, Nov. 1980, pp. 78–79; Nightingale, 'Women as audiences', p. 33

39 *True stories: 'Born to shop'*, ABC Television, 29 Sep. 1991

40 Kim Sawchuck, 'A tale of inscription/fashion statements', in *Body invaders: panic sex in America*, eds Arthur and Marilouise Kroker, St Martins Press, New York, 1987, pp. 61–62

41 Rebecca Piirto, 'The romantic sell', *American Demographics*, Aug. 1989, p. 38

42 See, for example, Marilyn Lake, 'Sexuality and feminism: some notes on their Australian history', and articles by Mary Spongberg and Katie Holmes, *Lilith*, 7, Winter 1991

43 Nightingale, 'Women as audiences', p. 36; John Fiske, 'Popular forces and the culture of everyday life', *Southern Review*, vol. 21, no. 3, Nov. 1988, p. 303

Conclusions

1 Carole Pateman, 'The marriage contract', in *Australian women: new feminist perspectives*, eds Norma Grieve and Ailsa Burns, Oxford University Press, Melbourne, 1986

2 See, for example, Luce Irigaray, 'Is the subject of science sexed?', *Cultural Critique*, vol. 1, 1985, pp. 73–89; Evelyn Fox-Keller, 'Gender and science', in *Discovering reality: feminist perspectives on epistemology, metaphysics, methodology and the philosophy of science*, eds Sandra Harding and Merrill B. Hintikka, D. Reidel,

Dordrecht, 1983; E.A. Grosz and Marie de Lepervanche, 'Feminism and Science', in *Crossing boundaries: feminisms and the critique of knowledge*, eds Barbara Caine, E.A. Grosz and Marie de Lepervanche, Allen & Unwin, Sydney, 1988

3 George Patterson Pty Ltd, *the Patterson report or 'wooing the Australian woman'*, G. Patterson, Sydney, 1972, n.p. (introduction)

4 *True stories: 'Born to shop'*, ABC Television, 29 Sep. 1991

5 John D'Emilio and Estelle B. Freedman, *Intimate matters: a history of sexuality in America*, Harper & Row, New York, 1988, pp. 233–34

6 Catharine McKinnon, 'Not a moral issue', 1983, in her *Feminism unmodified: discourses on life and law*, Harvard University Press, Cambridge, Mass., 1987, p. 154

7 Rosemary Pringle, *Secretaries talk: sexuality, power and work*, Allen & Unwin, Sydney, 1988, p. 152 and ch. 12

8 John Fiske, 'Popular forces and the culture of everyday life', *Southern Review*, 21, Nov. 1988, p. 293

Bibliography

Abbreviations

ABL	Australian National University, Archives of Business and Labour
APP	*Australian Parliamentary Papers*
CPP	*Commonwealth Parliamentary Papers*
DJA	David Jones Archives
GBA	Grace Brothers Archives
ML	Mitchell Library
NLA	National Library of Australia
NSWPP	*New South Wales Parliamentary Papers*
UMA	University of Melbourne Archives
VPNSWLA	*Votes and Proceedings of the New South Wales Legislative Assembly*
VPP	*Victorian Parliamentary Papers*

Primary sources

Store, wholesale and retail trade association records

Anthony Hordern & Sons

Anthony Hordern & Sons Ltd. *'While I live I'll grow': being an account of the foundation and growth of Australia's mammoth business*, Sydney, n.d. (?1907) (Articles reprinted from the *Australian Town and Country Journal*, 1906, and *Australia*, 1907) [ML]

Hordern family, newspaper cuttings and photographs, 1909–24 [ML]

Rawlings, Justly. 'Welfare work at Anthony Hordern & Sons Ltd', *Health*, vol. III, no. 3, May 1925, pp. 69–75

Redmond, Thomas J., *The history of Anthony Hordern & Sons Ltd*, Anthony Hordern & Sons printers, Sydney, 1938 [in Frank Clune, material for *The saga of Sydney*, ML]

Civil Service Co-operative Society Stores

'Civil Service Co-operative Society Stores', *Cyclopedia of New South Wales*, Sydney, 1907 [ML]

Civil Service Co-operative Society Stores of New South Wales, *Price List 1907*, [ML]

The Rendezvous of Sydney, 1927, [ML]

David Jones (in DJA unless otherwise stated)

Applications for employment, staff agreements and related correspondence, 1873–1906 (BRG 1/8). Also personnel files 1906–30.

Between Ourselves (David Jones' employees' magazine), 1919–21 [ML]

David Jones Ltd, Elizabeth Street store, 1922–38 (BRG 1/575) and circulars issued to staff and customers for the opening of the Elizabeth Street store, 1927 (BRG 1/574)

David Jones Ltd, *How time flies*, 1938 [ML]

David Jones Ltd, mail order catalogues 1899, 1902, 1903–4, c. 1910, 1916–17, 1919, 1920, 1924–30 (BRG 1/82–83)

David Jones Ltd, minute books, 1906–30 (BRG 1/32/1–4)

David Jones Ltd, *A Retrospect 1837–1897*, George Sands, Sydney, 1897 [ML]

David Jones & Company, Souvenir, 1887 (BRG 1/69)

Ford's Australian Almanac, 1851, in which is bound David Jones & Co. trade list (DJA Ref)

Harwood, A.R. Report to the directors of David Jones Ltd, 1913 (sighted 1985, accession number unavailable)

Lloyd Jones, Edward. Letters received from members of the firm, 1891–94 (BRG 1/24)

Lloyd Jones, Charles. 'The history of David Jones Limited', reprinted from the *Journal of the Royal Australian Historical Society*, vol. 41, no 5, 1955

Lloyd Jones, Charles and Robinson, Desmond. 'Customers are human' [Charles Lloyd Jones's autobiography], c. 1958 (PRG 2/80)

London office, letters received from, 1880–93 (BRG 1/13)

London office, memoranda concerning correspondence with, 1879–84 (BRG 1/16)

Miscellaneous correspondence and related papers, 1866–1907 (BRG 1/22)

Newspaper cuttings, 1919–21 (BRG 1/563), 1922–37 (BRG 1/X7), 1928, 1929 (BRG 1/X30)

Personnel Department, publications, Training Department, *Staff guide*, 1935 (BRG 1/121)

Secretary's office, 'History and policy of David Jones Limited', speech by Mr Stark to the Improvement Class, March 1925 (BRG 1/496)

Trading results, 1920–44 (BRG 1/140)

A visit to David Jones: reviewing the George Street store, the Country Order Department and the Marlborough Street Factory, 1923 (BRG 1/134)

Farmers

Farmer & Co., engagement book, 1873–81 [GBA]

Farmer & Co. Ltd, minute book, 1897 [GBA]

Farmer & Co., *Ninety-seven years*, Sydney, 1937 [NLA]

Taylor, Winifred. 'The application of intelligence tests to personnel in a retail store', *Australasian Journal of Psychology and Philosophy*, vol. III, no 3, Sep. 1925, pp. 211–18

Grace Brothers

Grace Brothers, employees' record cards ('blue cards') [GBA]

The Model Trader (catalogues), 1908–30 [GBA]

Hordern Brothers

'Sydney improvements', *Australian Town and Country Journal*, 24 Apr. 1886, p. 84

Lassetters

'A great business house: Lassetters, universal providers', *Australian Town and Country Journal*, 13 May, 1908, p. 38

'Lassetters: a great Australian business house' by the editor of *The Australian Field*, Sep. 1894, pp. 263–69

Ex-editor of the *Australian Field. Sixty years an employer, 1850–1910: written at the request of the staff and employees of F. Lassetter & Co.*, Marchant & Co., Sydney, 1910 [ML]

Marcus Clark (in Marcus Clark papers, ABL, unless otherwise stated)

General letterbooks, 1915–30 (74/2/1)
Minutes of meetings of Board of Directors, 1902–30 (microfilm M30/1 reel 1)
Details of bonus and deferred pay made to branch managers and other employees, 1903–38 (74/30)
Agreements and other papers concerning branch managers and other employees, 1909–24 (74/29)
Reports and papers presented at annual general meetings, 1929–31 (74/37)
Newspaper cuttings of the company's advertisements, 1922 (74/48)
Rules and Regulations [?1902–06], in material published by the company, 1893–1956 (74/49/27)
Newspaper clipping, 1913 (74/50)
Marcus Clark Ltd, *A souvenir of the success of Marcus Clark & Co. Ltd*, W.E. Smith, Sydney, n.d. (?1911) [ML]

Mark Foy's
Magnet, 1909–20 [ML]
The romance of the house of Foy: published in connection with the golden jubilee of Mark Foy's Ltd., Sydney, 1885–1935, 1935 [DJA BRG 1/209]

Nock & Kirby
Nock & Kirby Ltd, papers, profit and loss accounts etc. [ML MSS 4454]

Paterson, Laing & Bruce (wholesalers)
Paterson, Laing & Bruce papers, abstract of comparative trade, 1887–1946 [ABL N29/97]; A.B. Templeman's private record of departmental results, 1904–18 [ABL 38/24]

Peapes
Peapes & Co., records, 'Applications for engagement 1878–1902' [ML MSS 2161, Box Y812]
Illustrated Catalogues, 1897, 1904–05, 1907–30 [ML]
Article on Peapes & Co., *Sydney Mail*, 13 Sep. 1905, p. 678
'Peapes & Co. Ltd' in Sydney Chamber of Commerce, *Commerce in Congress*, Sydney, 1909 [ML]

Retail Traders' Association of New South Wales
Minutes of the Master Retailers' Association of New South Wales, 1903–21; minutes of the Retail Traders' Association of New

South Wales, 1921–30 [Archives of the Retail Traders' Association of New South Wales]

Journal of the Retail Traders' Association of New South Wales, 1919–30 (to 1921 *Journal of Master Retailers' Association of New South Wales*) [ML]

Robert Reid (wholesalers)
Robert Reid papers, price list 1911, and sale catalogues 1899–1912 [ABL 81/310]

Sargood Gardiner (wholesalers)
Sargood Gardiner papers, miscellaneous reports [UMA LS 4/5/2 Box 1]

Sydney Snow
Sydney Snow Pty Ltd papers, minutes 1920–30, in Cox Brothers papers [UMA]

Other manuscript material

Advertising Association of Australia and New Zealand, records, 1918–54 [NLA MS 1014]
Civic League, minute book, 1907–10 [ML MSS 2024/1]
Eleanor Hinder, papers [ML MSS 770]
Fell, Ian. 'Shops. The architectural treatment of modern shop design', B. Arch. thesis, University of Sydney, 1928 [Fisher Library]

Scott Family papers (Rose Scott papers):
Personal papers and correspondence, 1869–1925 (including speeches and notes on Early Closing) [ML MSS 38/20, 38/28 and 38/29]
Women's Political Educational League [ML MSS 38/43 items 1 and 2]
National Council of Women [ML MSS 38/50]
Collected papers 1852–1922 (including correspondence and speeches on Early Closing) [ML MSS 38/58X and 38/59]
Printed material, 1863–1924, item 5, newspaper cuttings on Early Closing [ML MSS 38/64]

Government records—Australia, Great Britain and Victoria

Census of the Commonwealth of Australia, 1911

Commonwealth Bureau of Census and Statistics, Labour and Industrial Branch, *Reports*, 1912–30

Great Britain and Ireland Home Office. *Report on the Acts for the Regulation of the Hours of Employment in Shops in Australia and New Zealand*, 1908

Interstate Commission of Australia, Prices Investigation No. 11 Report, Clothing, 1919, *CPP*, 1917–19, vol. 5

Interstate Commission of Australia, Tariff Investigation, Apparel—Corsets, 1915, *CPP,. 1914–17, vol. 6*

Parliament of the Commonwealth of Australia, *Report of the Royal Commission on the Basic Wage 1920*, Supplementary Report, 1921

Royal Commission on the Basic Wage, 1920, *APP*, 1920–21, vol. 4

Royal Commission on the Commonwealth Tariff, *APP*, 1905, vol. 2; 1906, vol. 4; 1907–08, vol. 4

Royal Commission on the Operation of the Factories and Shops Law of Victoria, 1901, *VPP*, 1902–03, vol. 2

Government records—New South Wales

Board of Trade. Cost of Living of Adult Female Workers, 1918, transcript of proceedings [AONSW 2/5768]

——Cost of Living for Adult Female Employees, 1919, transcript of proceedings [AONSW 2/5770]

——Cost of Living Enquiry—Males and Females General, 1920, transcript of proceedings [AONSW 2/5775]

——Cost of Living Enquiry (Females), 1920–21, [AONSW 2/5785]

——General Cost of Living Enquiry, 1920–21, transcript of proceedings [AONSW 2/5784]

——Cost of Living General and Exhibits, 1923, transcript of proceedings [AONSW 2/5799]

——*Bulletin: Living Wage (Adult Males)*, 1918

——*Compendium of Living Wage Declarations and Reports*, 1902–30

Census and Industrial Returns Act 1891, *VPNSWLA*, 1891–92, vol. 7

Census of New South Wales, 1891, 1901

Court of Arbitration, Shop Assistants Union of New South Wales v. Mark Foy, transcripts of proceedings, 1906, vol. 33 [AONSW 2/87]; 1907, vol. 42 [AONSW 2/95], vol. 43 [AONSW 2/96], vol. 44 [AONSW 2/97], vol. 45 [AONSW 2/98]

Department of the Attorney-General and of Justice, Special Correspondence bundles: Papers re Shoplifting, First Offenders

(Women) Act, and Women's Legal Status Bill 1905–39 [AONSW 3/3165]

Department of Labour and Industry, Necessary Commodities Control Commission, 1919–20, transcripts of proceedings [AONSW 2/5726–9]

——*Reports on the Working of the Factories and Shops Act*, 1897–1930

Early Closing Bill 1890

Factories and Shops Act 1896

Industrial Arbitration Reports, 1902–30

Industrial Commission, transcripts of proceedings, vol. 25, Shop Assistants (Metropolitan) Conciliation Committee, 17 Dec. 1928 [AONSW 2/412]

Royal Commission on the Alleged Shortage of Labour in the State of New South Wales, 1911, *NSWPP*, 1911, vol. 1, part 2

Royal Commission on the Hours and General Conditions of Employment of Female and Juvenile Labour in Factories and Shops, and the Effect on such Employees, 1912, *NSWPP*, 1911–12, 3rd session, vol. 2

Royal Commission on Industrial Arbitration in the State of New South Wales, Final Report, 1913, *NSWPP*, 1913, vol. 1

Royal Commission re Saturday Half-Holiday, New South Wales Legislative Assembly, 1909

Report of the Royal Commission on Strikes, New South Wales Government Printer, 1891

Select Committee on the Industrial Conciliation and Arbitration Bill, 1931, *NSWPP*, 1930–31–32, vol. 5

Sydney City and Suburban Sewage and Health Board Report, *VPNSWLA*, 1875–76, vol. 5

Books and other publications (all pre–1930 sources in ML)

Ackermann, Jessie. *Australia from a woman's point of view*, Cassell & Co., Melbourne, [1913] 1981

Australian Labor Party. *Minutes of Second Interstate Conference of Labor Women at Canberra, May 1930*

Beable, William H. *Behind the counter: a practical guide for shop assistants*, Angus & Robertson, Sydney, 1930

Belk, Russell W. and Coon, Gregory S. 'Can't buy me love: dating, money and gifts', *Advances in Consumer Research*, vol. 18, 1991

Berlei Ltd. *Fifty-two practical aids to better salesmanship* (collection of salesmen's manuals), 1926

Bray & Holliday Ltd. *Products of Bray & Holliday Ltd.*, Adshead Rose Publicity, Sydney, n.d., c.1924

Casson, Herbert N. *The art of customer-finding*, Cornstalk Pub. Co., Sydney, 1928

——*Better salesmanship and twelve tips on finance*, Cornstalk Pub. Co., Sydney, 1928

Coghlan, T.A. *Labour and industry in Australia from the first settlement in 1788 to the establishment of the Commonwealth in 1901*, Macmillan, Melbourne, 1969

——*The wealth and progress of New South Wales 1886–87*, Government Printer, Sydney, 1887 and 1902

——*General report on the eleventh census of New South Wales*, 1894

Commonwealth of Australia Advisory Council of Science and Industry, *Bulletin no. 15: welfare work*, 1919, and *Bulletin no. 17: industrial co-operation in Australia*, 1920

Country Women's Association of New South Wales, *Annual Reports*, 1928–31

Early Closing Association of New South Wales. *A few facts concerning the hours worked by shop assistants in Sydney and suburbs*, 1898

——*Early Closing Bill*, draft, ?1898

—— Leaflets and pamphlets, 1897–1900

Employers' Federation of New South Wales, *Annual Reports*, 1904–06, 1908–27

Foley, Alan. *The fight for trade: a series of articles prepared for the use of country traders who wish to combat the influence of mail order houses and city traders generally*, A. Foley, Bondi, NSW, ?1928

Foley, Alan & W.J. Hewett. *Text book of window dressing and display*, A. Lawrence & Co., Sydney and Melbourne, 1922–23

Forbes, George. *History of Sydney from the foundation of the city in 1788 up to the present time 1926*, William Brooks & Co., Sydney, 1926

Gewurz, E. *Wisdom and success in advertising*, T.C. Lothian, Melbourne, 1910

Hayes, J.W. *The draper and haberdasher: a guide to the general drapery trade*, Houlston & Sons, London, 1878

Lustre Hosiery Ltd. *The craft of retail selling: dedicated to the great army of men and women who fill a most important niche in the realm of merchandising*, Arthur McQuilty & Co., Sydney, n.d., ?1922

McLean, Robart (ed.). *The new atlas of Australia*, 5 vols., John Sands, Sydney, ?1886

Militant Women's Group, Sydney. *Woman's road to freedom*, Proletarian Press, Sydney, 1927

The modern draper: the draper's encyclopaedia, Caxton Pub. Co., London, 1927

National Council of Women of New South Wales. *Report of meeting held to establish the National Council of Women of New South Wales June 26 1896*

——*Two papers read at the Women's Council Meeting May 29 1919*

——*Biennial Reports*, 1913/14–1926/8

National Economy Exhibition, organised by the Women's Commonwealth Patriotic Association, official catalogue, 1917

Patterson, George Pty Ltd. *The Patterson report: or 'wooing the Australian woman'*, George Patterson Pty Ltd, Sydney, 1972

Piddington, A.B. *The next step: a family basic income*, Macmillan, Melbourne, 1921

Rydge's Business Journal. *Rydge's retail merchandising course*, Hogbin, Coker Ltd, Sydney, 1937

Scott, Rosemary. *The female consumer*, Associated Business Programmes, London, 1976

Shop Assistants Union of New South Wales. *Rules*, 1907

Shop Assistants and Warehouse Employees' Federation of Australia, New South Wales Branch. *Annual Reports*, 1927, 1932, 1933, 1934

Sinsheimer, Allen. *Retail advertising of men's and boys' wear*, Harper & Bros., London, 1926

Stopes, Marie. *Married love: a new contribution to the solution of sex difficulties*, Putnam, London, [1918] 1942

Swan, Annie S. *Courtship and marriage and the gentle art of home-making*, Hutchinson, London, 1894

Sydney Chamber of Commerce. *Annual Reports*, 1881, 1884, 1891–1930

Twopeny, R.E.N. *Town life in Australia*, Elliot Stock, London, 1883

Walker, A.W. *How to dress*, ed. by Samuel A. Mills, Sydney, 1906

Walker, R.R. *Communicators: people, practices, philosophies in Australian advertising, media and marketing*, Landsdowne Press, Melbourne, 1967

Women's Commonwealth Patriotic Association. *Series of pamphlets on thrift* 1915–17

Women's Co-operative Society Ltd. *Rules*, 1911

Young Women's Christian Association, Sydney. *Annual Reports*, 1885–1930

Articles

Annie, Edie. 'Nobody cares for me! The living wage for a working girl has been fixed in New South Wales at £1 19s 6d per week', *Women's World*, 1 Nov. 1922, p. 18

Anon. 'How to benefit by the summer sales: useful hints for bargain-hunters by one of them', *Everylady's Journal*, 6 Jan. 1919

Barker, J.V. 'The advertising art of Australia', *The Technical Gazette of New South Wales*, vol. 13, part 2, 1923, pp. 73–80

Buckingham, William. 'Retail merchandise control', *Blennerhassett's Commercial Educational Society of Australasia: business lectures for business men*, 1938

'Bunyip'. 'The sewing girls of Sydney', *The Australian*, vol. 4, Apr.-Sep. 1880, pp. 615–21

'Early history of the Housewives Progressive Association of New South Wales', by the editor of *The Housewife Magazine*, Feb.-Mar., Apr., May 1934

Gould, Stephen J. 'Toward a theory of sexuality and consumption: consumer lovemaps', *Advances in Consumer Research*, vol. 18, 1991, pp. 381–83

Irvine, E. Marie. 'Madam intervenes', *The Home*, Dec. 1920, pp. 90, 92

McConnell, W.K. 'Consumers' co-operation in New South Wales', *Economic Record*, Nov. 1929, pp. 263–74

McGuiness, Jan. 'Shoppers, take heart', *The Bulletin*, 18 June, 1991, pp. 96–98

Miss McKenny. 'Discussion of P.F. Rowland's case for early closing', *Australian Economist*, vol. 6, no. 1, 24 Nov. 1898, p. 86

'N.S.W. Federated Shop Assistants and Warehousemen's Association', *The Co-operator* (Eight Hour Souvenir and History of Trades Unionism), 7 Oct. 1912, p. 20

Piirto, Rebecca. 'The romantic sell', *American Demographics*, vol. 11, Aug. 1989, pp. 38–41

Ruehl, Peter. 'Advertising goes for new improved sexism', *Australian Financial Review*, 20 Sep. 1988, pp. 1, 8

Tracy, Beatrix. 'The shop girl', *The Lone Hand*, 1 Sep. 1908, pp. 523–30 [Reproduced in Beverley Kingston, *The world moves slowly: a documentary history of Australian women*, Cassell Australia, Stanmore NSW, 1977]

Webb, Ethel M. 'Keeping fit for business. The city girl's problem', *Woman's World*, 1 Mar. 1922, p. 25

Periodicals and newspapers

Advertiser's Monthly, 1929–30

Advertising in Australia (organ of the Victorian Institute of Advertising Men), 1921–22, 1927–29

Advertising in Australia (the national trade magazine of advertising and marketing), 1964–68

American Demographics, 1988–89

Association Woman (organ of the National YWCA of Australasia), 1917–25

Australasian Journal of Psychology and Philosophy (published by the Australasian Association of Psychology and Philosophy), 1923–30

Australian Economist (journal of the Australian Economic Association), 1888–98

Australian News of Ladies' Politics, 1905–06 (until Oct. 1906 *The Wardrobe*)

Australian Storekeepers' Journal (incorporating the *Draper and Warehouseman*), 1895–1901

Australian Worker (also *The Worker*), 1905–30

Block 14 Weekly, 1923

Commerce (organ of the Sydney Chamber of Commerce), 1912–30

Commonwealth Home, 1927–29

Dawn: a journal for the household, 1888–1905

Draper and Warehouseman, Clothiers' and Costumiers' Gazette (organ of the soft-goods trade in Australasia), 1892–94

Draper of Australasia, 1901–30

Draper of Australasia Diary, 1903

Happy Homes: a journal of pure literature for the household, 1891–92

Helen's Weekly, 1927–28
Herself, 1928–31
Home: an Australian quarterly, 1920–30
Journal of Marketing, 1977 (special issue on women)
Lone Hand, 1907–12
Mothers in Australia (organ of the Mothers' Union in Australia. After 1960 *Mia-Mia*), 1917–30
My Lady's Journal, 1905–06
Newspaper News, 1928–40
Ours: a paper for Australian homes (organ of the Housewives Association of New South Wales), 1921–22
Reason Why: a magazine for advertisers, 1908–09
Rydge's Business Journal, 1928–70
Shop Assistants' Magazine, Mar.–Dec. 1926, then *Steele Rudd's and Shop Assistants Magazine*, Jan. 1927–Aug. 1927 (subsequently incorporated as Steele Rudd's 'Shop Window' column in the *Commonwealth Home*, 1927–29)
S.P.C., The Official and Unconventional Organ of the Sydney Publicity Club, 1930–31
Sydney Morning Herald, 1880–1930
Sydney Technical College Handbooks, (before 1915, *Calendars)*
White Ribbon Signal (organ of the Woman's Christian Temperance Union of New South Wales), 1893–98, 1904–30
Woman, 1906, 1917–30 (1906 *Woman's Budget)*
Woman's News, 1905
Woman's Voice, 1894–95

Secondary sources

Books

Aaker, David A. and Day, George S. (eds). *Consumerism: search for the consumer interest*, 2nd edn, Macmillan, New York, 1974

Abelson, Elaine. *When ladies go a-thieving: middle-class shoplifters in the Victorian department store*, Oxford University Press, New York, 1989

Adams, Carole Elizabeth. *Women clerks in Wilhelmine Germany: issues of class and gender*, Cambridge University Press, Cambridge and Melbourne, 1988

Adburgham, Alison. *Shopping in style: London from the Restoration to Edwardian elegance*, Thames & Hudson, London, 1979
——*Shops and shopping 1800–1914: where and in what manner the well-dressed Englishwoman bought her clothes*, George Allen & Unwin, London, 1964
Allen, Judith A. *Sex and secrets: crimes involving Australian women since 1880*, Oxford University Press, Melbourne, 1990
Australian National Gallery. *The glamour show: studio photographs 1925–1955*, May-Sep., 1986
Bailey, Beth L. *From front porch to back seat: courtship in twentieth century America*, Johns Hopkins Press, Baltimore, 1988
Banner, Lois. *American beauty*, Alfred A. Knopf, New York, 1983
Baritz, Loren. *The servants of power: a history of the use of social science in American industry*, Greenwood Press, Westport, Conn., 1960
Barnard Eldershaw, M. *Tomorrow and tomorrow and tomorrow*, Virago, London [1947] 1983
Bartels, Robert. *The development of marketing thought*, Richard D. Irwin, Homewood, Ill., 1962
Barth, Gunther. *City people: the rise of modern city culture in nineteenth-century America*, Oxford University Press, New York, 1980
Barthes, Roland. *The fashion system*, translated by Matthew Ward and Richard Howard, Hill & Wang, New York, 1983
——*Mythologies*, translated by Annette Lavers, Paladin, London, 1973
Bartos, Rena. *Marketing to women around the world*, Harvard Business School Press, Boston, 1989
Baudrillard, Jean. *For a critique of the political economy of the sign*, translated by Charles Levin, Telos Press, St Louis, 1981
——*The mirror of production*, translated by Mark Poster, Telos Press, St Louis, 1975
Benson, Susan Porter. *Counter cultures: saleswomen, managers and customers in American department stores 1890–1940*, University of Illinois Press, Urbana, 1986
Boorstin, Daniel. *The Americans: the democratic experience*, Random House, New York, 1973
Bowlby, Rachel. *Just looking: consumer culture in Drieser, Gissing and Zola*, Methuen, New York and London, 1985
Brash, Nicholas, Anne Burke and Colette Hoeben. *The model store*

1885–1985, Kevin Weldon & Associates, McMahons Point, NSW, 1985

Bronner, Simon J. (ed.). *Consuming visions: accumulation and display of goods in America 1880–1920*, W.W. Norton, New York, 1989

Callery, Sean. *Harrods Knightsbridge: the story of society's favourite store*, Ebury Press, London, 1991

Davis, Dorothy. *Fairs, shops and supermarkets: a history of English shopping*, University of Toronto Press, Toronto, 1966

Deacon, Desley. *Managing gender: the state, the new middle-class and women workers 1830–1930*, Oxford University Press, Melbourne, 1990

D'Emilio, John and Freedman, Estelle B. *Intimate matters: a history of sexuality in America*, Harper & Row, New York, 1988

Dunstan, Keith. *The store on the hill*, Macmillan Co. of Australia, Melbourne, 1979

Edgar, Patricia and McPhee, Hilary. *Media she*, William Heinemann, Melbourne, 1974

Ewen, Stuart. *Captains of consciousness: advertising and the social roots of the consumer culture*, McGraw-Hill, New York, 1976

Ewen, Elizabeth and Ewen, Stuart. *Channels of desire: mass images and the shaping of American consciousness*, McGraw-Hill, New York, 1982

Fass, Paula. *The damned and the beautiful: American youth in the 1920s*, Oxford University Press, New York, 1978

Ferry, John William. *A history of the department store*, Macmillan, New York, 1960

Forty, Adrian. *Objects of desire: design and society 1750–1980*, Thames & Hudson, London, 1986

Fox-Keller, Evelyn. *Reflections on gender and science*, Yale University Press, New Haven, 1985

Fraser, Hamish. *The coming of the mass market 1850–1914*, Macmillan, London, 1981

Game, Ann and Pringle, Rosemary. *Gender at work*, George Allen & Unwin, Sydney, 1983

Gillis, John R. *For better, for worse: British marriages, 1600 to the present*, Oxford University Press, New York, 1985

Goffman, Erving. *Gender advertisements*, Macmilian, London, 1979

Harrison, Molly. *People and shopping: a social background*, Ernest Benn, London, 1975

Haug, Wolfgang Fritz. *Critique of commodity aesthetics: appearance, sexuality and advertising in capitalist society*, translated by Robert Bock, Polity Press, Cambridge, 1986

Hicks, Neville. *This sin and scandal: Australia's population debate 1891–1911*, Australian National University Press, Canberra, 1978

Holcombe, Lee. *Victorian ladies at work: middle-class working women in England and Wales 1850–1914*, David & Charles, Newton Abbott, 1973

Hordern, Lesley. *Children of one family: the story of Anthony and Ann Hordern and their descendants in Australia 1825–1925*, Retford Press, Sydney, 1985

Horowitz, Daniel. *The morality of spending: attitudes towards the consumer society in America 1875–1940*, Johns Hopkins University Press, Baltimore, 1985

Jefferys, James. *Retail trading in Britain 1850–1950: a study of trends in retailing with special reference to the development of co-operative, multiple shop and department store methods of trading*, Cambridge University Press, Cambridge, 1954

Jeffreys, Sheila. *Anti-climax: a feminist perspective on the sexual revolution*, Women's Press, London, 1990

——*The spinster and her enemies: feminism and sexuality 1880–1930*, Pandora, London, 1985

Joel, Alexandra. *Best dressed: 200 years of fashion in Australia*, Collins, Sydney, 1984

Kessler-Harris, Alice. *Out to work: a history of wage-earning women in the United States*, Oxford University Press, New York, 1982

Kingston, Beverley. *My wife, my daughter and poor Mary-Ann: women and work in Australia*, Thomas Nelson, West Melbourne, 1975

Lawson, Olive. *The first voice of Australian feminism: excerpts from Louisa Lawson's The Dawn 1888–1895*, Simon & Schuster, Brookvale, NSW, 1990

Leach, William. *True love and perfect union: the feminist reform of sex and society*, Basic Books, New York, 1980

Lees, Stella and June Senyard. *The 1950s ... How Australia became a modern society, and everyone got a house and a car*, Hyland House, Melbourne, 1987

Lewin, Miriam (ed.). *In the shadow of the past: psychology portrays the sexes. A social and intellectual history*, Columbia University Press, New York, 1984

Lloyd, Genevieve. *The man of reason: 'male' and 'female' in western philosophy*, Methuen, London, 1984

Lurie, Alison. *The language of clothes*, Random House, New York, 1981

McCalman, Janet. *Struggletown: public and private life in Richmond 1900–1965*, Melbourne University Press, Carlton, 1984

McCracken, Grant. *Culture and consumption: new approaches to the symbolic character of consumer goods and activities*, Indiana University Press, Bloomington, 1988

MacKinnon, Catharine. *Feminism unmodified: discourses on life and law*, Harvard University Press, Cambridge, Mass., 1987.

McNeil, Eugenie. *A bunyip close behind me: recollections of the nineties*, retold by her daugher Eugenie Crawford, Hawthorn Press, Melbourne, 1972

——*Ladies didn't: recollections of an Edwardian girlhood*, retold by her daughter Eugenie Crawford, Penguin, Ringwood, Vic., 1984

Marchand, Roland. *Advertising the American dream: making way for modernity 1920–1940*, University of California Press, Berkeley, 1985

Matthews, Glenna. *'Just a housewife': the rise and fall of domesticity in America*, Oxford University Press, New York, 1987

Matthews, Jill Julius. *Good and mad women: the historical construction of femininity in twentieth century Australia*, George Allen & Unwin, Sydney, 1984

Miller, Michael. *The Bon Marché: bourgeois culture and the department store 1869–1920*, Princeton University Press, Princeton, 1981

Neal, Lawrence. *Retailing and the public*, George Allen & Unwin, London, 1932

Pasdermadjian, H. *The department store: its origins, evolution and economics*, Newman Books, London, 1954

Pateman, Carole. *The sexual contract*, Polity Press, Cambridge, 1988

Pollon, Frances. *Shopkeepers and shoppers: a social history of retailing in New South Wales from 1788*, Retail Traders' Association of New South Wales, Sydney, 1989

Pollon, Frances and Philip Geeves. *A romance with retailing: an early history before 1900 and progress to 1913*, Retail Traders' Association of New South Wales, Sydney, 1983

Pratt, Ambrose. *Sidney Myer: a biography*, Quartet, Melbourne, 1978

Pringle, Rosemary. *Secretaries talk: sexuality, power and work*, Allen & Unwin, Sydney, 1988

Reiger, Kerreen. *The disenchantment of the home: modernizing the Australian family 1880–1940*, Oxford University Press, Melbourne, 1985

Rothman, Ellen K. *Hands and hearts: a history of courtship in America*, Basic Books, New York, 1984

Rubinstein, Helena. *My life for beauty*, Bodley Head, Sydney, 1964

Ryan, Edna. *Two-thirds of a man: women and arbitration in New South Wales 1902–1908*, Hale & Iremonger, Sydney, 1984

Santink, J. *Timothy Eaton and the rise of his department store*, University of Toronto Press, Toronto, 1990

Spearritt, Peter. *Sydney since the twenties*, Hale & Iremonger, Sydney, 1978

Steele, Valerie. *Fashion and eroticism*, Oxford University Press, New York, 1985

Strasser, Susan. *Satisfaction guaranteed: the making of the American mass market*, Pantheon, New York, 1989

Summers, Anne. *Damned whores and God's police: the colonization of women in Australia*, Penguin, Harmondsworth, 1975

Vamplew, Wray (ed.). *Australians: historical statistics*, Fairfax Syme & Weldon, Sydney, 1987

Walby, Sylvia. *Theorizing patriarchy*, Basil Blackwell, Oxford, 1990

Whitwell, Greg. *Making the market: the rise of consumer society*, McPhee Gribble, Melbourne, 1989

Williams, Juanita (ed.). *Psychology of women: selected readings*, Norton, New York, 1979

Williams, Rosalind. *Dream worlds: mass consumption in late nineteenth-century France*, University of California Press, Berkeley, 1982

Wilson, Elizabeth. *Adorned in dreams: fashion and modernity*, Virago Press, London, 1985

Wolf, Naomi. *The beauty myth*, Chatto & Windus, London, 1990

Zola, Emile. *Au bonheur des dames*, Hutchinson, London, 1895

Articles

Allen, Judith. 'Breaking into the public sphere. The struggle for women's citizenship in New South Wales 1890–1920', in *In pursuit of justice: Australian women and the law 1788–1979*, eds Judy Mackinolty and Heather Radi, Hale & Iremonger, Sydney, 1979

——'Evidence and silence: Feminism and the limits of history', in *Feminist challenges: social and political theory*, eds Carole Pateman and Elizabeth Gross, Allen & Unwin, Sydney, 1986

——' "Mundane" men: historians, masculinity and masculinism', *Historical Studies*, vol. 22, no. 89, Oct. 1987, pp. 617–28

——' "Our deeply degraded sex" and "the animal in man": Rose Scott, feminism and sexuality 1890–1925', *Australian Feminist Studies*, no. 7/8, Summer 1988, pp. 65–91

Auchmuty, Rosemary. 'The truth about sex', in *Australian Popular Culture*, eds Peter Spearritt and David Walker, George Allen & Unwin, Sydney, 1979

Baars, Anna Marie. 'The nature and distribution of retailing activities in the Perth central ward between 1888 and 1904', *Australia 1888 Bulletin*, no. 12, Nov. 1983, pp. 3–17

Bailey, Peter. 'Parasexuality and glamour: the Victorian barmaid as cultural prototype', *Gender and History*, vol. 2, no. 2, Summer 1990, pp. 148–72

Bartky, Sandra Lee. 'Foucault, femininity and the modernization of patriarchal power', in *Feminism and Foucault: reflections on resistance*, eds Irene Diamond and Lee Quinby, Northeastern University Press, Boston, 1988

Best, Sue. 'Foundations of femininity: Berlei corsets and the (un)making of the modern body', *Continuum*, vol. 5, no. 1, 1991, pp. 191–214

Bland, Lucy. 'Marriage laid bare: middle class women and marital sex', in *Labour and love: women's experiences of home and family 1850–1940*, ed. Jane Lewis, Basil Blackwell, Oxford, 1986

Bourke, Helen. 'Industrial unrest as social pathology: the Australian writings of Elton Mayo', *Historical Studies*, vol. 20, no. 79, Oct. 1982, pp. 217–33

Breckman, Warren G. 'Disciplining consumption: the debate about luxury in Wilhelmine Germany, 1890–1914', *Journal of Social History*, vol. 24, no. 3, 1990, pp. 485–505

Burnham, John Chynoweth. 'The new psychology: from narcissism to social control', in *Change and continuity in twentieth-century America: the 1920s*, eds John Braeman, Robert H. Bremner and David Brody, Ohio State University Press, Columbus, 1968

Cameron, Barbara. 'The flappers and the feminists: a study of women's emancipation in the 1920s', in *Worth her salt: women at work in Australia*, eds Margaret Bevege, Margaret James and Carmel Shute, Hale & Iremonger, Sydney, 1982

Chaney, David. 'The department store as a cultural form', *Theory, Culture and Society*, vol. 1, no. 3, 1983, pp. 22–43

Carrick, Jill. 'Turn of the century posters: representing women', *Arena*, no. 79, 1987, pp. 108–18

Collins, Anne-Maree. 'Woman or beast? Bestiality in Queensland 1870–1949', *Hecate*, vol. 17, no. 1, 1991, pp. 36–42

Crowley, F.K. 'The British contribution to the Australian population 1860–1919', *University Studies in History and Economics*, vol. 2, no. 2, July 1954, pp. 55–83

——'1901–1914', in *A new history of Australia*, ed. F.K. Crowley, Heinemann, Melbourne, 1974

Curthoys, Ann. 'Eugenics, feminism and birth control: the case of Marion Piddington', *Hecate*, vol. 15, no. 1, 1989, pp. 73–89

——'The sexual division of labour: theoretical arguments', in *Australian women: new feminist perspectives*, eds Norma Grieve and Ailsa Burns, Oxford University Press, Melbourne, 1986

Deacon, Desley. 'Taylorism in the home: the medical profession, the infant welfare movement and the deskilling of women', *Australian and New Zealand Journal of Sociology*, vol. 21, no 2, Jul. 1985, pp. 161–73

Ducrocq, Francoise. 'From poor law to jungle law: sexual relations and marital strategies (London 1850–1870)', in *Women in culture and politics: a century of change*, eds Judith Friedlander, Blanche Wiessen Cook, Alice Kessler-Harris and Carroll Smith-Rosenberg, Indiana University Press, Bloomington, 1986

Featherstone, Mike. 'The body in consumer culture', *Theory, Culture and Society*, vol. 1, no. 2, 1982, pp. 18–33

Fiske, John. 'Popular forces and the culture of everyday life', *Southern Review*, vol. 21, Nov. 1988, pp. 288–306

Forster, Colin. 'Aspects of Australian fertility, 1861–1901', *Australian Economic History Review*, vol. 14, no. 2, 1974, pp. 105–23

Fox-Keller, Evelyn. 'Gender and science', in *Discovering reality: feminist perspectives on epistemology, metaphysics, methodology and the philosophy of science*, eds Sandra Harding and Merrill B. Hintikka, D. Reidel, Dordrecht, 1983

Gardner, Deborah S. 'A paradise of fashion: A.T. Stewart's department store 1862–1875', in *A needle, a bobbin, a strike: women needleworkers in America*, eds Joan M. Jensen and Sue Davidson, Temple University Press, Philadelphia, 1985

Gatens, Moira. 'A critique of the sex/gender distinction', in *Beyond Marx? Interventions after Marx*, eds Judith Allen and Paul Patton, Intervention Publications, Sydney, 1983

Gilding, Michael. 'Economic relations in the bourgeois family, Sydney, 1870–1940', *Australia 1888 Bulletin*, no. 9, Apr. 1982, pp. 66–71

Glazer, Nona Y. 'Servants to capital: unpaid domestic labour and paid work', *Review of Radical Political Economics*, vol. 16, no. 1, 1984, pp. 61–87

Grahame, Peter R. 'Finding the reader: early consumer activism and the project of consumer literacy', *Continuum*, vol. 5, no. 1, 1991, pp. 215–27

Grosz, E.A. and de Lepervanche, Marie. 'Gender and science', in *Crossing boundaries: feminisms and the critique of knowledge*, eds Barbara Caine, E.A. Grosz and Marie de Lepervanche, Allen & Unwin, Sydney, 1988

Grosz, Elizabeth. 'Notes toward a corporeal feminism', *Australian Feminist Studies*, no. 5, Summer 1987, pp. 1–16

Halttunen, Karen. 'From parlor to living room: domestic space, interior decoration and the culture of personality', in *Consuming visions: accumulation and display of goods in America 1880–1920*, ed. Simon J. Bronner, W.W. Norton, New York, 1989

Harris, Neil. 'The drama of consumer desire', in *Yankee enterprise: the rise of the American system of manufactures*, eds Otto Mayr and Robert C. Post, Smithsonian Institution Press, Washington DC, 1981

——'Museums, merchandising and popular taste: the struggle for influence', in *Material culture and the study of American life*, ed. Ian M. Quinby, W.W. Norton, New York, 1978

Herbert, Ralph and Emmilson, Michael. 'Social contacts amongst suburban housewives', *Australian Journal of Social Issues*, vol. 12, no. 4, 1977, pp. 307–15

Irigaray, Luce. 'Is the subject of science sexed?', *Cultural Critique*, vol. 1, 1985, pp. 73–89

Jackson, Margaret. ' "Facts of life" or the eroticization of women's oppression? Sexology and the social construction of heterosexuality', in *The cultural construction of sexuality*, ed. Pat Caplan, Tavistock Publications, London, 1987

Jeffreys, Sheila. 'Indecent exposure', in *Women against violence against women*, eds Dusty Rhodes and Sandra McNeil, Onlywomen Press, London, 1985

Johnson, Lesley. 'The teenage girl: the social definition of growing up for young Australian women, 1950–1965', *History of Education Review*, vol. 18, no. 1, 1989, pp. 1–12

Jones, Elsie. 'Fertility decline in Australia and New Zealand 1861–1936', *Population Index*, 37, 1971, 301–25

Kelly, A.C. 'Demographic change and economic growth: Australia 1861–1911', *Explorations in Entrepreneurial History*, no. 5, 1967–68, pp. 207–77

Kunzle, David. 'Dress reform as anti-feminism', *Signs*, vol. 2, no. 3, 1977, pp. 570–79

Lake, Marilyn. 'Female desires: the meaning of World War II', *Australian Historical Studies*, vol. 24, no. 94, Oct. 1990, pp. 167–284

——'The politics of respectability: identifying the masculinist context', *Historical Studies*, vol. 22, no. 86, Apr. 1986, pp. 116–31

——'Sexuality and feminism. Some notes on their Australian history', *Lilith*, no. 7, Winter 1991, pp. 29–45

——'Socialism and manhood: the case of William Lane', *Labour History*, no. 50, May 1986, pp. 54–62

Langrehr, Frederick. 'Retail mall semiotics and hedonistic consumption', *Advances in Consumer Research*, vol. 18, 1991, pp. 428–33

Leach, William. 'Strategists of display and the production of desire', in *Consuming visions: accumulation and display of goods in America 1880–1920*, ed. Simon J. Bronner, W.W. Norton, New York, 1989

——'Transformations in a culture of consumption: women and department stores 1890–1925', *Journal of American History*, vol. 71, no. 2, Sep. 1984, 319–42

McBride, Theresa. 'A woman's world: department stores and the evolution of women's employment 1870–1920', *French Historical Studies*, vol. 10, no. 2, Fall 1978, pp. 664–83

Macarthy, P.G. 'Wages in Australia 1891 to 1914', *Australian Economic History Review*, vol. 10, no. 1, March 1970, pp. 56–76

MacCulloch, Jennifer. ' "This store is our world": female shop assistants in Sydney to 1930', in *Twentieth century Sydney: studies in urban and social history*, ed. Jill Roe, Hale & Iremonger, Sydney, 1980

MacKinnon, Alison and Bacchi, Carol. 'Sex, resistance and power: sex reform in South Australia c. 1905', *Australian Historical Studies*, vol. 23, no. 90, Apr. 1988, pp. 60–71

Mackinolty, John. 'The Married Women's Property Acts', in *In pursuit of justice: Australian women and the law 1788–1979*, eds Judy Mackinolty and Heather Radi, Hale & Iremonger, Sydney, 1979

McNeill, Sandra. 'Flashing: its effect on women', in *Women, violence and social control*, eds Jalna Hanmer and Mary Maynard, Macmillan, London, 1987

McQueen, Humphrey. 'Sale of the century', *Fremantle Arts Review*, vol. 3, no. 3, 1988, pp. 6–7

Matthews, Jill Julius. 'Building the body beautiful', *Australian Feminist Studies*, no. 5, Summer 1987, pp. 17–34

——'Educating for femininity: domestic arts education in South Australia', *Labour History*, no. 45, Nov. 1983, pp. 30–53

Morris, Meaghan. 'Things to do with shopping centres', in *Grafts: feminist cultural criticism*, ed. Susan Sheridan, Verso, London, 1988

Nightingale, Virginia. 'Women as audiences', in *Television and women's culture: the politics of the popular*, ed. Mary Ellen Brown, Currency Press, Sydney, 1990

O'Connor, John E. and Cummings, Charles F. 'Bamberger's department store, *Charm* magazine, and the culture of consumption in New Jersey 1924–1932', *New Jersey History*, no. 102, 1984, pp. 1–33

Pateman, Carol. 'The marriage contract', in *Australian women: new feminist perspectives*, eds Norma Grieve and Ailsa Burns, Oxford University Press, Melbourne, 1986

Peiss, Kathy. ' "Charity girls" and city pleasures: historical notes on working-class sexuality 1880–1920', in *Desire: the politics of sexuality*, eds Ann Snitow, Christine Stansell and Sharon Thompson, Virago, London, 1984

——'Making faces: the cosmetics industry and the cultural construction of gender 1890–1930', *Genders*, no. 7, Spring 1990, pp. 143–69

Pringle, Rosemary. 'Women and consumer capitalism', in *Women, social welfare and the state*, eds Cora V. Baldock and Bettina Cass, George Allen & Unwin, Sydney, 1983

Pumphrey, Martin. 'The flapper, the housewife and the making of modernity', *Cultural Studies*, vol. 1, no. 2, 1987, pp. 179–94

Radi, Heather. '1920–29', in *A new history of Australia*, ed. F.K. Crowley, Heinemann, Richmond, 1974

Reekie, Gail. 'Changes in the Adamless eden: the spatial and sexual transformation of a Brisbane department store 1930–1990', in *Life style shopping: the subject of consumption*, ed. Robert Shields, Routledge, London, in press

——'Decently dressed? Sexualised consumerism and the working woman's wardrobe 1918–1923', in *Women, work and the labour movement in Australia and Aotearoa/New Zealand*, eds Raelene Frances and Bruce Scates, special issue of *Labour History*, no. 61, Nov. 1991, pp. 42-56

——'Female office workers in Western Australia 1895–1920: the process of feminization and patterns of consciousness', in *The work place*, ed. Lenore Layman, *Time Remembered* special issue no. 5, Murdoch University, Perth, 1982

——' "Humanising industry": paternalism, welfarism and labour control in Sydney's big stores 1890–1930', *Labour History*, no. 53, Nov. 1987, pp. 1–19

——'Manufacturing gender: Sydney retailers and the clothing trade 1880–1930', in *Workers and Intellectuals*, eds Richard Nile and Barry York, Edward Blackwood, London, forthcoming

——'Market research and the post-war housewife', *Australian Feminist Studies*, no. 14, Summer 1991, pp. 15–27

——'The most beautiful store in the world', *Australian Left Review*, Feb./Mar. 1988, pp. 37–39

——'The sexual politics of selling and shopping', in *Contesting the 1890s: feminism rewrites history and culture*, eds Susan Sheridan, Susan Magarey and Sue Rowley, Allen & Unwin, Sydney, in press

——'The shop assistants case of 1907 and labour relations in

Sydney's retail industry', in *Foundations of arbitration: the origins and effects of state compulsory arbitration 1890–1914*, eds Stuart Macintyre and Richard Mitchell, Oxford University Press, Melbourne, 1989

Reiger, Kerreen. ' "Clean and comfortable and respectable": working-class aspirations and the Australian 1920 Royal Commission on the Basic Wage', *History Workshop Journal*, no. 27, Spring 1989, pp. 97–102

Rigg, Julie. 'The loneliness of the long distance housewife: Mrs Consumer', in *In her own right*, ed. Julie Rigg, Nelson, Melbourne, 1969

Roberts, Helene E. 'The exquisite slave: the role of clothes in the making of the Victorian woman', *Signs*, vol. 2, no. 3, 1977, pp. 554–69

Samson, Peter. 'The department store, its past and its future: a review article', *Business History Review*, vol. LV, no. 1, Spring 1981, pp. 26–34

Sawchuck, Kim. 'A tale of inscription/fashion statements', in *Body invaders: panic sex in America*, eds Arthur Kroker and Marilouise Kroker, St Martins Press, New York, 1987

Scott, Joan. 'Gender: a useful category of historical analysis', *American History Review*, vol. 91, no. 5, Dec. 1986, pp. 1053–75

Sinclair, W.A. 'Women and economic change in Melbourne 1871–1921', *Historical Studies*, vol. 20, no. 79, Oct. 1982, pp. 278–91

Smart, Judith. 'Feminists, food and the fair price: the cost of living demonstrations in Melbourne, August-September 1917', *Labour History*, no. 50, May 1986, pp. 113–31

Stephen, Ann. 'Agents of consumerism: the organisation of the Australian advertising industry 1918–1938', in *Media interventions*, eds Judith Allen et al, Intervention Publications, Leichhardt, 1981

——'Mass produced photography in Australia during the inter-war years', *Art Network*, no. 9, Autumn 1983, pp. 40–45

Stewart, Vivien. 'The way they were: a Sydney department store in the 1920s', *Heritage Australia*, vol. 9, no. 4, Summer 1990, pp. 20–23

Thompson, Janna. 'Women and the high priests of reason', *Radical Philosophy*, no. 34, Summer 1983, pp. 10–14

Thompson, Ruth. 'David Jones' centenary celebrations 1838–1938', *Australia 1938 Bulletin*, no. 3, Dec. 1980, pp. 11–18

Turnatori, Gabriella. 'Between public and private: the birth of the professional housewife and the female consumer', in *Women and the state: the shifting boundaries of public and private*, ed. Anne Showstack Sassoon, Hutchinson, London, 1987

Valverde, Mariana. 'The love of finery: fashion and the fallen woman in nineteenth century social discourse', *Victorian Studies*, vol. 32, no. 2, Winter 1989, pp. 169–88

Weinbaum, Batya and Bridges, Amy. 'The other side of the paycheck: monopoly capital and the structure of consumption', in *Capitalist patriarchy and the case for socialist feminism*, ed. Zillah R. Eisenstein, Monthly Review Press, New York, 1979

Windschuttle, Elizabeth (ed.). *Women, class and history: feminist perspectives on Australia 1788–1978*, Fontana, Melbourne, 1980

Wolfers, Howard. 'The big stores between the wars', in *Twentieth century Sydney: studies in urban and social history*, ed. Jill Roe, Hale & Iremonger, Sydney, 1980

Wolheter, Maralinda and Lammers, H. Bruce. 'An analysis of male roles in print advertisements over a 20 year span: 1958–1978', *Advances in Consumer Research*, vol. 7, 1980, pp. 760–61

Theses and unpublished works

ABC Television. *True stories: 'Born to shop'*, 29 Sep. 1991

Allen Judith, 'Women, crimes and policing in New South Wales 1880–1939', PhD thesis, Macquarie University, 1984

Cobb, Joan. 'The women's movement in New South Wales 1880–1914', MA Hons thesis, University of New England, 1966

Foley, Meredith. 'The women's movement in New South Wales and Victoria 1918–1938', PhD thesis, University of Sydney, 1985

Horton, Barbara. 'Brief history of David Jones Limited', 1985 [DJA]

Johnstone, Barbara. 'The selling machines: technologies of vision and the fine art of selling', BA Hons thesis, Griffith University, 1991

Little, Barbara. 'Retail trade and distribution in Sydney 1880–1914', PhD thesis, University of Sydney, 1979

Lucy, Mary. 'History of David Jones Ltd', 1976 [DJA]

MacCulloch, Jennifer. 'Female shop assistants in Sydney c.1890–1929', BA Hons thesis, Macquarie University, 1978

Malino, Sarah Smith. 'Faces across the counter: a social history of female department store employees 1870–1920', PhD dissertation, Columbia University, 1982

McEwen, Ellen. 'The Newcastle coalmining district of New South Wales 1860–1900', PhD thesis, University of Sydney, 1980

Raftery, Paul. 'The house built on service: David Jones Limited during the inter-war years, 1919–1939', Bachelor of Economics Hons thesis, University of Sydney, 1980

Reekie, Gail. 'Sydney's big stores: gender and mass marketing', PhD thesis, University of Sydney, 1987

Roberts, Denise. 'The movement for the early closing of shops in New South Wales 1890–1899', BA Hons thesis, University of New South Wales, 1981

Shute, Carmel. 'Australian women and the Great War: aspects of ideological change, with particular emphasis on Queensland', BA Hons thesis, University of Queensland, 1973

Spierings, John. 'Magic and science: aspects of Australian business, management, advertising and retailing, 1918–40', PhD thesis, University of Melbourne, 1989

——'Realising dreams: elements of advertising in Australia between the wars', unpub. paper, University of Melbourne, 1986

Thompson, Ruth. 'David Jones in war and peace', BA Hons thesis, Macquarie University, 1980

Index

Page numbers in italics refer to illustrations